American Furniture

AMERICAN FURNITURE 2020

Edited by Luke Beckerdite

Published by the CHIPSTONE FOUNDATION

Milwaukee

Distributed by Oxbow Books

Cover   Indian head, door pediment in the first floor, central hall of the Pennsylvania State House. (Courtesy, Historic American Buildings Survey, Library of Congress; photo, Jack E. Boucher, 1959).

Endpapers   Francis Guy (1760–1820), *The Tontine Coffee House*, New York, New York, ca. 1797. Oil on linen. H. 43", W. 65". (Purchase, the Louis Durr Fund, New-York Historical Society.)

Design and production   Wynne Patterson,
Copyediting   Richard Lindemann,
Typesetting   Jo Ann Langone

Published by the Chipstone Foundation
Distributed by Oxbow Books
oxbowbooks.com

Contents

Editorial Statement

American Furniture is an interdisciplinary journal dedicated to advancing knowledge of furniture made or used in the Americas from the seventeenth century to the present. Authors are encouraged to submit articles on any aspect of furniture history, essays on conservation and historic technology, reproductions or transcripts of documents, annotated photographs of new furniture discoveries, and book and exhibition reviews. References for compiling an annual bibliography also are welcome.

Manuscripts must be double-spaced, illustrated with black-and-white prints, transparencies, or high resolution digital images, and prepared in accordance with the Chipstone style guide. The Foundation will offer significant honoraria for manuscripts accepted for publication and reimburse authors for all photography approved in writing by the editor.

Luke Beckerdite

American Furniture

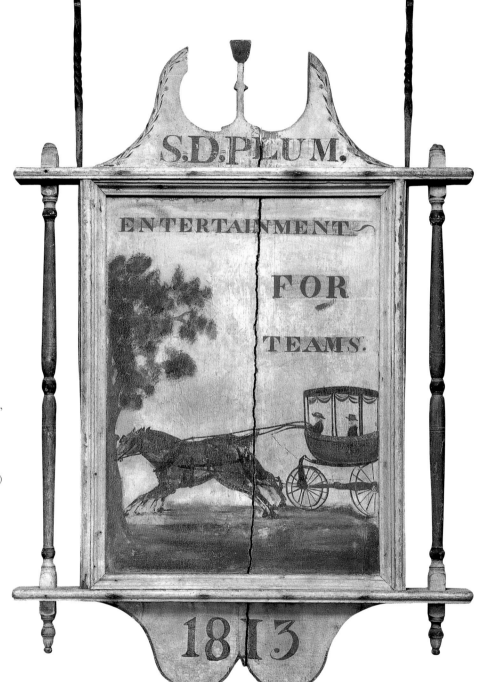

Figure 1 S. D. Plum tavern sign (double-sided, recto), probably Meriden, Connecticut, 1813. Paint on pine with iron. H. 51", W. 34", D. 3". (Courtesy, American Folk Art Museum, gift of Ralph Esmerian, acc. 2013.1.55; photo, 2000 John Bigelow Taylor; Art Resource, New York.)

Nancy Goyne Evans

From Craft Shop to Countinghouse: The Interaction of Woodworkers and Allied Artisans with the Business Community in the Late Colonial and Federal Periods

▼ THIS STUDY IS BASED ON a large body of written material providing insight into the myriad jobs performed by cabinetmakers, carpenters, painters, and allied artisans to meet the needs of fellow craftsmen, retail businesses, the professions, merchants, and the maritime community during a period of growth, expansion, and technological change in America. Location frequently played a part in a woodworker's success, whether in a rural or an urban environment. The rural craftsman frequently possessed a homestead and farmed his land to help support his family. His land might supply timber used in his trade or as barter in supplement to foodstuffs and other commodities. Frequently his customer base was limited, however, and his distribution area relatively modest. Handyman skills could broaden his income. The urban craftsman had other opportunities and faced somewhat different circumstances. His customer pool often was larger, and in a coastal area it often extended to the maritime community. He frequently lived and worked in rented space without sufficient ground to make a garden, acquiring foodstuffs to feed his family by purchase, sometimes by barter. To pursue his trade, he purchased wood from a local board yard or independent supplier and other materials from specialty shops. Competition frequently was keen, and it increased markedly during the early nineteenth century.

Identifying the Business Site
Integral to establishing a new business was the need to acquaint potential customers with its location. This could be achieved by word of mouth in a small community. In a large urban area, however, even a published notice might not suffice. Jacques-Pierre Brissot de Warville described a common problem when visiting Philadelphia in 1788: "the streets are not inscribed and the doors not numbered." A business newcomer of modest means might identify his location relative to an established business, public building, or the residence of a prominent individual. Many owners identified their place of business with a sign. Early signs frequently were suspended from the facade of the business structure; later signs usually were installed flat against the front of the building.[1]

The common material of the sign was a wooden board, frequently fitted with a plain or decorative framework. A white pine board was the common choice in New England; yellow (tulip) poplar was more prevalent in the Middle Atlantic region and parts of the South. Secondary woods in the framing might include ash, oak, chestnut, or maple. Signs of the late colonial and early federal periods often were of vertical rectangular form, many with a pediment at the top and a shaped skirt at the bottom (fig. 1). Somewhat less common was the horizontal rectangular sign; oval or shield-shape signs were rarer choices. In 1812 William Chappel of Danbury, Connecticut, made special note when he produced an "Ovil sign" for a customer. Relatively uncommon until the early nineteenth century was "painting a sign on tin," a job recorded in 1816 by Allen Holcomb of New Lisbon, New York, for Dr. Walter Wing. By the early nineteenth century the broad distribution of large sheets of tinned iron made this option possible.[2]

Business signs of the late colonial and early federal periods frequently were pictorial. Aside from the occasional name or business of the proprietor, lettering was minimal, since literacy was not universal. The pictorial subject of the sign usually identified the nature of the business. For instance, in 1751 at Philadelphia the sign of the "Tent" identified the shop of Thomas Lawrence, an upholsterer on Second Street, who supplied both household furnishings and military equipment. Ironmonger Peter T. Curtenius of New York chose a "Golden Anvil and Hammer"; elsewhere in the city baker William Mucklevain displayed a sign depicting "Three Biskets." An unusual request by Truman and Company, apothecaries of Providence, Rhode Island, was recorded by William Allen, a local painter and gilder. After "Painting a Sign board" in May 1785, Allen also painted "an Owl to stand on ditto." The complete job cost the proprietors 24s. ($4.00 in later decimal currency). In the following decade Boston painters Daniel Rea Jr. and George Davidson had calls to paint signs identifying a variety of trades (fig. 2). Simon Hall visited Rea in July 1791 for a job described as "painting a Beauro . . . mehogony and Writ'g S. Hall, Cabinet maker on the Sides," indicating the sign was a board for hanging, the printed letters and image visible from

Figure 2   Shop of the Painter and Glazier, in Edward Hazen, *The Panorama of Professions and Trades* (Philadelphia: U. Hunt, 1839), p. 215. (Courtesy, Winterthur Library, Printed Book and Periodical Collection.)

Figure 3 Jeweler's trade sign, Louis Fremeau, Burlington, Vermont, nineteenth century. Carved and painted wood. H. 22″, Diam. 15″. (Courtesy, Collection of Shelburne Museum, gift of Mrs. Louis Fremeau, acc. 1958-5.2; photo, Andy Duback.)

either side, a common practice. William Williams engaged Davidson several years later to paint his "Sine hat Boxes and a Wooden Hatt." The wooden hat appears to have been three-dimensional and was either fixed to the top of the signboard or suspended from the bottom. The cost at £5.2.0 ($17.00 in decimal currency) was relatively substantial. Windsor chair maker Reuben Sanborn also engaged Davidson to prepare his sign featuring a "gold chair." The cost at £5.8.0 ($18.00 in decimal currency) identified work executed in gold leaf, probably on two sides of a suspended board rather than as a three-dimensional object. Sanborn's business site at this date (1799) was Doane's Wharf, a location where he could easily participate in the export trade in vernacular chairs.[3]

Pictorial symbols painted on hanging boards and the occasional suspended three-dimensional object continued in use for business signs into the early nineteenth century. Thomas Boynton of Windsor, Vermont, painted and gilded a sign for silversmiths Johonnot and Smith in September 1815 and then made a "label" lettered "Walk In." The partners called on Boynton again in December, paying $6.00 for a job of "painting and gilding a watch for a Sign" (fig. 3). A popular insignia of the barber's trade was the white-painted pole spirally ornamented with a red band, the red color describing the earlier historical role of barbers as surgeons and bloodletters. Samuel and Daniel Proud of Providence, Rhode Island, recorded "making a Barber Pole" for Phillip Lewis, and a pole valued at $1.50 was in the 1832 estate of William Taylor, a barber of Boston. Pifer Washington Case of Johnstown, New York, had occasion to paint a barber pole for a customer several years later. Whereas cylindrical barber poles were shaped on a turning lathe, George Ritter, a cabinetmaker of Philadelphia, used hewing and shaping tools to fashion a large boot in 1835 for Levick and Jenkins, shoe dealers. The boot, made of yellow poplar, is described as "2 feet 3 [inches] long, the foot 18 inches long . . . 8 in[ches] thick." The job would have required one or two sizable pieces of timber. Given its dimensions, the boot probably functioned as an outdoor sign rather than as an indoor feature. It may have hung suspended from the second story or been fixed on a ledge above the entrance. By this date flat, lettered signs fastened to the business facade had become common advertising pieces, and street names and numbered buildings were common in communities of reasonable size.[4]

Following the War of 1812 use of signage fixed to a building facade, and sometimes along a side, increased measurably as trade began to grow and flourish (fig. 4). Nevertheless, the hanging sign still remained a choice in some locations for several decades. As late as 1820, when William Wood Thackara visited the small community of Tisbury, Massachusetts, on Martha's Vineyard, he remarked that the "sign boards over the shop doors hang out as ostentatiously as though the place contained many thousand inhabitants."[5]

Most fixed signs were wider than their depth, the size determined by the message. A sign made by Timothy Gladding for Peter Gansevoort in 1831 at Albany, New York, for a charge of $1.25 was of modest length and contained the client's name and occupation: "Examiner in Chancery." Requiring more extensive work was a sign constructed at Philadelphia in 1828 by George Ritter for John Jordan, a grocer (see fig. 2). The job, which cost $4.00, was described as "a sign Board 8 feet 3 inches Long [wide] by 18 inches wide [tall] with Walnut Doughftails in Back side & two mouldings on the edge." The dovetails were dovetail keys inserted across the narrow dimension of the wood in shallow slots to strengthen the board and control warping. The moldings on the edges addressed the same issues besides adding a decorative element. Ritter later made a small sign with "moulded edges" for Dr. George F. Alberti. The "4 rose blocks for sine board" turned in the shop of Thomas J. Moyers and Fleming K. Rich at Wythe Court House, Virginia, in January 1838 at a cost of fifty cents were either for the four corners of new work or to refurbish an older sign. The actual surface pattern of the "rose" is unknown, although the modest cost and production method suggest a simple design, likely of concentric circles rather than carved petals.[6]

Once a proper board for a sign was in hand, decoration began with a "priming" coat of paint to cover any irregularities in the wood, followed by one or two coats of the desired ground color. A simple painted border could serve to frame the lettering and any images on the signboard. Although most grounds were plain, there were ornamental options. Grounds could

Figure 4   Drug and paint store, J. & J. Reakirt, Philadelphia, Pennsylvania, ca. 1844. Lithograph drawn by Mathias S. Weaver, printed by Thomas Sinclair. H. 16", W. 13". (Courtesy, The Library Company of Philadelphia.) The building exhibits several types of signs: informational boards fixed flat against the external structure, information painted directly on an exterior surface, and a three-dimensional mortar and pestle suspended at the second-story level at a corner of the building.

be enhanced with smalt, a pigment made principally of finely pulverized cobalt blue glass strewed "on any ground of oil-paint while wet, where it makes a bright warm blue shining surface." George Rutter, a painter of Philadelphia, advertised in 1791 "Signs done with the best Strewing Smaltz." Frédéric Louis Moreau de Saint-Méry, a temporary resident of Philadelphia in the mid-1790s, commented on the city's artisans "who make a specialty of painting remarkably beautiful signboards with backgrounds of different colors, speckled with gold or silver." While in Philadelphia, Moreau de St. Méry opened a printing, stationery, and bookshop at the corner of First and Walnut Streets and commissioned a signboard in English and French.[7]

Most signs were printed with serif letters (see figs. 1, 2, and 4); a few employed cursive lettering that resembled handwriting. Lettering was executed in plain paint contrasting in color with the ground, or in gilt. The charge for the work frequently was calculated by the number of letters. In two separate transactions, William Gray of Salem, Massachusetts, charged 2d. per painted letter and 9d. per gold letter, although prices for both types of work were variable, based on letter size. "Shading," recorded in Vermont by Thomas Boynton, made letters bolder by creating a sense of depth achieved by bordering parts of the letters with a contrasting color

Figure 5 Books of gold leaf, probably England, 1800–1830. Gold leaf interfaced with laid paper. H. 3⁹⁄₁₆", W. 3¹³⁄₁₆" (closed booklet). (Courtesy, Monmouth County Historical Association, Freehold, New Jersey; photo, Winterthur Museum.)

(see fig. 36). On occasion a finished sign was priced by the foot, as occurred in 1837 when William Wilson of Lowell, Massachusetts, charged 3s. per foot for a twenty-four-foot sign. John Doggett of Roxbury, Massachusetts, upon completing a job of gilding a sign, appears to have priced his work by the number of gold leaves or books that were used. His bill of $5.50 to Captain Jesse Doggett in 1808 for gilding his tavern sign, the "Ball and Pin" (skittle), was based on the five and one half books of gold leaf the job required (fig. 5). Doggett's tavern may have been accompanied by sufficient exterior grounds to accommodate the game of ninepins in fair weather.[8]

Little is written about the application of a protective varnish coat to a sign once painting and gilding (if present) were complete. Sparse evidence still remains on some preserved signs, although the practice probably was more common than indicated. The cost was minimal, and it probably was included as part of the cost of overall decorative work. Windsor and fancy seating, except perhaps for the cheapest production, was routinely finished with a coat of "chairmaker's varnish," whether plain painted in the eighteenth century or decorated in the early nineteenth century. Varnish protected the chair's finished surfaces from the wear of use just as a varnish coat could protect an outdoor sign from the abuse of weather. Luke Houghton, a cabinetmaker and chair maker of Barre, Massachusetts, recorded a fifty-cent charge to Kendall and Baker in 1816 for varnishing a sign, probably one already in use and in need of minor refurbishing.[9]

Once a signboard was completed, it required installation. Craft accounts and other records suggest how this was accomplished. Jacob Mordecai, when recalling his youth in pre-revolutionary Philadelphia, described a sign for the fashionable retail shop of George Bartram: "the Golden Fleece, a gilt lamb suspended half way across the pavements in 2d Street near Carter's Alley." The support appears to have been a horizontal arm fixed to the building (fig. 6). A similar arrangement was recorded in 1815 by Thomas Boynton at Windsor, Vermont. After supplying Frederick Pettes, innkeeper, with a

Figure 6   Detail of a delegation of Native Americans to Philadelphia, *New Lutheran Church, in Fourth Street Philadelphia*, drawn, engraved, and colored by William Russell Birch (1755–1844) and Thomas Birch (1779–1851), published in *The City of Philadelphia . . . as It Appeared in the Year 1800* [hereafter *Birch's Views of Philadelphia*] (Philadelphia: W. Birch and Son, 1800), plate 6. (Courtesy, Winterthur Library, Printed Book and Periodical Collection.) The scene describes a method of hanging shop signs above the walkways of the city. The male figure with an outstretched arm at the right front is said to be Frederick Augustus Muhlenberg, speaker of the U.S. House of Representatives.

"Sign Stage House" for $3.00, Boynton added another fifty-cent charge for "painting arm and hanging d[itt]o." Not identified but part of this work were "the Irons" necessary for hanging the sign. These metal straps with eyelets at the top to engage metal hooks on the arm were fixed to the side edges or the top of the sign (see fig. 1). An alternative method of installation involved a freestanding post with or without an arm at the top (see fig. 7). An early record is Joseph Bolton's work in 1762 of hanging a sign from a post in front of the shop of Stephen Collins, an up-and-coming storekeeper/merchant in Philadelphia. Later, in 1789, Gershom Jones, a pewterer of Providence, Rhode Island, hired Job Danforth Sr. to make a signpost and install his sign.[10]

Two methods of preparing posts are indicated in records. Paul Jenkins of Kennebunk, Maine, recorded hewing a signpost, whereas Moses Parkhurst of Paxton, Massachusetts, described "turning sign posts." An indication of the time required to prepare some signposts is noted in the accounts of William Fifield of Lyme, New Hampshire, when in 1821 he recorded "1 Day work on Sign post." Installation of a long, flat sign to be mounted flush against a building was a different challenge. After William Wilson made a ten-foot sign for customer W. C. Burrows at Lowell, Massachusetts, in 1837, he used a "Crain" to help secure it in place. At this date the crane would have been a human-powered hoisting device. Not all signs were as professional as those described. John Bernard, a Briton traveling in the Carolinas about 1800, commented on the common rural ordinary (tavern): "You might

Figure 7 Detail of *Virtue and Vice, Sobriety and Drunkenness*, Thomas Birch, Philadelphia, ca. 1830. Ink and watercolor on paper. H. 10¹⁄₁₆", W. 14⁷⁄₁₆". (Courtesy, Winterthur Museum, acc. 67.0131.)

always know an ordinary, on emerging from the woods, by an earthen jug suspended by the handle from a pole . . . or a score of black hogs luxuriating in the sunshine and mud before the door" (fig. 7).[11]

Maintenance at the Business Site

Miscellaneous woodworking and related work at the business site was an ongoing call; many jobs were incidental in nature, while others were more extensive. An infrequent request was for "moving" the shop. Of two recorded late eighteenth-century jobs—one in Hartford, the other in Danbury, Connecticut—one required a full day and the other a half day of the craftsman's time. The modest costs indicate the moves involved transferring shop contents to other facilities rather than physically moving the structures. If the work had represented physical moves of the shops, the craftsmen involved probably would have provided "roolers [rollers] for moooving bildings," such as those purchased in 1820 by Zachariah Chafee, a mason of Providence, Rhode Island, from Samuel and Daniel Proud (fig. 8). An extensive job of a different type, completed by Thomas Christy at Boston, Massachusetts, in 1782 for Moses Grant, an upholsterer and shopkeeper, involved "putt'g a new front To the shop he improved

belonging to his Father." Outdoor activity by craftsmen in other locations included work on a shop roof and a job that required "three days a
Shingling Store" accompanied by "pa[i]nting Coving." Constructing new
or replacement steps at a business site was a recurring request in all areas,
from Gloucester, Massachusetts, to Newport, Rhode Island, to Middletown, New Jersey. Some steps were painted; others, apparently, were left
in the wood. Henry Wansey, an English visitor to America during the
mid-1790s, commented when visiting Philadelphia: "Almost every house of
trade has an assent of steps to enter, and a sloping cellar window or door
to receive goods" (see figs. 4 and 9).[12]

Two unusual references of mid-eighteenth-century date posed an initial
interpretative challenge. A customer at Reading, Massachusetts, requested
Peter Emerson to make "Bords for Shop winders [windows]," the cost
amounting to a significant £1.5.0 ($4.17 in later decimal currency). Abraham
Dennis of Newport, Rhode Island, engaged Job Townsend Jr. for a similar job:
"Fixing a Board on his Shop window." What was the purpose of the boards?
Both references became clearer in the early nineteenth-century accounts
of George Ritter of Philadelphia when Abel Wyman, a shoe dealer, engaged
the cabinetmaker for "Making, painting & fixing two show Brackets at front

Figure 9 Detail of shop facades adjacent to Christ Church, Philadelphia, from *Christ Church, 1811*, by William Strickland (1787–1854), Philadelphia, Pennsylvania, 1811. Oil on canvas. Overall H. 48", W. 52". (Courtesy, Historical Society of Pennsylvania Collection, Bridgeman Images.) The shop facades detail a show box next to the shop door at the left and interior display shelves at transom levels in the bow window and the windows of the adjacent building at the right.

door of Store." Made of pine, these tall, slim boxlike containers with shelves were used to display merchandise similar to that available in the store. A single show box at the front door of a shop is depicted in figure 9, where it is accompanied by a large bowed shop window, describing in its particular character the purpose of the boards for shop windows. Horizontal shelves for displaying merchandise were fixed to the interior woodwork, each shelf positioned at a transom level of the window. In 1791 when working for the local merchant Charles Shoemaker, Philadelphian David Evans described a similar job as "4 Shelves for Store Windows." Two shelves for displaying footwear are installed at transom level in a large window viewed from inside a shoemaking shop (see fig. 14).[13]

Aside from carpentry, exterior shop and store work called for painting. A substantial job of "painting Shop twice over" for John Munroe of Barnstable, Massachusetts, at a cost of $7.50, probably engaged the painter Nathaniel Holmes the better part of one week (see fig. 2). The work was accompanied by priming a blind, or outside shutter, and "finding paint." After "grinding green and puting it on," Holmes continued by painting the door, shop steps, and pump, probably with the same green. Of particular note because of its rare mention is work undertaken by Thomas Boynton in painting and then "Pencilling Store front" for G. W. and C. F. Merrifield, printers at Windsor, Vermont. The principal tool used for this work was a fine-tipped camel's-hair brush, called a pencil, with which a skilled painter could create decorative work consisting of thin straight or curved lines to emphasize structural features, such as a doorway or window, or create the illusion of paneled features.[14]

A cheap way of brightening outdoor walls or common structures was by using whitewash, a mixture of lime and water. A better quality of work employed Spanish whiting or oyster-shell white mixed with size and water. Frederick K. Coady, a craftsman of upstate Ogdensburg, New York, recorded at least two instances of whitewashing, one at a customer's store, the other at a shop. Miscellaneous jobs performed by woodworking craftsmen included a variety of incidental tasks. Job E. Townsend installed a lock on the "Store Door" of Phillip Morss (Morse?) in 1788 at Newport, Rhode Island, and William Wilson supplied "1 Door plate" priced at twenty-five cents some years later for the shop and office of A. W. Moulton at Lowell, Massachusetts. The plate may have resembled those advertised in 1791 at Philadelphia: "Japanned Plates for Window Shutters, Doors, &c. elegantly wrote or printed in Gold Letters."[15]

Interior work at the business site was as varied as exterior work. Grocer Richard P. Foulke of Philadelphia had substantial "Carpenters work" done at his store at the "Corner of filbert street and 8th" in 1822 by Joseph Dives. Record of an exact business address for a customer, as here, is a rarity in craftsmen's records. Jobs involving windows and doors actually fall into a category of inside-outside work. Richard Blow, a storekeeper and merchant in Norfolk, Virginia, engaged Hatter and Miller in 1783 for a job at the store that included glazing eighty-five lights (window panes), for which the workmen cut sixty-four new panes of glass and supplied the putty (see fig. 2). Similar jobs elsewhere were more modest by comparison. Pease and Fowler of Middletown, Connecticut, engaged Elizur Barnes to set two squares of glass in the shop door. A rowdy youth led Silas E. Cheney, a cabinetmaker of Litchfield, Connecticut, to charge the father twelve cents for "your boy breaking Glass out [of] Shop." Owners of facilities other than stores and shops also called on skilled artisans for related work. Proprietors of the Levi Shephard and Sons factory at Northampton, Massachusetts, employed Harris Beckwith in 1805 to make "two Window frames and Sashes for the factory." Two years earlier Beckwith had worked for Job White making "A Door for your Shop" then "Caseing and hanging the same."[16]

Structural work within the shop accounted for a variety of other jobs. A customer of Job E. Townsend at Newport, Rhode Island, hired him for "Putting up a Pertiation in the Shop." Another customer requested that he move a partition to another location in the shop. Both jobs were priced in the general range of three dollars, aside from materials, and likely required several days of the craftsman's time. During the same period (ca. 1800), Townsend also worked at the shop of Edward Stanhope "Cutting a hole for a Stove Pipe." The dimensions of this type of job were stated in more detail by Job Danforth Sr. at Providence, Rhode Island, when working at the shop of Robert Adam: "cutting holes in the floor and Roof . . . for your Stove pipe." Dur-

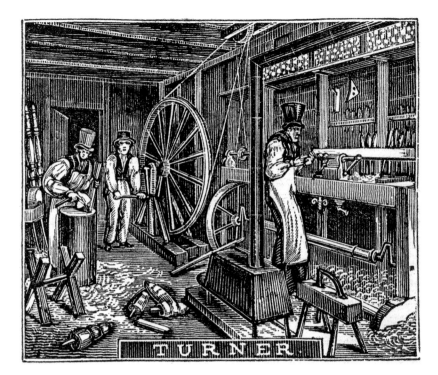

ing the late eighteenth century, metal stoves rapidly replaced the hearth as
the heat source for craft shops and stores. Metal stoves burned fuel more
efficiently, were freestanding, and radiated heat in all directions (fig. 10; also
see fig. 47). Another job, described by Horace Beckwith of Northampton,
Massachusetts, as "two days Work in your Blacksmith Shop Laying floor,"
cost Charles Chapman twelve shillings. The six-shilling wage per day, as
indicated, was a good average pay for a skilled craftsman during much of
the period under discussion. When the British currency system was replaced
with a decimal system in the 1790s, six shillings were equated with one dollar throughout the United States, except for New York, where the figure
frequently was eight shillings New York currency.[17]

Interior painting was a recurring need in many places of business. After
the extensive glazing work at Richards Blow's commercial facility in Virginia, Hatton and Miller followed with "painting ye inside of ye Store."
Successful retailers found that their premises required periodic refurbishing, much as proprietors of well frequented inns and taverns needed to
remain alert to the maintenance of their properties. During the early 1840s
several facilities in the town of Windsor, Vermont, a flourishing and handsome commercial center on the Connecticut River, benefitted from the services of Thomas Boynton. Innkeeper Samuel Patrick hired him to paint the
"south room and dining room floor in [the] Tavern." The $4.50 charge was
covered in part by an earlier credit for Patrick who had supplied Boynton
with "1 Cord of wood, 1/2 Bass wood" and "a turkey for thanksgiving."
A substantial job took Boynton to the Windsor Tavern Company, where he
was engaged in a process he termed "Stamp painting" in the "2d & 3d Entry
Halls" and the "Dining room and setting room." This work was followed by
"varnishing [the] 2d Hall" and "Varnishing [the] Dining room and reading

room floors with 3 gall[on]s [of] varnish." While on the premises, Boynton also lettered and numbered doors, hung bells, and provided a "Sign Windsor House." The complete job amounted to $68.68. At Ogdensburg, New York, in 1842 Frederick K. Coady painted the floor twice at G. N. Seymour's store. An uncommon call earlier the same year found him papering the shop of S. B. Strickland.[18]

Supplying the Specific Needs of Business

The accounts of foreign visitors to America and commentary by residents attest to the substantial variety of trades practiced in the American colonies prior to the Revolutionary War. Following the conflict, corresponding documents describe the rapid expansion and proliferation of craft shops and large and small businesses in concert with the expansion of mercantile activity, both domestic and foreign. This section will focus on the activities cited most frequently in the material gathered for this study—whether pertaining to trades, shops, stores, professions, merchandising, or commerce—to understand better the woodworker's critical role in supporting and shaping the business community.

Craft Shops

Hatters

Work for hatters, and to a lesser extent for milliners, was a frequent call at the woodworking shop. George G. Channing of Newport, Rhode Island, grandson of William Ellery, a signer of the Declaration of Independence, recalled the early nineteenth-century years of his youth and noted that beaver hats were costly and worn only by a few gentlemen. Continuing, he identified the felt hat made from less costly fur "stiffened with paste and glue" (later with gum shellac) as the common head wear of men and boys. Wind, dampness, and rain took their toll, and under those conditions, owners were required to "block out" the bodies and rims of their hats or they assumed "the most grotesque and forlorn shapes imaginable."[19]

In June 1773 Samuel Williams, a Philadelphia "joiner" with a board yard on Fourth Street between Market and Chestnut, advertised "4 inch poplar plank for hatters," describing the material of hat blocks used locally. Purchased individually or by the dozens from woodworkers everywhere, the cylindrical hat block was an essential commodity. Hatters used them in large numbers: blocks to shape the body of the hat; separate blocks for the dyeing process; other blocks for the finishing process. The more than 200 "Colouring Blocks" purchased by hatter William Washburn of Kingston, Massachusetts, between 1824 and 1827 from Nathan Lucas were for use in the dye bath. Two Connecticut woodworkers, Jeduthern Avery and Samuel Durand, specifically identified a "hat block for finishing hats on." Sales of hat blocks to Thomas Tilestone, a hatter of Windham, Connecticut, by Amos D. Allen identify block size and fabrication methods: "6 Hatblocks sawed 7 In across at the band, 7½ at top, 5 In high" and "1 Hatblock made of seasoned stuf glued and Turned 6½ Deep, 7 by 7⅞." The cost of a hat block ranged from fifteen to fifty cents depending on size, fabrication, use, and other factors. On occasion, alterations were made to hat blocks already in use, as recorded in Maine by Paul Jenkins.[20]

The hatter's bow, a rod with an attached string, was an essential tool in creating the body of a hat. The bow string, plucked through use of a wooden pin, created vibrations aligning the foundation fibers into a pad. Covered with a damp piece of linen and compressed with a hatter's basket—a flat piece of woven work—the pad was exposed to moisture and heat and the fibers gradually matted by hand into a felt forming the body of the hat. The hatter then applied the stiffening, which was solidified in a steam box. One or more layers of fur for the nap were prepared in the same manner, following which the nap was raised with a brush or toothed instrument. The hat was then placed in the dye bath, after which it was washed and dried and turned over to a finisher. Figure 11 provides a visual description of the hat-

Figure 11 *Shop of the Hatter*, in Edward Hazen, *The Panorama of Professions and Trades* (Philadelphia: U. Hunt, 1839), p. 52. (Courtesy, Winterthur Library, Printed Book and Periodical Collection.)

making process. In the right foreground a workman uses a hatter's bow, while the background shows other workmen shaping mats in hot water baths. The large wheel is the dyeing mechanism fitted with many blocks on which the hats are hung. The wheel, turned with a crank, immerses part of the hats at a time in the dye bath until they are properly colored. Beyond hat blocks, craftsmen supplied several tools of hat making. Samuel Wing of Sandwich and Abner Taylor of Lee, Massachusetts, made hatter's bows; Taylor also bored blocks for brushes used in raising the nap. The Proud brothers of Providence and Job Townsend Jr. of Newport, Rhode Island, recorded sales of bow pins. At Philadelphia the accounts of Daniel Trotter list sales of hatter's baskets and bows.[21]

Although bonnet making was a trade that gave employ and even owner-ship of a business to many women, the craft was dominated by men. Just as wooden hat blocks were critical to fabricating male head wear, shaped wooden blocks for forming the crowns of women's cloth hats were criti-cal tools of the millinery trade. Buckram, made of hemp or coarse linen stiffened with sizing, was the common choice for the crown. To this was attached pasteboard or buckram edged with wire to form the front part of the hat, according to prevailing fashion. A cloth lining and a finish cover of silk, satin, muslin, or the like, completed the basic work prior to the applica-tion of ornament, such as ribbons, lace, artificial flowers, feathers, and other materials (fig. 12). Many women's hats were made of straw; some were of domestic fabrication, although Leghorn hats imported from the vicinity of Livorno, Italy, were exceedingly popular. Straw for use in hats was cut to length, whitened (bleached), split, and pressed using a simple machine. The splits were braided into plaits, which were then sewed together to

form a hat. American merchants imported both finished hats and plaits for domestic assembly.[22]

Documents identify a variety of woodworking shops that supplied tools and materials for the milliner's trade. Elizur Barnes of Middletown, Con-necticut, sold a customer "Bonnet blocks For Daughter" in 1822. The same decade Deborah Chamberlain purchased "2 bunet blocks" directly from Allen Holcomb at New Lisbon, New York. Two craftsmen, George Landon of Erie, Pennsylvania, and John Cate of Wolfeboro, New Hampshire, sold bonnet blocks produced on turning lathes. Accounts of other craftsmen address the woven hat trade. Solomon Cole of Connecticut provided several customers at Glastonbury with "splits" for bonnets. Two accounts identify a machine to process straw splits: Abner Haven of Framingham, Massachusetts, repaired a machine already in use, whereas Elisha Blossom Jr. of New York constructed a "Mill for pressing split straw" priced at $8.00 for Miss Zebiah Richards. The mill likely had rollers operated by a hand crank. Elizur Barnes went a step further in "Fixing a Box for Bleaching Bonets" for Miss Johnson, milliner. Edward Hazen notes in his discussion of the milliner's trade that "great quantities of straw are . . . plaited in families, especially in the New-England states, and sold to neighboring merchants, who, in turn, dispose of it to those who form it into hats." The accounts of Abner Taylor of Lee, Massachusetts, may actually reference this cottage industry in an 1812 charge of $1.75 to a customer for "womens work on bonnets."[23]

Whereas both hatters and milliners sold many hats individually to customers—and occasionally small boxes to store them—a significant part of the hat business was in quantity sales, which required boxes or cases to transport the merchandise to retail facilities. At about thirty cents apiece, individual boxes for women's hats were cheaper than those for men, which cost approximately fifty cents apiece, probably reflecting the differences in size of the products. Several hat boxes made of chestnut in eastern Connecticut by Perez Austin cost seventy-five cents apiece, although it is possible that each held more than one hat. Reflecting quantity sales, Austin also charged Joseph Simms $2.50 for "Carrin [carrying] Hats to Norwich," likely for deposit at a retail facility for distribution or with a coastal trader (fig. 13). The dimensions of a large box to hold men's hats for broad distribution was recorded by George Ritter at Philadelphia in the 1820s: "a Hatt Box 3 feet 8 long by 2 feet 2 high and 2 feet wide having eight divisions to contain 2 doz Hatts." In the same decade Nathan Cleaveland of Franklin, Massachusetts, made a significant number of bonnet cases, large and small, for Davis Thayer

Figure 13 Detail of the *Hat Store of C. and J. H. Bulkley*, Philadelphia, Pennsylvania, ca. 1833. Lithograph printed by Childs and Inman. H. 7½", W. 10½". (Courtesy, The Library Company of Philadelphia.) The right-side return of the sign reads "BEAVER HATS."

and Company, charging by the box or the time spent making boxes. On one occasion Cleaveland charged fifty-six cents for "half a days work making Bonnet Cases." A month later he posted a ninety-two-cent charge for "half a days work myself and Apprentice makeing Cases." If similar conditions are represented, simple arithmetic indicates the apprentice's time was charged at thirty-six cents per half day. The accounts of William Wilson, a painter at Lowell, shed light on the further accommodation of bonnets. For one customer he varnished, or stained and varnished, more than a dozen bonnet stands (see fig. 12). Another patron requested that he varnish a "Bonnet tree." Whether the tree furnished a retail facility or a domestic setting, it served its purpose: display or temporary storage.[24]

Figure 14   *The Shoemakers*, New York, ca. 1855. Chromolithograph printed by E. B. and E. C. Kellogg. H. 8½", W. 12½". (Courtesy, Connecticut Historical Society, acc. 1982.7.8.)

Shoemakers

Many references to making a "shoemaker's bench" or a "shoemaker's seat" appear in woodworkers' accounts, and comparison of the pricing suggests the terms identify the same equipment. Common pricing varies from 6s. to 7s. 6p. ($1.00 to $1.25), a few prices lower and several higher, including "a Shoemakers seat with a drawer" at 9s. ($1.50) made by Titus Preston of Wallingford, Connecticut, in 1807 for Phineas Pond. Three shoemaker's seats, each with a drawer, are pictured in figure 14. Boards abutting the shop window display finished footwear, lasts (foot models) are scattered on the floor or secured in a wall rack, and a songbird in a cage presages piped-in music of a later era. Tools and pieces of leather are scattered about the room. Edward Hazen described the shop activity in general terms: "The materials are cut out and fitted by the foreman, or by the person who carries on the business [right], whilst the pieces are stitched together and the work finished by workmen who sit upon the bench." Insight into the preparation of the wooden lasts is recorded by David Pritchard of Wallingford, Connecticut, relative to customer James Harrison: "for the use of my Shop in part to Turn Lasts three weeks."[25]

In making a boot or shoe of leather, the parts forming the "uppers," precut to size, were stitched together and attached to a sole, which approximated the length and width of the customer's foot. Inner and outer soles were attached by sewing and nailing. The workman at left is preparing a leather outer sole on a smooth stone known as a lapstone, which is balanced on his lap. Using the broad face of the shoemaker's hammer, the leather sole is condensed and made more durable by pounding it. Either this workman or the workman facing him would have presoaked the leather they are working in the stave-formed bucket in the foreground. The workman at center left holds an awl in his right hand to punch holes in a sole to accommodate stitching. The third benchman, his back to the viewer, has shoe thread wrapped around one hand and holds a sewing "needle" fashioned from a hog's bristle in the other hand. Common shoe thread was made from waxed flax; a stronger variety was made of hemp. The work at hand was placed between the craftsman's knees and held fast using a shoemaker's stirrup, a leather loop placed around the work and one knee and held taut by the foot. The benchmen at the right and center use stirrups. A quicker alternative method of fastening soles and uppers of shoes and boots employed wooden pegs, although footwear made by this system was not as durable or as easy to repair. Philip Deland, a woodworker of West Brookfield, Massachusetts, furnished "one peg bench with a drawer &c." at $3.00 to a shoemaking customer in 1829 along with "one pegsett first rate" at thirty-four cents and a "doubble peg sett." Deland supplied another shoemaking customer with six awl helves (handles). In Rhode Island Job E. Townsend charged 2s. 3d. (37½¢) for "a Mallet for Pounding Leather." Useful to the trade were "Boot Trees" for preserving boot shape, which Lemuel Tobey sold to a customer at Dartmouth, Massachusetts (see fig. 14, near right wall) along with a "Sho[e]makers Bench." A "small Candle stick for shoemaker" made by Robert Whitelaw of Ryegate, Vermont, was useful in winter, when craftsmen of many trades frequently were at the bench before sunrise or after sunset.[26]

The accounts of Wait Stoddard, tanner, currier, and cordwainer (shoemaker), of Windham, Connecticut, with Amos D. Allen, cabinetmaker and chair maker, provide insight into the business of supplying a family with new footwear during a three-year period. A pair of "Calf skin Shoes" bought by Allen for himself at 10s. ($1.67) in January 1800 is described more completely in a later ten-shilling purchase: "1 pair Calf skin Shoes Lin[e]d and bound." The binding was a thin strip of leather sewed around the top edge. A pair of "Womans Shoes" listed at 7s. ($1.17) may have been fabricated of prunella, a "twilled, worsted cloth" popular for women's footwear, although the soles were made of leather. Slippers also are listed, one entry describing "4 pair of green slips" at 3s. 6d. (58¢). These may resemble the footwear of the workers seated on the benches in figure 14. Other entries address repairs: "new topping pair [of] boots" or "Soalling pair boots." If an entire new sole or heel was not required, a piece of leather know as a tap might be used to renew a worn heel or sole. Stoddard supplied Allen with leather for other purposes: calf, morocco, lamb and sheep skins, and "1 Side harness leather" weighing ten pounds. Allen repaid Stoddard for services and materials with a variety of barter goods: bushels of grain, a silver watch, furniture and furniture repairs, and use of his wagon. In the early nineteenth century several communities became shoe manufacturing centers, supplying in part the export market, including Lynn, Massachusetts, where "scarcely a house . . . is not inhabited by a shoemaker," and Newark, New Jersey, where one manufacturer employed from 300 to 400 workmen.[27]

Other Crafts

References to the interactions between woodworkers and other members of the craft community in the material at hand are scattered, although they document the nature of those contacts. Most common are references to individuals in the metal-working trades. George Ritter of Philadelphia repaired "a T-square" in 1837 for the journeyman of Nicholas Kohlencamp, a tinsmith. Several references focus on iron processing. In 1790 Job Danforth Sr. of Providence, Rhode Island, billed Amos Throop for "work Done on y[ou]r black smiths shop." Danforth returned three years later for a job of "diging and puting a pipe to [the] water works," identifying the power source used to operate the bellows in Throop's forge. Water, apparently, was the power that operated the large trip hammer that William Fifield serviced two decades later at James Proctor's iron works at Lyme, New Hampshire, a town watered by three streams that empty into the Connecticut River. At Atsion Furnace in the pine barrens of central New Jersey, work often focused on patterns for stoves and chimney backs. Two Philadelphia craftsmen, John Folwell in the 1770s and Daniel Trotter in the 1780s, supplied some of the "molds" necessary for casting. Trotter also furnished patterns for sash weights and andirons.[28]

The button, a fastener for clothing, was an item of popular request. Crafted from many materials—base or precious metal, bone, mother-of-pearl, glass, wood—the button represented a basic convenience or a fashion statement. Merchants imported quantities of buttons, and by 1798 Timothy Dwight, president of Yale College and commentator on New England society of the early republic, noted a substantial manufacture of "gilt buttons" in the town of Waterbury, Connecticut. Before the widespread availability of manufactured buttons, however, inexpensive turned wooden button molds were in the market. Ranging in price from slightly more than 1d. to 3d. (1½–4¢), these disks were covered with cloth appropriate to their use. A notice for a runaway "Irish Servant Man" in the *New York Weekly Journal* of March 22, 1742, describes the clothes worn by the absconder: "a Felt Hat, a blue drab jacket, an outside Jacket black and white homespun drugget [a coarse common cloth] shorter than the blue one, Buttons covered with the same." Thomas Pratt of Malden, Massachusetts, sold "fifteen buttonmolds" to a customer in the following decade for one pence apiece, but that quantity was eclipsed some years later by purchases made at Ipswich by Benjamin Ross, who likely was a tailor. From 1781 to 1783 Ross acquired 237 dozen molds at two pence per mold and thirty-four and one half dozen at three pence. He also purchased a "but[to]n hole board," probably a gauge to size buttonholes to buttons.[29]

Figure 15 Lewis Miller (1796–1882), *Jacob Nell, Barber, Shaving Nicklas Huber*, York, Pennsylvania, ca. 1815–1825. Small ink and watercolor drawing and text on paper. (Courtesy, York County History Center, York, Pa.)

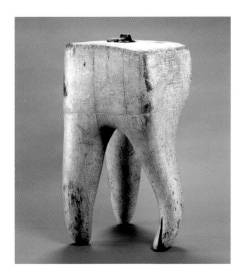

Figure 16 Dental trade sign of large tooth, date unknown. Carved and painted wood. H. 23¾", W. 12½", D. 13½". (Courtesy, Collection of Shelburne Museum, gift of Julius Jarvis, acc. 1962-181.)

Barbers and Dentists

Specialized seating for barbers and dentists was uncommon until the early nineteenth century. Prior to that time chairs with tall backs to support the head were pressed into service when needed. "Elbows" to support the arms, although convenient, were not necessarily present. As dedicated chairs came onto the market, an adjustable headrest became a feature (fig. 15). Some chairs also had legs of extra length. George Landon, a cabinetmaker of Erie, Pennsylvania, sold a "Barber Chair" in August 1821 to a customer for $2.50. The cost included the 62½¢ Landon credited to another individual in that month for "irons for [back of] barber chair." Shaving customers was as important a function of the barber as was cutting and dressing hair. Smith and Lippins, black barbers at 365 Broad Street in Newark, New Jersey, near David Alling's chair manufactory, placed an order with Alling in 1837 for a barber chair, four Windsor chairs, and two low stools to furnish or expand the seating at their place of business. A low stool could support a customer's feet when "in the chair." Another customer ordered a caned curled-maple barber's chair and a "morocco" seat cushion en suite. One focus of George Ritter's cabinetmaking business at 72 North Fourth Street, Philadelphia, a few years earlier was chairs for dentists. McElheney and Van Pelt purchased "a Dentists portable mah[ogan]y chair with fall Back hung with quadrants, & [a] circular Screw seat" at $15.00. The seat was similar to a piano stool, and the quadrants were quarter-circle metal hinges for adjusting the chair back. A related "mahagany Dentists operating chair" made for another customer for $25.00 had a "screw circular seat stuffed with curled hair & covered with black hair cloth." Samuel C. Bunting, a merchant on Third Street, placed an unusual order for a mahogany dentist's chair with quadrants and revolving seat that stood on a board 3 feet, 5 inches long and was equipped with a "Mah[ogan]y toe board [and] irens underneth" the seat. The chair was not unlike a seat for an invalid without the large wheels. Bunting also requested a packing box, special packing, and portage to his shipping location at 28 South Wharves, where the chair was forwarded to the customer. Shopping in urban areas in this period was accomplished principally on foot. Proximity of location and the high level of Ritter's skill, as attested in his accounts, attracted Bunting and others to his shop. Whether in an urban setting or a town location, however, a hanging trade sign at a dentist's door, such as that illustrated in figure 16, could be quite direct.[30]

Physicians and Apothecaries

Prior to the mid-eighteenth century gaining a medical education in America was accomplished by serving an apprenticeship with a practicing physician or surgeon. Medical ranks were strengthened in urban areas by the arrival of individuals trained in the centers of learning in Europe. Gradually the study and practice of medicine in America became systematized, with marked improvement of professional standards. Philadelphia, for example,

Figure 17 William Jennys (1774–1858), *Portrait of Dr. John Brickett* [1774–1848], Newburyport, Massachusetts, ca. 1805–1807. Oil on canvas. H. 29½", W. 25". (Courtesy, Collections of the Museum of Old Newbury.) Dr. Brickett also was an apothecary and is portrayed holding a leather-bound volume of *Materia Medica*.

became a center of medical activity where young men were encouraged to travel abroad to study at the important centers of Edinburgh, London, and, occasionally, Paris. Medical lectures, papers, and research began to be published regularly and disseminated. By 1756 the city's medical profession realized a long-held goal of opening a hospital to serve the community. There followed in the 1760s the establishment of a medical school at the Pennsylvania Hospital and another at King's College (later Columbia), New York. Members of the associated craft of apothecary specialized in preparing "different ingredients to form [medicinal] compounds," and besides serving physicians they could prescribe treatment and distribute remedies to their own clientele. When an area was without an apothecary, local physicians supplied the medicinal needs of patients (fig. 17). Dr. John Brickett, who also was an apothecary, is seen holding a leather-bound copy of *Materia Medica*, describing the natural and compounded substances used in treating diseases. Colleges of pharmacy were established in Philadelphia and New York during the early nineteenth century.[31]

Nests of drawers, or cases, were common at the business site of both the physician and the apothecary. As early as 1759 Dr. John Newman ordered "a Case with 40 small Draws" for £1.12.0 ($5.33) from a member of the Lunt family at Newbury, Massachusetts. Many decades later, in 1824, Dr. Charles Dyer of Middletown, Connecticut, paid Elizur Barnes $68.00 for "a Case of apothacary in 4 parts—34 Draws in Each, Total 136 Draws at 50 ct" each. Whereas nests of drawers were popular with members of the medical community throughout New England, they also were in use in the Middle Atlantic and other regions. Wilmer Worthington of West Chester, Pennsylvania, probably an apothecary, acquired "A Medacine Case (27 Draws)" in 1826 from Amos Darlington Jr. Upon installation of a case of drawers, the proprietor of a shop arranged to have the contents labeled. Daniel Rea Jr., ornamental painter of Boston, had several calls of note. "Paint[in]g & Lableing" for Dr. William Jackson in 1792 included sixty large drawers and seventy of smaller size. A job for Samuel Miller, an apothecary, included painting, ornamenting, and labeling fifty-seven drawers. Miller also requested Rea to paint, gild, and label thirty-one bottles. Truman and Company was hired by William Allen of Providence, Rhode Island, in 1784 to paint "Specia Bottles," large containers used for storage. The same year Samuel Blythe painted and gilded two "Canisters," or small boxes, possibly made of metal, at Boston for Dr. William Sterns. Wooden boxes were particularly useful in the medical business for drugs, pills, salts, and the like. Robert Rantoul, an apothecary and minor merchant of Beverly Massachusetts, engaged Ebenezer Smith Jr. in 1812 to cut "14 lb Quasha wood," a medicinal bark or wood from Surinam (formerly Dutch Guiana) used to make a tonic. A storage box would have been useful, or perhaps Rantoul had a "pair of large Drawers for Drugs," as found on the premises of David Eaton in Chester County, Pennsylvania. By the 1840s wholesale druggists were established in commercial centers such as Philadelphia, where J. and J. Reakirt occupied a prominent corner location and displayed a hanging mortar and pestle along with the flat signage on their building (see fig. 4).[32]

When details are unavailable, the medicine chest is distinguished from the medicine case by its price, which centered in the one-dollar range. That was the cost of Dr. Dyers' chest; his case, with its many drawers, cost $68.00, as indicated. Dr. Burley Smart ordered a "medicen chest with Lock" at Kennebunk, Maine, for $1.00 from Paul Jenkins. A more particular account of a chest describes one made for Dr. Jonathan Easton in 1798 at Newport, Rhode Island, by Job E. Townsend: "To A medeson Chest 20 Inches Long and 14 Inches Wide & 7 Deepe, In the clear [open interior] 12 Partings [partitions]." The 15s. charge ($2.50) reflects the overall size of the case and the extra work of installing the partitions. Dr. Dyer's patronage of Elizur Barnes extended to the purchase of furniture for his establishment in the form of "a Cherry Show Case" at $6.50. Some physicians placed emphasis on other forms (fig. 18). Dr. John Morris of York, Pennsylvania, used a sturdy paneled cupboard and shelving to support his labeled bottles, large and small, and a long chest with tiers of drawers both for other medical storage and as a support for a distillation apparatus. A "large pine book case with 2 drass [drawers] & painted in Side & out" purchased by Dr. Smart from Paul Jenkins was a form found in other physicians' offices. The 1838 estate

Figure 18 Lewis Miller, *Office of Dr. Johan*
[John] *Morris*, York, Pennsylvania, 1800.
Ink and watercolor drawing and text on paper.
(Courtesy, York County History Center, York,
Pa.) Pictured are Dr. Morris, Lewis Miller Sr., and
his young son Lewis, later the chronicler of York.

papers of Dr. Jacob Ehrenzeller at West Chester, Pennsylvania, list a "Book
case" in the "Office" valued at $10.00 and "Books in Book case" estimated
at $50.00, describing a substantial medical library. A desk and portable desk
also furnished Dr. Ehrenzeller's office. Throughout the period of this study,
the desk was considered essential equipment for a physician. A "Wrighting
Desk & Stool" purchased from David Evans in 1790 at Philadelphia cost
Dr. John H. Gibbons £2.12.6 ($8.75). With Evans's cabinet shop being at
115 Mulberry (Arch) Street, Gibbons office at 103 Mulberry was just a short
walk away.[33]

STORES AND SHOPS

The terms *store* and *shop* frequently are defined as interchangeable words,
each representing a place where goods are kept for sale. Occasionally the
store is identified as a shop of large size. The following discussion will
focus principally on businesses described as stores in recorded transactions
with members of the woodworking community. Shops are included when
the nature of their business purchases suggests, or as a directory listing or
other information signifies, that substantial retail activity was pursued.

    In most cases a moderate retail business is identified when either or both
of two types of business furniture is indicated—the counter, such as that
in the store of Captain Andrew Johnson (fig. 19), or the showcase. Peter
Marselis's work at New York in 1779 for the firm of Taylor and Bayard
involved "making a Dish Counter & Shelves in their Store." In many cases
the counter may have been no more than a sturdy box open at the back, with
or without a bottom. That would explain storekeeper William Barrell's hir-
ing John Hall, a carpenter of Philadelphia, to install a bottom in his counter,
or Job E. Townsend's work for a customer at Newport, Rhode Island, in

Figure 19 Lewis Miller, *Store of Captain Andrew
Johnson, Merchant*, York, Pennsylvania, 1800.
Ink and watercolor drawing and text on paper.
(Courtesy, York County History Center, York, Pa.)

constructing "a Draw for his Counter in Shop." George Ritter of Philadelphia made a special drawer accommodation described as a "patent Spring thimble-drawer lock with two Keys for counter drawer," and at Litchfield, Connecticut, Silas E. Cheney recorded another occasional job as "putting railing to Counter." Cherry is identified in one instance as the material of the counter, although the variety of finishes described in accounts indicates that cheaper woods were more common for counter construction. Thomas Boynton recorded painting a "Counter mahogany" at Windsor, Vermont. The material of Boynton's counter may have been white pine, a wood he is known to have used in his shop. Pifer Washington Case of Johnstown, New York, employed "Stain for Counter Tops," although he also used "graining Color," as did William Wilson, a painter of Lowell, Massachusetts. Both craftsmen applied a final varnish coat to protect the grained surfaces.[34]

A "Glass show Case" ordered from Philomon Robbins of Hartford, Connecticut, in 1834 by Colton and Williams cost $30.00 for the work. That was a relatively high price, although the showcase form represented a more expensive piece of equipment than the counter. Construction of Robbins's showcase involved building sections of window sash and incorporating them into the overall design of the case. Providing some insight into the appearance of a showcase is Elizur Barnes's description of a job undertaken the previous decade for a customer at Middletown, Connecticut: "To a Show Case with Cherry Sash front & top." After initial construction of the showcase, there still remained the work—and sometimes the expense—of glazing the sash. Accounts suggest that some glazing was carried out by someone other than the builder. For example, Frederick Coady of Ogdensburg, New York, charged Hecock and Curry eighty cents to set "8 Lights in Show Case." At Newport, Rhode Island, Job E. Townsend recorded "Putting Railing on his Glass Case" for Harvey Sessions. Other tasks mimic those in finishing the counter, such as "Painting a Show Case mehogony Colour" or "Staining," with varnish as a final coat.[35]

Temporary storage was necessary in stores and shops, and installing drawers and shelves was a convenient way to accommodate some types of merchandise. Following the practice of apothecaries, William Barrell and Christopher Champlin, merchants respectively of Philadelphia and Newport, Rhode Island, installed nests of drawers. In other circumstances larger drawers were more useful. Christopher H. Talcott of Coventry, Connecticut, paid $5.00 to have drawers made for his store, and Elias Redfield of Essex acquired "six draws for shop" at a cost of $4.50. The exact purpose of the drawers is rarely identified. Edward Jenner Carpenter, apprentice cabinetmaker in the Greenfield, Massachusetts, shop of Miles and Lyons, commented in his journal in November 1844 on a job for the store of Dewey and Clark when "making 28 drawers for them to keep their groceries in." Painting and lettering, or painting and graining, frequently followed drawer installation. For a client's store in Albany, New York, Ezra Ames, artist and ornamental painter, completed a sizable job in 1796 described as "painting [and] lettering 70 draws" at £1.12.0, "painting & lettering 8 boxes" at 4s., and "lettering 10 barrels" at 5s., for a total cost of 41s. ($5.12 1/2, New York cur-

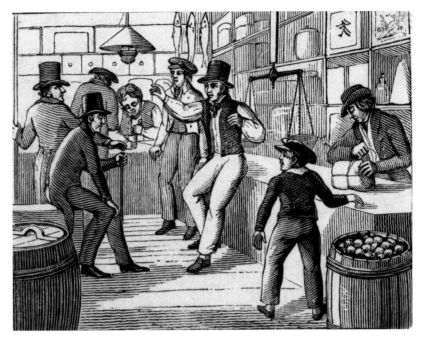

Figure 20   Alexander Anderson (1775–1870), [*A Rural Grocery Store*], northeastern United States, ca. 1825–1850. Wood engraving. (Courtesy, The Miriam and Ira D. Wallach Division of Art, Prints, and Photographs: Print Collection, "Scenes of daily life in nineteenth-century America," The New York Public Library Digital Collections, 1794–1870.)

rency). By contrast, the cost of putting shelves in a store or shop frequently was more modest (fig. 20). Day and Pollard, storekeepers of Washington County, Vermont, paid William Ripley $1.00 for installing shelves, a typical cost for many jobs. Specific dimensions are rarely given because shelf length and number varied depending on interior space and the kinds of goods to be shelved. An 1815 account of Silas E. Cheney for Sophia Jones, proprietress of a shop at Litchfield, Connecticut, describes "makeing shelves," supplying a "Counter," and "fixeing Draws" all for $5.00. Apart from drawers and shelves, Job E. Townsend assisted customer Harvey Sessions in December 1821 with a "Cloth Roller" at his store in Newport, Rhode Island, by making a "New Exeltree" for the roller. The following August, Townsend was back for a job of "Putting up his Meshene for Rolling Cloth," probably the same cloth roller assembled and used only periodically when new merchandise arrived. A third call in April 1823 found Townsend mending the "Roling Mesheene frame."[36]

On occasion one of several case pieces stood in a store or shop to supplement the counter or showcase. Proprietors of stores doing a substantial business would have found a desk convenient (fig. 21). Three woods are mentioned for the desk in the records at hand: locust, cherry, and pine, the cherry desk the most expensive at $10.00. Minor related work included repairing a lock, replacing a desk fall (lid), or supplying a stool to use at the desk. A table could also serve as a desk or as a surface to hold merchandise. A bookcase would have been an appropriate companion to the desk. A "Book Case in ye Shop" made by carpenter Samuel Hall for David Sage at Middletown, Connecticut, in 1788 required "3 Days & half" of labor and consumed "21 feet of Pine Bords" and "80 Brads and Nailes," with "9d worth of Glue." Major Nathan Dillingham of Lee, Massachusetts, ordered a "deep Cupboard" for his shop in 1815 from Abner Taylor, likely as a supplement to the "large drawer & cletes" (handles) acquired two years earlier. Incidental

Figure 21   Shop of the Tailor, in Edward Hazen, *The Panorama of Professions and Trades* (Philadelphia: U. Hunt, 1839), p. 59. (Courtesy, Winterthur Library, Printed Book and Periodical Collection.) The owner of the shop or a clerk is using a desk at the extreme left.

Figure 22   Shop of the Bookseller, in Edward Hazen, *The Panorama of Professions and Trades* (Philadelphia: U. Hunt, 1839), p. 195. (Courtesy, Winterthur Library, Printed Book and Periodical Collection.)

seating in stores and shops usually consisted of a few inexpensive chairs or stools, but occasionally there was a notable exception. Amos Bradley of East Haven, Connecticut, supplied Abram and Jared Bradley, owners of a store and packet, with three chairs in 1807 priced at $1.50 each, identifying either Windsor or fancy chairs. Some thirty years later the firm of Smith and Wright, saddle and harness manufacturers at Newark, New Jersey, made an attractive choice in "6 curld [maple] counter stool[s]" purchased from David Alling.[37]

Two unusual countertop items are worthy of note. A purchase made by Benjamin Dyer from Amos D. Allen at Windham, Connecticut, in 1802 at a cost of $4.00 is described as "a Casket for shop counter, door with 12 Panes of glass 6 by 8." Webster defines a casket as "a small chest or box for items of value." The casket had a horizontal orientation, and given the number of glass panes and their size, the door consisted of two rows of five panes, the overall length (frame and mullions) being approximately 35 to 45 inches depending on the orientation of the panes. The "door" with lock was hinged to be raised. A similar "glass" casket of substantial size sits atop the counter near the door in the bookstore pictured in figure 22. The second countertop item was more a curiosity then a functional piece, or in the words of Webster "fitted to excite attention." George Ritter of Philadelphia crafted the object in 1834 for $5.00 to the specification of the customer, a close neighbor identified as Mr. Clark "Bookseller 2d below Arch." The work involved "Making a Show Book 3 feet long by 2 feet wide & 6 inches thick." The finished product, in the form of an open book, would have been placed on a flat elevated surface to attract attention somewhere in Mr. Clark's bookstore. Several items made for other shops assisted in day-to-day activity, including a "Letter box" described in another account as "1 Letter case with glass door." It was made by Elisha H. Holmes for $2.75 for a shop-keeper at Essex, Connecticut. A free-standing form, probably of larger size, was a "Paper Case with Draws & Doors" priced at £2.5.0 ($7.50), made in 1790 by David Evans for a client in Philadelphia. Incidental items, such as a "Step Lather for Store" made by Evans or "candlesticks for shop" made by Holmes improved efficiency and maximized shop time, particularly in the nineteenth century when business expanded rapidly in urban centers. During his travels in North America in 1853, William Chambers, a British citizen, noted when visiting Philadelphia "the unexpected splendour of the shops—large stores shewing a long vista of elegant counters, shelving, and glass-cases."[38]

COUNTINGHOUSES AND COUNTING ROOMS

These terms, in part, describe the business center of the merchant whose occupation was importing merchandise for domestic distribution and exporting goods appropriate for distant markets (fig. 23). The export business was conducted in several ways: directly with another merchant house abroad, through an agent (supercargo), or by the captain of the vessel containing the merchandise to be sold. In large urban centers, individuals dealing exclusively in groceries or specializing in particular foodstuffs, such as flour, frequently rose to the status of merchant in the volume of

Figure 23 Counting House of the Merchant, in Edward Hazen, *The Panorama of Professions and Trades* (Philadelphia: U. Hunt, 1839), p. 109. (Courtesy, Winterthur Library, Printed Book and Periodical Collection.) The double-sided slant-top desk on tall legs was of a size to accommodate up to four clerks. A small portable desk with slanted writing surface and pigeonholes on the table below was available for additional use. The large case mounted on the wall held ledgers and other account books for easy reference at a counter along the wall.

their business, requiring both specialized furniture and adequate staff. The countinghouse also was the business center of the attorney at law with a substantial practice in transacting legal business for clients before a public court of law and in drawing up individual legal documents, such as wills and deeds (fig. 24). In an economy where coin and paper money were frequently in short supply, particularly in rural areas, the merchant, large retailer, or attorney might find barter an acceptable medium of exchange.[39]

The principal furniture form of the countinghouse was the desk and its accompanying seat. Woodworking craftsmen used several terms to identify this desk; equally popular were *countinghouse desk* and *writing desk*. Two terms used much less frequently were *high desk* and *large desk*. Records at hand identify the primary wood of construction more than a dozen times within a date range extending mainly from 1784 to 1837. An exception in date is the work of Job Townsend Jr. at Newport, Rhode Island, in building a "Writeing Desk" in 1754 for John Wanton (son of Governor Gideon Wanton), whose account with Townsend was credited with mahogany. Mahogany construction is identified twice again, cherry occurs three times, and walnut and yellow poplar are mentioned once each. The most common material, with five references, is pine, a wood probably also identified in two accounts of Daniel Rea Jr., ornamental painter of Boston, who painted writing desks for a merchant and an attorney during the 1790s, one in mahogany color and the other, with its frame, in green.[40]

Documents provide insight into the appearance of the countinghouse desk through details given for building a single and a double unit. Elisha Blossom, a journeyman cabinetmaker in New York, worked at times for his uncle David Loring, a master cabinetmaker on Beekman Street, where in 1813 Blossom crafted a "Single counting house Desk" and recorded details

Figure 24 Horace Bundy (1814–1883), *Vermont Lawyer*, Manchester, Vermont, 1841. Oil on canvas. H. 44″, W. 35½″. (Courtesy, National Gallery of Art, acc. 1953.5.4.) The anonymous lawyer's law books are handy in the bookcase behind him. His writing equipment is at hand: a sharpened quill pen, an inkpot with an additional quill pen, a tall cup-shaped sander containing blotting sand to dry his writing, a small pot containing red sealing wax, and a personal seal with a bulbous handle, the seal at the opposite end containing the lawyer's initials or a device.

of the job. The construction material was either pine or whitewood (yellow poplar), wood recorded in Blossom's dealings with Loring. The "starting" cost at £2 ($5.00, New York currency) identifies a basic frame of unstated length, although probably about 3 feet, 6 inches, the "starting" size in the 1810 *New-York Revised Prices for Manufacturing Cabinet and Chair Work*. The desk consisted of a rectangular stand with four tall legs connected by stretchers, which supported the writing unit (see fig. 23). To the starting size Blossom added eighteen inches in length. The writing unit, or case, had a flat top at the back to which "1 flap," or sloped writing board, was attached. The center interior of the case was reinforced by a "middle end" (partition), which also provided extra support for the writing flap. Inside the divided case at the back were a total of "8 letter holes" with "8 arches," or valances, above four small drawers. Mounted on the flat exterior top was a low gallery supported on "14 pillars." Six screws, the heads "cov[ere]d," secured the writing box to the stand. The finished surfaces were stained, then polished, and a lock installed. Given its approximate five-foot length and the two interior compartments, the desk would have accommodated two clerks. Blossom's charge to Loring was £4.15.0 ($11.88, New York currency).[41]

A MERCHANTS COUNTING HOUSE

Figure 25 Detail of *A Merchant's Counting House*, Philadelphia, Pennsylvania, ca. 1790–1800. Engraved by Alexander Lawson (1773–1846), published by T. Dobson, PR 031. (Courtesy, Bella C. Landauer Collection of Business and Advertising Ephemera, New-York Historical Society, 98124d.) A desk with a double-sided slant top accommodates four clerks within a gated enclosure. Small writing tables are attached to the gated wall, and two large cases on the back wall hold account books.

Almost a quarter century later George Ritter of Philadelphia was engaged by William Boller, a merchant located on Front Street adjacent to the shipping wharves, to build a large two-sided countinghouse desk that cost the merchant $25.00 (fig. 25). Ritter subcontracted some of the work to carpenter Isaac Smyth, who made "the Stand for a counting house desk" with turned legs of yellow poplar scantling (see fig. 10). Smyth followed work on the stand with "plaining up the stuff for the desk & assisting in all, say one Day & half." The "pine" desk "beveled on Both sides" was 5 feet, 8 inches long and five feet in depth. It contained "five Drawers, with locks on the four side drawers." Two each of the side drawers with locks were located in the desk proper immediately below either beveled writing surface. The overall length and width indicate that the desk could accommodate four clerks, two on each side. The "Top of [the] Desk [was] covered with cloth & edged with a bead." The frame supporting the desk proper was "secured together with 14 screws." Use of two woods in the construction of Boller's desk, yellow poplar and pine, would have been concealed when "Stained & varnished."[42]

Other references to single and double countinghouse desks occur in records, although the documents lack the details of construction found in the cited examples. More insight is present regarding the placement and appearance of the cloth cover used on desks. Stephen Girard hired Henry Connelly at Philadelphia in 1811 to cover the "Writing flap" of his desk with cloth. The appropriate cloth was identified several years earlier at Providence, Rhode Island, when the firm of Almy and Brown paid a local craftsman to cover its "Writing Table & Desk" with baize, a woolen felted and napped fabric used on writing surfaces. The common color of the baize is described in the inventory of the business premises of John Mifflin, Esq., of Philadelphia, which itemizes "A Counting ho[use] Desk covered w[i]th Green Cloth" (see fig. 26). The same document addresses the subject of a seat to accompany the desk: "a stool & steps belong[in]g to the Desk." Two separate items appear to be identified, suggesting the stool was exceptionally high or the user was of short stature (see fig. 25). Alternative seating identified by John Eastmond, commission merchant of Albany, New York, describes "1 double Writing desk & benches." Not all writing desks ordered from craftsmen were for local use. In 1823 Elizur Barnes of Middletown, Connecticut, recorded an order from Josiah Williams and Company for "3 Counting Room Desks," the total cost $42.00, with another charge of $3.50 for "Boxing 3 Desks." Middletown's location on a navigable section of the Connecticut River gave local merchants access to coastal and distant markets. Two Philadelphia customers of David Evans, proprietors of substantial stores in 1791, required specialized furniture. Charles Shoemaker, flour merchant, and Joseph Miller, grocer, ordered desks for their businesses, Miller's purchase described as "a Large Pine wrighting Desk" for £4.10.0 ($15.00). Both customers and Evans were located within a short walk of each other's place of business.[43]

Supplemental furniture providing for the smooth functioning of the countinghouse was varied—some forms more essential than others—depending on the circumstances. Countinghouse counters, cupboards, and bookcases constituted the large furniture forms. The countinghouse counter, although uncommon, appears from descriptions to have been particularly useful. William Boller, the Philadelphia merchant who purchased a large double-sided countinghouse desk to accommodate four clerks, also purchased a large twelve-dollar pine counter from George Ritter described as "6 feet long by 2 feet wide [deep] & 3 feet high containing Six Drawers 22 in long by 9 in deep, Stained & Varnished, & containing 120 feet of pine." For a counter in place in the sizable Vermont store of Isaac Greene, Hezekiah Healy was hired to make "a Change Drawer & fix in a board for shelf." A corner cupboard of moderate size, judging by the cost at £3.5.0 ($10.83), was built and installed in the store of merchant Richard Blow at Norfolk, Virginia, in 1783 by the partners Hatton and Miller, the craftsmen who had painted the store after extensive window glazing. Continuing their work, the men constructed a "Sq[ua]r[e] Table with 2 Drawers" for £1.14.0 ($5.67). Eight years later the partners Bonner and Lindsey built a "Counter Desk" for the store priced at £1.8.0 ($4.67).[44]

Another purchase made by Richard Blow for his store was a "Writing Desk & Book Case" for £8.16.0 ($29.33). This purchase may have been a combination stand-up writing desk with a series of open bookshelves below for ledgers. In 1789 Ralph Earl painted a portrait of dry goods merchant Elijah Boardman of New Milford, Connecticut, standing at a sturdy model of the suggested type filled with heavy business ledgers (fig. 26). Other bookcases were constructed without a desk unit. Records at hand make no mention of hardwood frames, although they describe several units with painted and stained surfaces. John Codman, a Boston merchant with an office on Codman's Wharf, hired Daniel Rea Jr. in 1797 to paint his bookcase mahogany color. In that city several decades later Andrew Dunlap, district attorney with an office in the Old Court House, called on John Treadwell to build five bookcases at a cost of $25.00. Treadwell subcontracted the finishing to Eben Jackson, a painter, who following the then current trend grained the bookcases in imitation "Maple & Mahogany 22 yds at 50 cts [per yard] & Varnishing the same," all at an additional charge of $11.00. Several other bookcases purchased in the 1830s appear to have been of substantial size, judging by the cost. The structure of a "Library Book Case" acquired by Owen Stover, Esq., of West Chester, Pennsylvania, for $18.00 from Amos Darlington Jr. is speculative. It likely was a broad open unit without doors or cupboard. Probably similar, with the addition of a pair of doors, was a "Book Cass for His Offis with Pannald Doors" built for John Cadwalader, Esq., later Judge Cadwalader. William Cragg of Philadelphia fabricated the case and finished it in stain and varnish for $20.00.[45]

Absent from the records at hand dealing with the countinghouse bookcase is any reference to a horizontal rectangular hanging wall case containing multiple vertical partitions for the convenient storage of current business ledgers and journals. Yet these open storage cases are pictured in active use in illustrations of the countinghouse (see figs. 23 and 25). A small bookcase made for a modest 8s. ($1.33) for Isaac Greene, who kept a large store at Windsor, Vermont, may reference this type of bookcase. Another option at first appeared viable. Boston merchant John Codman employed Daniel Rea Jr. in November 1801 and January 1802 to paint a total of six "Book Chests mehogony" color for $5.00. A chest being a box with a lid, that type of storage would appear impractical for account books in daily use. Discovery of a cogent reference in Samuel Eliot Morison's *Maritime History* clarified Codman's purchase. Within a sizeable merchant house, the author describes how clerks might at times delve into the "neat wooden chests that enclosed the records of each particular vessel."[46]

The well-equipped countinghouse also had a case or other container to hold papers and letters. George Ritter of Philadelphia, whose account-book entries are considerably more comprehensive than the typical business record, noted dimensions for a pair of paper cases he made at $3.00 each for William Boller, merchant, in 1837: "14 inch[s] high by 14 deep & 12 inches

Figure 26 Ralph Earl (1751–1801), *Portrait of Elijah Boardman* (1760–1846), New Milford, Connecticut, 1789. Oil on canvas. H. 83″, W. 51″. (Copyright © The Metropolitan Museum of Art, bequest of Susan W. Tyler, 1979, acc. 1979.395; Art Resource, New York.) Boardman was a dry goods merchant in Connecticut. Green baize covers the slanted writing surface of his tall bookcase-desk.

wide, each having six pidgeon holes, Stained & varnished." The dimensions determined the arrangement of the pigeon holes, which were stacked three over three, each opening approximately 3½ inches by 6½ inches, a common size since papers and letters were routinely folded and identified on the outside (see fig. 24). Several other accounts cite cases of pigeon holes, expanding the range in date and number of holes. Nicholas Skull of Philadelphia, surveyor and mapmaker, did business with John Gillingham in March 1750 to the sum of £8.12.6 ($28.75 in later decimal currency), obtaining seven cases with a combined total of 138 pigeon holes, plus two presses (cupboards) to house them. During the 1790s Robert R. Livingston, chancellor of New York State, patronized Thomas Burling and Son in the City, acquiring "a Mohog'y Paper Case of Pigeon Holes" for which he paid £4.10.0 ($11.25, New York currency). On occasion a paper case was fitted with containers. William Wragg, Esq., interacting in 1799 with Nicholas Silberg, cabinetmaker of Charleston, South Carolina, paid him to make "a large liquor case," subsequently altered to "a paper Case with two inside Boxes." Some "papers" housed in cases were identified as letters, as indicated in the records of Arthur Bronson, a broker on Wall Street, New York.[47]

Another storage unit found in some countinghouses was a rack. When Arthur Bronson had his letter case repaired, cleaned, and varnished in 1838, his "Check Rack" underwent the same treatment. Other records list racks for letters, a rack for a desk, and a "Book Rack for a Safe," all priced in a moderate range. To this list is added a "mahogany rack for the seales" ordered in 1828 from George Ritter by attorney William Biddle at his business location on Walnut Street, Philadelphia. Window shades also were a necessity at many places of business, particularly during the summer season, and venetian blinds were popular with the business crowd. John Rea, specialist in upholstery and venetian blind making at Philadelphia, accommodated merchant John Slesman in 1800 by making and hanging "2 Venetian Blinds for [the] Compting house Windows." As a specialty sideline, city cabinetmaker David Evans also made venetian blinds. Baker and Commeges placed an order in 1800 for "a blind [for] the Circular Window" at their "Compting Room" that cost $10.00 and a blind for the window fronting their store for $9.00. Evans's business in venetian blinds continued, and in 1808 Simon Gratz and Company purchased three "Mohogony Blinds" for their counting room windows for the substantial sum of £15 ($50.00). The cost reflects the fabrication material, installation, and difficult business times during this period, when President Thomas Jefferson's Embargo Act was in force, curtailing normal waterborne trade. Not all venetian blinds were made with mahogany slats. Painted slats were just as popular, especially those painted green, the color John Codman directed Daniel Rea Jr. to use when "Paint'g four pair of Venetian shades" for his store at Boston. The two-pound charge describes shades of modest size already in use. Amos Darlington Jr. made an unusual installation described in 1825 as "hanging gate in office" at the business premises of Joseph Peirce, Esq., of West Chester, Pennsylvania (see fig. 25). The fifty-cent charge for the work indicates that the gate was either rehung or was new and obtained from another source. Many counting rooms were not of a size to have a railing enclose the counting-room desk and the clerks who kept the accounts and correspondence of the business. A railing created a space apart from the hustle and bustle of daily activity and general business on the premises.[48]

OTHER CENTERS OF BUSINESS

Banks

In 1781 the Second Continental Congress appointed the wealthy Philadelphia merchant Robert Morris as superintendent of finance. Morris immediately set about controlling waste and unnecessary spending and introducing proper administrative methods. He also recognized the need for financial flexibility and obtained a charter for the Bank of North America. David Evans supplied "Venetian Blinds" for the building almost a decade later, followed by "6 blinds for windows" in 1793 for the Bank of Pennsylvania (fig. 27). Meanwhile, with the move of the national seat of govern-

Figure 27   *Bank of Pennsylvania, South Second Street, Philadelphia*, drawn, engraved, and colored by William Russell Birch and Thomas Birch, published in *Birch's Views of Philadelphia*, plate 27. (Courtesy, Winterthur Library, Printed Book and Periodical Collection.) The bank was designed by Benjamin Henry Latrobe (1764–1820) in the new Greek Revival style and built between 1798 and 1801. The building to the left with the front awning is City Tavern which, like the Tontine Coffee House in New York, served as a merchant's exchange.

ment from New York to Philadelphia, Congress chartered the First Bank of the United States in 1791, and in the same year Evans was contracted to make a "Clock Case Painted & put up in the Directors Room." Banks were also established in other centers throughout the young and maturing nation. At Roxbury, Massachusetts, Simon Willard engaged John Doggett in 1804 to gild a "clock case for [the] Boston Bank" at a charge of $28.00. A decade later Silas E. Cheney was hired by Lucius Smith and Company of Litchfield, Connecticut, to make a "large table" for the local bank. More substantial work was carried out for the Exchange Bank on State Street, Hartford, during the 1830s by Philemon Robbins. He installed a mahogany counter top and twenty-two feet of railing and supplied two mahogany desks, the complete job billed at $46.50. The counter may have resembled the substantial specimen that furnished the bank at York, Pennsylvania,

Figure 28 Lewis Miller, *Interior of York Bank*, York, Pennsylvania, 1812. Ink and watercolor drawing and text on paper. (Courtesy, York County History Center, York, Pa.) Pictured are John Schmitd [*sic*], cashier, and the Reverend Daniel Dunn, patron.

earlier in the century (fig. 28). Still other craftsmen undertook varied work for banks during the early nineteenth century. Amos Darlington Jr. of West Chester, Pennsylvania, made a small box and two venetian blinds for a local bank in 1824, followed six years later by two desks, one priced at $6.00 and the other at $12.00. Chairs purchased at the factory of Henry W. Miller in 1830 for the "Central Bank" of Worcester, Massachusetts, for $16.33 indicates they were either Windsor or fancy seating.[49]

Inns

The American inn, a public house of small to moderate size for the lodging of travelers, also included a tavern where food and drink were available. A tavern also functioned as an inn, although sometimes it was no more than a house where liquor was served, with light fare available occasionally. When domestic travelers or visitors from abroad made stops for lodging, they frequently found a mixed bag of accommodations, leading to frequent comment. The Reverend William Bentley of Salem, Massachusetts, during travel in western New England in 1793, stopped at a new house in Bernardston to which he and his party had been referred. The pastor quickly pronounced the accommodations "mean," describing "rooms without partitions, without clean linen, & without knowledge of the persons who slept near us." Bentley "lodged upon the bed" but "in no sense in it." British and other European travelers were also keen observers, among them John Lambert, who with traveling companions stopped at an upstate inn at Granville, New York, in 1807, where they "were supplied with an excellent supper." Following the meal, the party retired upstairs to:

one large room . . . [that] contained above a dozen beds, so that we each had a separate one; a thing not always to be met with at every tavern in the States. But the practice of putting two or three in a bed is now little exercised, except at very indifferent taverns, and they are chiefly confined to the back parts of the country.

The enactment of controls improved conditions. Timothy Dwight, president of Yale College, described regulation of the inns in Connecticut in 1796, where "every innkeeper . . . must be recommended by the selectmen and civil authority . . . of the town in which he resides and then licensed at the discretion of the court of common pleas."[50]

Still, conditions were far from optimum in developing regions, as Dwight's young niece, Margaret Van Horn Dwight, found out in 1810 when traveling from New Haven, Connecticut, to Ohio (fig. 29). The journey was rugged, with poor roads, rain, and snow; it was unpleasant, with poor

Figure 29 *American Stage Waggon*, drawn by Isaac Weld, engraved by James Storer, published by I. Stockdale, London, 1798. Illustrated in Isaac Weld, *Travels through the States of North America and the Provinces of Upper Canada and Lower Canada . . . 1795, 1796, and 1797*, 2 vols. (London: John Stockdale, 1800), 1: frontispiece. (Courtesy, Winterthur Library, Printed Book and Periodical Collection.)

accommodations in dirty conditions, sometimes sleeping on the floor. The roads, inns, and taverns were crowded with wagoners who swore and drank excessively. Writing about this period in Ohio's early development, a later commentator noted that community institutions offered "opportunities for social intercourse" and became a "focal point for cultural development." The four institutions critical to this development in the "pioneer communities" of the Ohio Valley were "the tavern, the church, the school, and the county court." The tavern often also served as a stop for the mail coach. In contrast to Miss Dwight's experience, the duc de La Rochefoucauld Liancourt, when stopping in coastal New England in the mid-1790s in what later became the state of Maine, "was surprised to find the inns so decent and well kept, in a part of the country so remote, and so rarely visited by travellers." Another Frenchman, the marquis de Chastellux, traveling in America during the previous decade, found on entering an inn at Morristown, New Jersey, "a dining-room adorned with looking glasses and handsome mahogany furniture," and a table spread for dining. Near the end of his American travels, Chastellux and his party made an unexpected stop at Baron's tavern in coastal New Hampshire due to heavy rain. They dried themselves "by a good fire, in a very handsome apartment, adorned with good prints" and mahogany furniture.[51]

The size of an inn and the type and variety of its furnishings were dictated by the nature and volume of its business. At Windsor, Vermont, a town of almost 3,000 inhabitants in 1810, patronage was good at Frederick Pettes's coffee house and inn. The town, which was surrounded by fertile lands that supported sheep and cattle, was a center of trade along the upper Connecticut River. Its citizens were prosperous, and the town was distinguished by its sophisticated architecture. The Pettes inn and coffee house served as a community meeting place for several organizations, including the Masonic Lodge. Because the premises also functioned as a stage house, it was assured a steady stream of patrons. Furnishings appropriate for dining and lodging in the public house were supplied originally in 1801 when the building was erected. By 1813 some refurbishing, repairs, and replacements to the furnishings were required. On October 8 of that year Thomas Boynton, a cabinetmaker newly returned to his native area from Boston, painted a fireboard for Pettes. Still developing his new business in Windsor, Boynton boarded with Pettes from October through December before setting up his own household. Additional work for Pettes followed in 1814 through 1815. Miscellaneous tasks included scraping and varnishing a portable desk, painting four kegs, and mending a light stand and a cricket (low stool). Boynton also constructed a "money draw[er] with a lock" and supplied newly fashionable seating: "6 gilt fancy bamboo chairs" (probably Windsors) at $18.00, "12 rush Bottom elegant" fancy chairs at $72.00, and a "B[oar]d top rocking Chair," a relatively new form in comfort seating at $3.75.[52]

Documented purchases made from cabinetmaker Silas E. Cheney and an estate inventory describe the furnishings of Grove Catlin's inn in the town of Litchfield, Connecticut, the seat of Litchfield County. The area was prosperous, with soil well suited for grazing cattle, the land dotted with scenic lakes, and small rivers providing waterpower for nascent manufactures of textiles and iron. The town was the site of a law school "of great respectability" that flourished there for almost thirty years from its founding in 1784 by the Honorable Tapping Reeve, a judge in the Supreme Court of Connecticut. Both Reeve and Catlin were significant customers of Cheney, and Cheney boarded with Catlin for several months in 1801. Catlin's interaction with Cheney principally documents furniture maintenance and replacement for an active lodging and dining facility. In June 1809 Catlin purchased new fireboards for two hearths, although whether plain painted or ornamented is unknown. They do not appear in Catlin's inventory of 1829, although they may have been considered part of the building. In 1811 Catlin directed major attention to the inn's seating furniture, which comprised Windsor and fancy chairs, and he paid for minor repairs to a rocking chair. Fifteen Windsor chairs required new backs at 41½¢ apiece. The repairs were followed by three coats of paint at 25¢ the chair and ornament at 10¢ apiece.

Another group of fourteen chairs was repainted and ornamented at the same charges. The following year Catlin purchased one dozen new fancy chairs for the inn: ten side chairs were $2.50 apiece and two armchairs en suite were $3.50 each. In an additional purchase in 1814 Catlin acquired two spitting boxes for $1.50. These were low rectangular wooden boxes filled with sand to accommodate the popular habit among men of chewing tobacco. Catlin died in 1829; Cheney predeceased him in 1821 at about age forty-five. Listed in Catlin's estate inventory are seventy-two chairs and two settees along with "10 sand boxes." Lodgers and innkeeper were accommodated for sleeping by "5 high Post Bedsteads" and "10 Common d[itt] o." A brief selection of other listed items speaks to the sophistication of the inn: "16 Bed Valances" $12.00; "17 Calico Window Curtains" (printed cotton) $4.25; "1 Good Looking Glass" $6.00; "14 Common d[itt]o" $10.50; "6 Common Cherry Dining Tables" $13.50; "3 Ditto Tea Tables" $5.25; and "1 Mahogany Tea Table" $10.00.[53]

Figure 30 Francis Guy (1760–1820), *The Tontine Coffee House*, New York, New York, ca. 1797. Oil on linen. H. 43", W. 65". (Purchase, the Louis Durr Fund, New-York Historical Society, acc. 1907.32.) The Coffee House was located at the intersection of Wall and Water Streets adjacent to the East River.

During a summer visit to New York in 1794, Henry Wansey, a British traveler, observed that the new Tontine Coffee House was modeled after London prototypes. The "handsome large brick building" at the corner of Wall and Water Streets (fig. 30, left) was entered through a raised portico. Inside, "a large public room" functioned as "the Stock Exchange of New York, where all bargains are made." Records were kept of ship arrivals

Figure 31 The Sun Inn, Bethlehem, Pennsylvania, in William C. Reichel, *The Old Sun Inn at Bethlehem, Pa., 1758* (Doylestown, Pa.: W. W. H. Davis, 1876), frontispiece. (Courtesy, Moravian Archives, Bethlehem, Pennsylvania; photo, Winterthur Museum.)

and clearances "as at Lloyds" of London. Financed by shares, the "house was built for the accommodation of the merchants." Lodging was available with boarding "at a common table" for "ten shillings currency a day." Stores on the premises, although not visible from the street as in London, were available for rent. Fabricating the house furniture engaged a number of woodworking craftsmen residing in lower Manhattan in the vicinity of the new structure, although many items are not particularized. Craftsmen Peter Shackerly, Gifford and Scotland, and Nicholas Carmer provided furniture specifically identified as mahogany in the amount of £173 ($432.50, New York currency). Samuel Richards itemized his production as "1 writing Desk, 1 Table, & F[urniture] Brackets" plus "Venetian Blinds," the latter charged at £40 ($100.00). Clock and watchmaker Effingham Embree produced a timepiece billed at £16 ($40.00). Upholsterer John Brower submitted two bills totaling £98.13.0 ($246.63), presumably for work independent of finish covers for the above mahogany furniture. Looking glasses and chandeliers were provided by William Wilmerding from his store on Maiden Lane at a charge of £98.18.0 ($247.25). Longtime proprietors of a chair-making shop on John Street, Thomas and William Ash, submitted two bills together amounting to £87.4.0 ($218.00), presumably for Windsor seating since fancy chairs were still uncommon and Windsors were the practical choice for lodging and dining areas. Outside the building all was hustle and bustle, with drays parked in all directions and the tall masts of vessels along the East River visible in the immediate distance. Traveling to New York in 1801, Thomas P. Cope, a Philadelphia Quaker businessman, commented: "there are no houses in N. York which answer to the Inns in Philad. for the accommodation of travellers, excepting the Tontine Coffee House may be ranked as of that class."[54]

Construction of the Sun Inn in the Moravian community of Bethlehem, Pennsylvania, began in 1758, and it was sufficiently complete to receive travelers in autumn 1760. The central-hall building consisted of a basement and three floors above ground (fig. 31). The first floor contained a large common room, the innkeeper's quarters, a large kitchen and adjacent pantry, and a three-room apartment consisting of a sitting room and two bedrooms. The second floor contained three similar apartments surrounding a large hall (room) for dining. The attic story, divided into four sleeping rooms each accommodating four bedsteads, was lighted, in part, by German-style shed-roofed dormers. Rooms throughout the building were heated either by a large hearth or a German-style tile stove. When the inn opened for business, Bethlehem was already on the main travel route between the Carolinas and coastal Massachusetts. The hostelry quickly gained a reputation for its hospitality, excellent management, and cuisine (fig. 32), a reflection of the town's original communal economy and the continuing oversight of the church. Johann David Schöpf, a German traveler in America in 1783–84, noted that "in addition to transient travelers, Philadelphians are wont to make excursions hither," to view "the institutions and social arrangements of the congregations" and enjoy "the superior entertainment afforded by

Figure 32 Lewis Miller, *Mrs. Hersh's Tavern*, York, Pennsylvania, 1809. Ink and watercolor drawing and text on paper. (Courtesy, York County History Center, York, Pa.) Pictured is a kitchen in a hostelry of German-American background. Food is being prepared in large kettles, long-handled frying skillets, and a bake oven, where the cook-proprietor is using a long-handled wooden peel to insert a loaf of bread for baking after the dough has risen in its cloth-covered basket like those in the middle ground.

this house." Visitors to the inn in the late eighteenth century included the "great and near-great," activity being particularly brisk during the Revolutionary War. When the Englishman Isaac Weld visited in 1796, he was lavish in his praise, proclaiming the inn to be the "neatest and best conducted one . . . that I ever met with in any part of America." Initially £157.1.3 ($523.54) was spent on furniture for the inn. Following Moravian business practice, annual inventories were made in English or German. Furnishings in 1763 included "6 wallnut chairs" and "24 woven seat chairs," the latter probably of slat-back design, augmented in number and described in 1781 as fifty-one chairs with "woven straw seats." By 1800 five green armchairs, each valued at 6s. ($1.00), were accompanied by forty-five chairs valued at 5s. 6d. (92¢), the entire group identified in 1805 as Windsor seating. There also were "34 sundrie Chairs part moldit," describing remnants of previous

Figure 33   Indian Queen Hotel, Philadelphia, ca. 1831. Lithograph printed by Childs and Inman. H. 12⅜", W. 11½". (Courtesy, The Library Company of Philadelphia.) Several decades after the visit of Francisco de Miranda to Philadelphia, the Indian Queen Inn became a hotel at the same location, Fourth and Chestnut Streets.

seating, the "moldit" ones probably joined chairs. Four benches were in the "public Roome," or first-floor common room. By 1816 Windsor chairs had taken over the inn: two dozen, half described as "new," were accompanied by eighteen more in the common room, now called the "Great Parlor," and forty more were scattered about the "Haus." The "30 Schr[e]iner Stuhle" (cabinetmaker's chairs) may have furnished the dining hall. There were two specialized seats: a rocking chair and "1 grosse Lähm Stuhl," or invalid's chair, valued at $4.50. Other furnishings, purchased at various times into the early nineteenth century, included bedsteads of single and double size, 8-day and 24-hour timepieces, walnut and cherry tables (some folding), a writing desk, two large looking glasses, "a moldit dresser with glass windows" (cabinetmaker's cupboard with glass doors), and a walnut chest "with flowers" (painted or inlaid ornament).[55]

When Thomas P. Cope visited New York in 1801 and found only the Tontine Coffee House comparable to the inns of Philadelphia, one Philadelphia facility he had in mind was the City Tavern (see fig. 27), near the intersection of Second and Walnut Streets, which like the Tontine served as a merchant's exchange. Another city landmark of the late eighteenth century was the Indian Queen Inn, or Tavern, on Fourth Street at Chestnut, where Francisco de Miranda, a South American patriot, found excellent accommodations (fig. 33). The Golden Tun Tavern likely would have achieved comparable renown had it not been for the premature death of the innkeeper. Opened in mid-1795 at 59 South Water Street, its proprietor, Samuel Fraunces, was a tavern- and innkeeper of considerable experience. He had emigrated from the West Indies to New York in the 1750s and established an inn eventually known as Fraunce's Tavern, where he earned a reputation as an excellent steward. General Washington was acquainted with Fraunces long before he bade farewell to his officers at the tavern in 1783, and when the general became president, Fraunces became his household steward. When the national government relocated to Philadelphia in June 1790, Fraunces followed and continued to serve the first family until June 1794, when he returned to inn-keeping. The following midyear Fraunces became proprietor of the Tun Tavern, renamed the Golden Tun. The inn was furnished in style, as attested by the comprehensive inventory of the premises made on October 24, 1795, shortly after Fraunces's death at age seventy-two on the tenth day of the month.[56]

The item "Golden Tun and sign" describes the identification of the two-story inn: a board bearing the name in printed or cursive letters and the gilded miniature of a tun (a large cask probably used for wine) supported above or suspended below the signboard. Inside the inn, painted structures and furniture, consisting of a bar, seven tables, and five boxes, or wooden stalls, furnished an informal area that probably served as a small coffee house—a popular center for news and conversation in the eighteenth and nineteenth centuries. The three-sided stalls likely had attached side benches (none otherwise mentioned) for seating and structural stability. Each stall was furnished with a painted table; "Green Curtains and rods" completed the scheme to provide privacy, as desired (fig. 34). Facilitating service were

Figure 34   Richard Caton Woodville (1825–1856), *Politics in an Oyster House*, painted in Düsseldorf for a Baltimore patron, 1848. Oil on canvas. H. 16″, W. 13″. (Courtesy, The Walters Art Museum, Baltimore.) The setting here closely matches the description of the three-sided booths in the Golden Tun Tavern, Philadelphia, each booth also furnished with two benches and a table and a curtain on a rod at the front that could be drawn for privacy. The lighting fixture is an intrusion of the later period of the canvas.

four pounds of coffee, a coffee mill, two tin biggins (drip-type coffee urns), tin coffee pots, and a dozen coffee cups and saucers. Another informal area, located beyond the "entry Cloth 11½ [feet] long" was a "Bar & shelves" stocked with wine glasses, tumblers, decanters, and punch bowls for dispensing the wines, spirits, ales, cider, and mixed drinks of the house. Other public areas on the first floor contained mahogany furniture: tables, some in sets of three or five, others described as large or round; two pier tables; two "square" card tables with green baize playing surfaces and "76 packs of Cards"; a large sideboard supporting "2 Knive Cases Cont[ainin]g White handle K[nives] & [Forks]"; and a "Cellaret" sideboard with a central arch to accommodate one of "2 Wine Coolers." The placement of several other sizable pieces of mahogany furniture is uncertain: a wardrobe, a "desk & drawers," and a bureau. Seating throughout the inn consisted of a dozen mahogany chairs with "worked" bottoms; six dozen Windsor side chairs, probably used for dining, drinking, and as bedroom furniture; and five rush-bottom chairs servicing the well-equipped kitchen areas. The item "Stair case Carpet & Rods" identifies the presence of the second story, although the inventory has no distinctive order. Thirteen bedsteads and a green couch, each with a full complement of bedding, provided comfortable sleeping.

Among the bedstead frames were seven with low posts, two with high posts (one painted), two with either a canopy top or tent top, and two mahogany frames, one each with round posts or grooved posts. In addition are listings for bedstead and window curtains, one "full set" containing hangings of both types. Fabrics for windows included red damask, green baize, and "New Chintz." Many floors were covered with carpets, rugs, or painted floor cloths in square patterns. When Fraunces assumed proprietorship of the inn, many furnishings were already in place, although the new innkeeper likely made changes. With Philadelphia the center of the federal government, parts of the local population were constantly in flux, making household furnishings readily available at moderate cost at one or more local auctions.[57]

Several unusual items appear in the appraisal of the Golden Tun furnishings: "3 wooden cases Cont[ainin]g Shells" valued at £16.10.0 ($55.00) and "a M[ahogan]y box cont'g shells &c." valued at £7.10.0 ($25.00). The valuations indicate these were no ordinary items. Rather than collections of loose shells, the cases contained decorative compositions of shells fixed to a backing or ground. The mahogany box contained something more than shells, indicated by "&c." It may have held a three-dimensional scene that included costumed waxwork figures accompanied by small waxwork animals, ornamental paperwork, and other appropriate materials. Fraunces is known to have been proficient in the art of shellwork, having made and gifted to Martha Washington about 1783 a shell and waxwork tableau portraying the Trojan warrior Hector and his wife Andromache. The tableau was purchased at the sale of Martha Washington's estate by her granddaughter Martha Custis Peter, who took it to Tudor Place, the Peter family home in Washington, D.C., where it remains.[58]

MILLS

From the time of early settlement in America sawmills and gristmills—powered by water, or occasionally by wind—were essential to establishing communities. Timber, some of it sawed into planks and boards, was necessary for erecting buildings, providing modest household furnishings, building fences, and supplying fuel for cooking and heating. Wood was the material of staves for barrel making, and it was used in constructing the small watercraft that plied the waters before the establishment of a major shipbuilding and naval stores' industry. Gristmills provided for the sustenance of a community, grinding wheat into flour and corn into meal.[59]

Sawmills

Apart from local sawmills that handled routine work, other mills were located near large timber sources where considerable wood was precut into planks, boards, clapboards, shingles, and staves destined for distant lumber markets. When Yale College was in recess, President Timothy Dwight frequently made journeys of exploration throughout New England and New York state, recording his observations. During the mid-1790s he noted "there is scarcely a township in New England which has not a complete set of gristmills and sawmills," the millstreams being "so numerously and

Figure 35 South View of Trenton, N.J., in John Warner Barber and Henry Howe, *Historical Collections of the State of New Jersey* (Newark, N.J.: Benjamin Olds, 1844), facing p. 280. (Courtesy, Winterthur Library, Printed Book and Periodical Collection.) The two rafts of timber manned by helmsmen on the Delaware River probably are destined for a Philadelphia market.

universally dispersed." When visiting near the mouth of the White River in Vermont several years later, he further observed that "a great quantity of lumber sawn at this place is conveyed in rafts down the Connecticut [River]." Several other travelers commented on the practice of floating quantities of wood down rivers by raft to urban markets from the forests where it had been cut by lumbermen. Francisco de Miranda, traveling along the Hudson River in upstate New York, remarked: "It is incredible the quantity of sawed wood . . . upon this river on rafts" being transported "to New York at very little cost." Observations by Henry Wansey were similar as he made his way toward Philadelphia along the Delaware River, where he saw "vast rafts of timber of a quarter of a mile in length . . . floating down the stream." Some rafts contained "a hut erected for a family to lodge in, and a stable with a horse and cow at its entrance." Figure 35 depicts two log rafts guided by helmsmen on the Delaware River opposite Trenton, New Jersey.[60]

During a trip in 1776 along the Hudson River north of Albany, Charles Carroll of Carrollton, Maryland, remarked "two saw mills (one of them carrying fourteen saws)" on the Saratoga, New York, estate of General Philip Schuyler. This may have been the same mill visited by Timothy Dwight some years later, in 1799, in the village of Stillwater, where a "gang of saws" converted "a log into boards by a single operation." At some sites it was possible to harness the power of a waterfall to operate the machinery of a mill. John Lambert noted the force of a waterfall used to operate several sawmills in the vicinity of Middlebury, Vermont. Following the opening of the Erie Canal, Rochester, New York, became an important manufacturing center because of the "immense water-power formed by the falls of the Genesee." Among the many businesses using this power were twelve devoted to saw-milling (see fig. 38).[61]

References to work on customers' mills occur in the accounts of wood-working craftsmen, although the entries do not always identify the type of mill cited. A direct reference to sawmill work is entered in the accounts of William Chappel of Danbury, Connecticut, who worked a day in 1794 at the facility of John McLean. Extensive work by Nathaniel Dominy V on a "Saw Mill 22 Days" for customer Captain William J. Rysam, a "retired master mariner," was recorded either at East Hampton, Long Island, or nearby at Sag Harbor, where Rysam owned business facilities. The work appears to identify a new mill, since another job described as "22 Days building Fulling Mill" for two business partners at Sag Harbor required similar time and cost just a pound more. Dominy himself owned a sawmill, recording "boards sawed at our mill" on several occasions. Across Long Island Sound at Windham, Connecticut, William Fuller, owner of a sawmill and gristmill, occasionally called on Nathaniel F. Martin to service his facility. General work at the sawmill in March 1795 was followed in November by "4 & 1/2 Days making floom at Saw mill," a flume being an inclined channel to carry water from a source to the waterwheel of a mill. Five years later Martin spent "5 Days making [a] water whell" for Fuller. As other records suggest, it was not uncommon on occasion to replace a worn or underperforming waterwheel. Martin may have exchanged an undershot wheel for a more powerful overshot example. (The breast wheel became dominant later with the development of manufacturing-type mills.) If the flume built earlier brought water from the Shetucket River or a swift minor stream, a new waterwheel would have further increased the mill's power, an asset since Fuller also operated a gristmill. Payment to Martin often was in barter goods: oak and chestnut boards, corn, and in 1804 use of Fuller's sawmill "to Saw 1865 feet [of] bords and slitwork [long narrow strips] & 180 feet [of] posts, and Rafters at 400 feet."[62]

At coastal Kingston, Massachusetts, Nathan Lucas undertook work on another mill flume, recording 4½ days charged at one dollar per day. Inland at Charlton, Asa Clemens hired Chapman Lee in 1813 for a job of "making

[a] Sawmill Gate," a rectangular frame supporting one or more long vertical saw blades placed side by side for cutting one or more boards or planks simultaneously, as required. Sometimes a mill dam was the power source for a waterwheel. After William Fifield of Lyme, New Hampshire, spent time in November 1813 working on the sawmill of Daniel Smith, Esq., at New Hampton, he spent another day working on Smith's mill dam. Another dam, located at the head of the Acushnet River, served as the power source to operate the sawmill and gristmill of Ebenezer Allen Jr., a successful cabinetmaker at New Bedford, Massachusetts, prior to his premature death in 1793. Demand for lumber continued to grow during the early nineteenth century. Some yards established in metropolitan areas achieved substantial size, as demonstrated in the facility operated by G. and E. Green at New York (fig. 36). Located at West and Horatio Streets adjacent to the Hudson River, the yard relied on water transport to obtain its stock, as attested by the sailing vessels tied up at its wharves.[63]

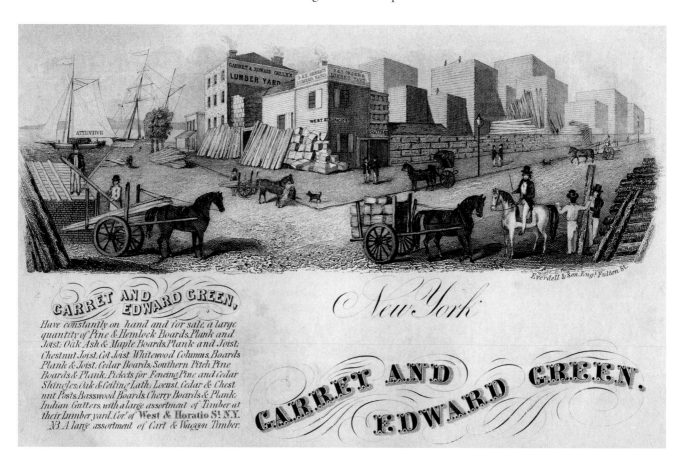

Figure 36 Handbill, Garrett and Edward Green, New York, New York, ca. 1845. Engraved by Everdell and Son. H. 5¼", W. 8⅜". The mammoth size of this facility speaks to the rapid expansion of the city before the mid-nineteenth century.

Figure 37 Alexander Anderson (1775–1870), [*A Rural Gristmill*], northeastern United States, ca. 1825–1850. Wood engraving. (Courtesy, The Miriam and Ira D. Wallach Division of Art, Prints, and Photographs: Print Collection, "Scenes of daily life in nineteenth-century America," The New York Public Library Digital Collections, 1794–1870.) The power source for the gristmill is just visible behind the building: a large vertical overshot waterwheel placed in motion by water carried to it in an elevated millrace from the water source.

Gristmills

Wheat milled into flour and corn ground into meal were staple commodities in American society. Small community gristmills, such as that illustrated in figure 37, were familiar throughout New England and in rural areas everywhere. The common gristmill became a merchant mill only where wheat and corn were cultivated extensively and most of the product was destined for export. Much of New England was hilly and with rocky soil not conducive to agriculture, except for an occasional fertile meadow or cattle-raising area. The region was well-endowed with waterpower, however: hillside streams, durable falls, innumerable lakes and ponds, and a variety of river systems. These resources eventually became productive for other types of industrial development. The eastern Middle Atlantic region and adjacent areas as far south as Virginia comprised the major merchant milling district, where the vertical overshot waterwheel became the mainstay. Moderate to large milling centers with access to export centers, such as Philadelphia and the Chesapeake Bay region, were developed by the late eighteenth century along rivers and streams with strong currents, rapids, or dams, including the Delaware, Wissahickon, Brandywine, Jones Falls, and Potomac. After completion of the Erie Canal in New York state in 1825,

Figure 38   The Upper Falls of the Genesee River at Rochester, N. Y., from the East Bank Looking N.W., Rochester, New York, 1835. Drawn by J. Young, lithographed by J. H. Bufford, published by C. and M. Morse, PR 020. (Courtesy, Collection of Geographic Images, New-York Historical Society, 98180d.) From a small village established at the start of the nineteenth century, Rochester increased rapidly in area and population after 1825 following the opening of the Erie Canal. Wheat, already being grown in the Genesee Valley, quickly became a leading crop when the power of the falls of the Genesee River was harnessed. That power supported the vast flour milling complex shown here, among other businesses.

Genesee Falls near Rochester became prominent as a flour milling site supported by wheat from the Genesee Valley (fig. 38). A principal destination for American flour was the West Indies, although American ships carried the product far afield.[64]

The large vertical overshot waterwheel that became an important power source of the gristmill permitted "the high rotating speeds required in grain milling." Maintenance was a recurring concern, however, because the wooden gear wheels, composed of cogs and rounds, were subject to friction and wear. A 1792 account entry by Lemuel Tobey at Dartmouth, Massachusetts, addresses the subject of maintenance: "Turning 14 Rounds fore the Grist Mill," a facility owned by Stephen Table. Providing more insight into the dimensions of this work is a charge made several decades later when James Geer of Groton, Connecticut, billed Peleg Rose $4.32 for "turning 72 Mill rounds," for his pinion, or lantern, mill gear. Another aspect of millwork focused on the waterwheel shaft, which conveyed power to the cogwheel. In 1808 William Chappel of Danbury supplied "1 Stick Timber for [the] water wheel shaft" at the Red Mill. The facility may have been new, although there is no indication that Chappel was the craftsman who actually made the installation. Work on a mill flume was undertaken at Kingston, Massachusetts, in September 1820 when Nathan Lucas, with previous experience, charged Stephen Bradford $8.00 for the job. Lucas's usual rate of one dollar a day suggests the work could have required more than a week to complete, unless the fee also included the cost of replacement timbers. A month later Lucas returned for a job of "diging Sluceway 1½ Rods" (24¾ feet). The work may have related to the job on the flume, although it could have identified a channel, or tailrace, to carry off surplus water from the pit under the millwheel. Some years later Lucas was called to work on the "Grist Mill Wheel" at Bradford's mill complex, a site that also included a "Clay Mill." As payment for his services Lucas accepted a variety of barter, including "corn at the mill" and "Sundry of Earthen Ware." Nathaniel F. Martin, who had carried out earlier work on the sawmill of William Fuller at Windham, Connecticut, returned to the mill site in 1805 for a job described as "putting in box to grist mill." The reference is not specific, but it could describe a gear box or a container that received bolted (sieved) flour from milled grain for transfer to sacks or barrels.[65]

The quality of the pair of millstones used in grinding grain related directly to the efficient operation of a gristmill. French siliceous buhrstones were considered the best. Quality stones were also obtained from England and the Continent in the Rhine region around Cologne. Native granite, hard sandstone, and other types of stone were alternatives. A stone dresser prepared a stone for milling using a pick, or mill bill, to cut furrows on the face forming ridges with sharp edges extending obliquely from the center of the stone to the circumference. With use, a pair of stones required periodic redressing. An observer describing the extensive merchant milling complex along the Brandywine (fig. 39) near the community of Wilmington, Delaware, where Thomas Shipley operated a mill with an overshot wheel, wrote in 1789:

Figure 39   Bass Otis (1784–1861), *Brandywine Mills*, Wilmington, Delaware, ca. 1840. Oil on canvas. H. 31¼", W. 40⅜" (framed). (Courtesy, Delaware Historical Society, gift of H. Fletcher Brown, 1941.051.)

> There are in one view on the Brandywine, ten mills with not less than twenty pair of stones, capable of grinding two thousand bushels a day. One set of gears serves two pair of stones, not for both pair to run at once, but when one pair is up dressing or cooling, the other to run; and thus in active or busy times, the mill grinds perpetually day and night.

The complex had tidewater access to the Delaware River and Philadelphia, from where large vessels conveyed the product to markets in the West Indies and Europe. Within six years Oliver Evans, a young engineer born in Delaware, and his collaborator Thomas Ellicott published *The Young Mill-Wright and Miller's Guide* (1795), an influential book on American water milling that provided information on planning, building, and equipping a mill so that "all the operations—cleaning, grinding, and bolting" required no "human intervention" except to "set the different machines in motion."[66]

Cider Mills

The cider mill, a lower key installation than the sawmill or gristmill, and the popular drink cider, were noted by various travelers in America. Jedidiah Morse, passing through the Narragansett region in 1797, commented that both East Greenwich and Warwick, Rhode Island, were known for "making good cider." John Lambert found that cider was a favorite beverage in Connecticut and further explained that "large orchards crowded with an immense variety of fruit-trees are attached to every farm in the State." While traveling in New Jersey during autumn in the mid-1790s, William Strickland, a British agriculturist, took note of the woods and orchards on his way to Newark, where he learned that Newark cider was considered among the best in the nation. He found that "the people are now busily employed in the first crushing of the apple" and added "but this is only for common use, the best Cyder being made later in the Season." Another Briton, Thomas Anburey, a soldier in America during the Revolutionary War, noted cider-making equipment in use when passing through eastern Pennsylvania: "in almost every farm there is a press, . . . some make use of a wheel made of thick oak plank, which turns upon a wooden axis, by means of a horse drawing it, and some have stone wheels." Perhaps some of the stone wheels were made from millstones no longer fit for grinding. Lewis Miller, the chronicler of York, Pennsylvania, made a sketch of an "Apple mill" on the local farm of George Spangler showing piles of apples and a horse providing the operating power.[67]

Anburey noted only part of the equipment necessary for cider making. He described a circular vat with a narrow trough inside an outer rim, where the fresh fruit was dumped to be crushed by a horse-drawn wheel (fig. 40). The fruit, reduced to pomace, was scooped up into open pails with the wooden shovels seen on the canvas and taken to the cylindrical press at the right. The press, its floor grooved in channels, was filled with pomace arranged in layers separated by clean straw, woven horsehair, or some other porous material. A cover, or heavy wooden frame, was placed on top and a screw, operated by a long wooden hand lever as shown, lowered the cover on the pomace until all juice was extracted and placed in barrels. Records of woodworking craftsmen describe the interaction of various artisans with

Figure 40 William Moore Davis (1829–1920), *Cider-Making on Long Island*, ca. 1865–1875. Oil on canvas. H. 19¾", W. 29¾". (Courtesy, Fennimore Art Museum, Cooperstown, New York, gift of Stephen C. Clark, acc. 368.1955; photo, Richard Walker.)

cider mill owners. Shortly after moving from Amherst to New Salem, Massachusetts, Nathaniel Bangs recorded "work Done to your Sieder mil" for Lieutenant Jeffe Peirce, a new customer. At Cornish, New Hampshire, Stephen Tracy performed unknown "work on the Cider mill" of Simon Smith, although credits in his accounts add a dimension. For this and other jobs in 1826, Smith was credited by Tracy with "use of his mill to make . . . cider" on at least three occasions. Scattered throughout Tracy's accounts, both when in Connecticut and later in New Hampshire, are references to his accepting as barter apples and barrels of cider. At East Hampton, on eastern Long Island, Nathaniel Dominy V also accepted cider as barter. His recorded work on a cider mill belonging to David Scoy in 1807 lists "Nuts & Screws" for the mill. Representing significant time is Nathan Lucas's "6 days work on a Cider Mill" for Nathan Chandler at Kingston, Massachusetts. The time involved and the words "a mill" rather than "the mill" suggest the facility was new. Chandler, who already owned salt meadows, appears to have been expanding his farm holdings, as he also paid one of Lucas's workmen to build a "Hen House."[68]

MARITIME TRADES

Shipbuilding began at an early date in the American colonies. Long before there were thoughts of independence, shipbuilding had become an exceedingly profitable business. The market was twofold: the greater part of busi-

SLOOP OF 1776

TWO-MASTED SCHOONER

SNOW RIG

BRIG

BARK

SHIP OF THE 18TH CENTURY

Figure 41 Principal types of American sailing vessels, 1760–1840. Composite from Charles G. Davis, *Shipping and Craft in Silhouette* (Salem, Mass.: Marine Research Society, 1929), figs. 8, 17, 23, 28, 51. (Courtesy, Peabody Essex Museum.) The distinctive shape, number, and arrangement of sails and masts differentiate types of vessels without reference to the hull.

ness served colonial customers, but a sizable market also existed for British buyers. An abundance of raw material close at hand favored the American builder, who could construct a vessel for half to two-thirds the cost of one built in England. Colonial yards constructed two classes of vessels: large ships of between one hundred and more than four hundred tons for transatlantic voyages; and single-masted sloops for coastal traders and fishermen, including the somewhat larger schooner for the Caribbean and North Atlantic trades (fig. 41). It was not unknown, however, for seasoned masters of sloops to venture a voyage across the North Atlantic to the Cape Verde or Madeira Islands with cargoes of common chairs and woodenwares. The Verdes, relatively treeless, welcomed wooden products; the Madeiras were the source of a popular wine of the same name. The overall market for small vessels was twice that of large ships. The Atlantic seaboard was dotted with features that encouraged both coastal and foreign commerce—sizable natural ports, navigable rivers, and countless bays, coves, and inlets. The prodigious number of vessels, large and small, on the waters gave employ not only to seamen but to craftsmen in ancillary trades, such as rope and sailmakers, carpenters, carvers, and painters.[69]

Considerable destruction of American shipping occurred during the Revolution. The whaling fleets of Nantucket and New Bedford were decimated. The marquis de Chastellux indicated that "the English had not left a

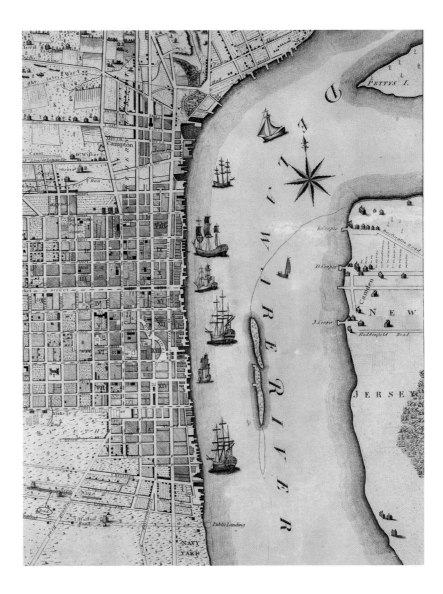

Figure 42   Detail of a *Plan of the City of Philadelphia and Its Environs*, Pierre Charles Varlé, cartographer, Robert Scot, engraver, Philadelphia, Pennsylvania, 1802. Line etching on laid paper (state two). Overall H. 20½", W. 27". (Courtesy, Winterthur Museum, acc. 1960.0358.001 A.) The city's many shipping wharves along the Delaware River, including parts of the Northern Liberties and Southwark, speak to the flourishing state of Philadelphia when it served as the national capital from 1790 to 1800.

single bark" in the harbor at Philadelphia in 1778; however, two years later he noted the changed scene along Front Street "out of which open upwards of two hundred quays" (fig. 42), where he saw "about three hundred vessels in the harbour." South of Philadelphia in the postwar period, Baltimore, with access to Chesapeake Bay, experienced exceptionally rapid growth in size and in trade with the back country, which proffered grain, tobacco, and produce in exchange for manufactured goods. Large vessels loaded and unloaded their cargoes at Fell's Point, although business was conducted nearby in town at the merchants' countinghouses. Continued growth and territorial expansion soon joined the two areas by land into a single commu-

Figure 43   *South St. from Maiden Lane,*
New York, New York, ca. 1834. Aquatint
drawn and etched by William J. Bennett
(1787–1844) after the engraver's painting,
published by Henry J. Megarey. (Courtesy,
The Miriam and Ira D. Wallach Division
of Art, Prints, and Photographs: The I.
N. Phelps Stokes Collection of American
Historical Prints, The New York Public

Library Digital Collections.) The site on
South Street is on the East River looking
south from Maiden Lane, where two
blocks farther along the waterfront the
observer could view the Tontine Coffee
House a short distance up Wall Street
and perceive the full impact of America's
leading business center.

nity. During the following decade William Strickland arrived at New York "in
the midst of a forest of masts, some hundreds of vessels . . . , more in number
and in closer tier than I ever before saw, except on the Thames below London bridge" (fig. 43). Contemporary visitors to New York described the
depth of the water in the East River as "sufficient for the largest merchant
vessels" to dock and remarked on the rarity of the water freezing due to "the
saltness of the sound and the bay" as well as the "greater ebb and flow of the
tide" and the "rapidity of the currents." At Boston the Englishman Henry
Wansey, when visiting in 1794, noted that State Street was a center of trade,
its terminus at Long Wharf adjacent to a "noble capacious" harbor filled
with wharves. Estimates of the size of Long Wharf varied, although a length

of 1,200 to 1,500 feet probably was close to the mark. Wansey described its width at about eighty feet and was intrigued that "in the middle of it stands a long row of store houses, from end to end, which forms a very convenient arrangement for ships . . . to load and unload at opposite sides of the same warehouse at the same time" (fig. 44). A decade earlier Francisco de Miranda had noted that at low tide there were seventeen feet of water at the head of the wharf. Commercial activity in Boston Harbor was huge, approximately three times that of its neighbor Salem.[70]

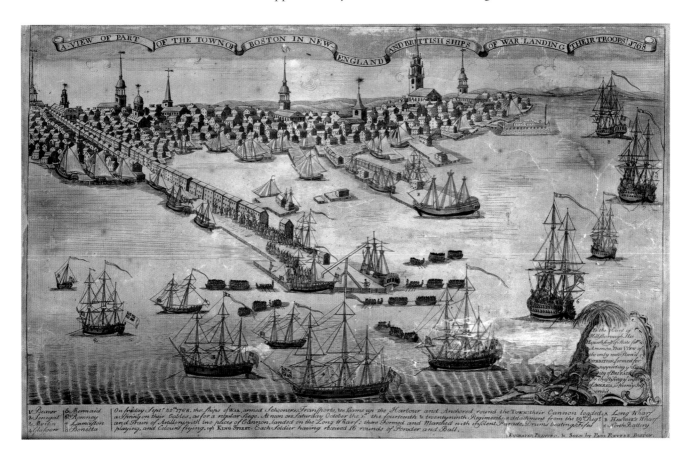

Figure 44 A View of Part of the Town of Boston in New-England and Brittish [*sic*] Ships of War Landing Their Troops!, Boston, 1770. Line engraving by Paul Revere (1735–1818). H. 8⅝", W. 15⅜". (Courtesy, Boston Athenaeum, George Francis Parkman Fund purchase, 1955, acc. 1955.2.) A sizeable row of storehouses stood on Long Wharf from before the Revolution.

Just as trade and commerce were important to the economic life of the colonies, so both became critical to the prosperity of the new nation. Following the war, trading terms with England were altered by the infamous Orders in Council. Raw materials from America could be carried directly to Britain in American or British vessels, as formerly, although direct American trade with Canada and the British West Indies was now forbidden. Dutch and, for the most part, French ports in the West Indies remained open to American shipping. Eventually the continuing turmoil and war in Europe altered ownership of some Caribbean islands or prevented critical provisioning of others, temporarily opening some islands to American shipping and closing others. Some Spanish islands not open earlier also became available for trade with American vessels, and American interests found additional new areas of the globe to explore: the Mediterranean and Baltic regions, the Far East, and after 1800 Central and South America.[71]

The maritime business of the country was far from smooth sailing, however. From the mid-1790s into the new century the French preyed on neutral American shipping, a reflection of the excesses of their revolution and the later aggressiveness of the Directory under Napoleon Bonaparte.

Despite treaties with Great Britain and efforts to have the Orders in Council repealed, the English in their war with France found numerous excuses to ignore American neutrality. Spoliation excesses came to a head in December 1807 when Congress, at President Jefferson's urging, passed the Embargo Act forbidding all clearances of American vessels for foreign ports and barring British vessels from American ports. The act was highly unpopular with American shipping interests, and fourteen months later, in March 1809, it was nullified. James Madison, after assuming the American presidency in 1809, made another attempt to have the Orders in Council rescinded, although his efforts came to naught.[72]

Trade resumed, adapting to new conditions, but prosperity was short lived. Napoleon tricked Madison into believing the British were ready to repeal the Orders in Council, leading Madison to give the British three months to comply. When no action took place by February 1811, Madison forbade further trade with Great Britain. Matters dragged on until finally, in June 1812, Congress issued a declaration of war, unaware that the British planned to suspend the Orders effective two days later. The British retaliated with a blockade of much of the American coast and by mobilizing ground forces. Whereas American encounters with British ground forces did not go well, spectacular American victories on the water helped to boost American morale. Abdication of Napoleon in 1814 permitted the British to focus on the war in America, and they launched a four-part invasion. One site was the Chesapeake region, which in August resulted in the destruction of the national capitol, the president's house, and other public buildings in Washington. Another site targeted by the British was New Orleans, where in January 1815 the British were defeated by a new military leader, General Andrew Jackson. The battle was something of an empty victory for America. Peace talks had begun shortly after America declared war, but the British had bided their time, expecting that decisive victories would strengthen their position. The Treaty of Ghent ending the war actually was signed on December 24, 1814. The years of commercial turbulence during the embargoes and war encouraged some far-sighted merchant families in New England to become "pioneer manufacturers," although significant interest continued in waterborne trade and shipping.[73]

Small sloops plying the coast from landing to landing and port to port were common from colonial days. The Duke de la Rochefoucauld Liancourt, writing in the late 1790s, noted that the town of New Castle on the Delaware River "confines itself to the coasting trade with Philadelphia." On a visit to New York more than a decade later Timothy Dwight claimed "the coasting vessels of the Hudson, New England, and New Jersey appear to the eye to be numberless." Captains of coasting and other vessels to the South found good trade in carrying raw cotton from large and small coastal and gulf ports to newly established spinning and weaving mills in New

England and other locations. During the early post-revolutionary period part of the coasting business became regularized, introducing fixed sailing times for the carriage of both passengers and freight. In 1788 Brissot de Warville noted packets from the southern New England towns "going to New-York," and another commentator remarked on packets from eastern Long Island "plying to Boston." Many packets out of Philadelphia headed south for Norfolk, Charleston, New Orleans, and other ports. The packet business also extended to transatlantic sailings of square-rigged ships. The Black Ball Line of New York, which began operation in 1818, was the pioneer transatlantic packet line to Liverpool, sailing the first of every month during fair weather or foul. New York's population by the 1810s exceeded that of other American cities, and this center of business achieved financial dominance. The city's relatively ice-free coastal location established the port as the nation's premier entrepôt. Thomas P. Cope, a prominent businessman and merchant of Philadelphia, established a packet line in 1821 between that city and Liverpool, and the next year packets began sailing from Boston to Liverpool. The British established packet lines to America, too, although American vessels captured the market. An Englishman "on a walk through the docks at Liverpool" noted the reason: American ships were "long, sharp built, beautifully painted and rigged," whereas the English vessels were "short, round and dirty, resembling great black tubs." The whaling business picked up where it had left off after the upheaval of the Revolutionary War, extending its expeditions farther into the Pacific. American trading vessels in Pacific waters made contacts with the western coast of South America, the northwest coast of America, China, the East Indies, and India.[74]

Meanwhile, new developments in water travel occurred on American rivers. Robert Fulton, although not the earliest designer of a steamboat, demonstrated in 1807 steam's practical application when he piloted a steamboat, later known as the *Clermont*, up the Hudson River from New York to Albany. Four years later Timothy Dwight could declare: "Hardly any sight is more rare or more beautiful than the steamboats which move on the waters connected with New York, and which began their first operation deserving of any notice at this place." Progress was rapid, and steamboat service expanded during the 1810s beyond the Hudson to adjacent New Jersey and Long Island Sound. Vessels grew in number and size, and they extended their range of travel. The principal function of the steamboat on eastern waters was to carry passengers. Carl David Arfwedson, a Swedish traveler in America, recorded boarding the steamboat *President* at Providence, Rhode Island, in 1832 for a journey to New York. Later the same year he undertook another trip by steam from Philadelphia to Baltimore, the city of monuments. Although discussion of steamboats on the western rivers is outside the scope of this study, several points are notable. The application of steam to river travel revolutionized business in the West, where carriage of freight upriver was now possible on the Mississippi and other waterways of swift current. The shallow beds of these waterways dictated a new shallow hull design with a flat bottom, which also permitted travel into the many subordinate rivers of the West.[75]

Fabrication of Sea Chests

A young man planning to go to sea equipped himself with a container of some type, often a wooden sea chest, to hold his clothes and personal gear. The long rectangular chest had a lift lid and a loop handle, or becket, at either end made of rope or another woven material, each handle secured to the box by a wooden bracket. The sides of the box were straight or canted and the corners dovetailed. A bumper around the bottom protected the construction from shocks at sea. The chest also served as a chair or seat. The interior was plain or fitted with a till or one or more other convenient compartments. The exterior frequently was unpainted. Minor embellishments sometimes included initials or a date. Some decoration was whimsical, while other ornament might take the form of a vessel in full sail painted on the front panel or inside or outside the lid. Decoration likely was acquired along the way rather than at the start of a mariner's career. Craftsmen in Connecticut and Rhode Island who recorded making sea chests charged somewhat more or less than a pound ($3.33) for the work. Amos D. Allen of Windham, Connecticut, constructed a sea chest in 1799 described as "1 Chest for sea 3 [feet] 9 Ins long, 19 or 20 wide [front to back] with a case." The work was paid for by Gideon Hoxey, the young seaman, or perhaps by his father. Whether the outer "case" was made of wood or heavy cloth, such as sail duck, is unknown. Proper clothing for wear at sea and other gear, known as slops, were available from ship chandlers in seaport communities. David W. Williams, a ship chandler of Essex, placed an order in 1828 with Elisha H. Holmes for "1 Slop table with draw[er] 2 ft 9 in long 3 ft 8 Wide" and payed $4.50.[76]

Sailmakers and Rope makers

Prior to the Revolution, many maritime communities were unable to produce the quantities of canvas and cordage required by the shipyards, necessitating the importation of this type of ships' chandlery from England at high prices. Following independence, the ancillary maritime trades in America began to increase in number and size. Traveling in New England in the 1790s, the Duke de la Rochefoucauld Liancourt noted "a sail-cloth manufactory, which employs a great number of skilful hands" at Salem, Massachusetts. Sailcloth at that date was a strong, coarse cloth of closely woven hemp yarns produced on a rope-maker's wheel. Daniel Trotter, a cabinet-maker of Philadelphia, mended a sailmaker's bench and added a drawer in 1790 for John Dowers, whose shop was on Water Street near the docks. Several decades later a sailmaker at Essex, Connecticut, ordered a new bench with a drawer from Elisha H. Holmes and paid him $1.25. The low bench, with its drawer for thread, needles, and other tools, was a convenient support for a sailmaker, who stitched seams and hems with the heavy cloth draped across his knees (fig. 45). The strong thread, or twine, used for sewing was formed from two strands of hemp yarn twisted together. An individual pursuing the craft of sailmaker also was known as a ship's tailor.[77]

Visitors to America commented more frequently on the ropewalk than the sailmaker's shop, probably due to the physical size of the former. By

Figure 45 Sailmakers, in Jan Joris van der Vliet, [*Book of Crafts and Trades*] (Holland, 1635; reprinted in Harry Bober, *Jan Van Vliet's Book of Crafts and Trades* [Albany, N.Y.: Early American Industries Association, 1981])), pl. 11. (Photo, Winterthur Library.) Although this is an early representation of the craft of sail making, craft procedure was not significantly changed by use of a sailmaker's bench for seating and easy access to the tools of the trade.

the mid-eighteenth century Boston's largest ropewalk could produce rope in lengths of 600 feet at an inside facility and 780 feet at a facility outside. "Yarns and small stuff" were made in an adjacent building. In total, the work consisted of all types of "cordage, white rope, tarred rope, and twine." By 1774 Philadelphia had six or more ropewalks, complemented by facilities for other shipbuilding trades, including thirteen sailmaker's shops. John Fanning Watson, a chronicler of early Philadelphia, noted that shipbuilding and related trades once located within the city had migrated to the outskirts by the late eighteenth century. In his journal, Dr. Robert Honyman described a visit to Salem, Massachusetts, early in 1775 and his amazement to find "some of the longest & finest Rope walks & spinning houses I ever saw . . . making large ropes and cables." Many other New England towns, including Portsmouth, New Hampshire, and Newport, Rhode Island, were active shipbuilding and outfitting communities. On a journey to New York City in the 1790s, shortly after erection of the Tontine Coffee House with its merchant's exchange, Moreau de St. Méry commented on a relatively new ropewalk across the East River in Brooklyn, part of it erected on pilings at the river's edge. He estimated its length at slightly more than 1,000 feet and stated "it employs forty people." A visit to South Carolina in 1808 prompted John Lambert to comment on the commerce of the state, which included ropewalks to support shipping established near Charleston.[78]

To process yarn used in making rope, a spinner filled a sack with hemp fibers, attached some to a hook behind a spinning machine, and walked backward to the other end of the ropewalk holding the yarn firmly to maintain equal tension throughout (see fig. 46). Meanwhile, another workman (in the foreground) turned a large wheel to provide the twist. This process formed one strand, which the spinner held on to while proceeding back up

Figure 46 *Facility of the Rope Maker*, in Edward Hazen, *The Panorama of Professions and Trades* (Philadelphia: U. Hunt, 1839), p. 56. (Courtesy, Winterthur Library, Printed Book and Periodical Collection.)

Figure 47 *Office of Humphrey Hathaway,*
at the Head of Rotch's Wharf, New Bedford,
Massachusetts, ca. 1873, depicting a scene of 1819
or later. Pencil sketch on paper by Edward S.
Russell. From Horatio Hathaway, *A New Bedford*
Merchant (Boston: Merrymount Press, 1930).
(Courtesy, New Bedford Whaling Museum,
Estate of Thomas S. Hathaway.) This counting
room adjacent to the wharves probably was
typical of a moderate to large coastal facility of the
early nineteenth century. The two long desks with
their bookcases and slanted writing surfaces could
accommodate two or three clerks each. By the late
eighteenth century iron stoves had replaced the
hearth as the heat source. Here, the forward area
of the room with its Windsor seating, maps, and
a telescope provided a convenient place for sea
captains, clients, and others to meet and acquire
news about markets, shipping conditions, and
related subjects.

the walk while the yarn was wound on a reel. Sailmaker's thread, or twine, required two strands twisted together, and three strands twisted together formed a light rope. Strands used in heavy ropes and cables required hardening, the twist applied by a crank of considerable force. Cordage exposed to air and water, such as a ship's rigging, usually was tarred. The accounts of woodworking craftsmen identify their interaction with the rope-making trade. For "Work at ye Rope Walk Self an[d] Boy 5 Day" in 1758, Joseph Lindsey of Marblehead, Massachusetts, charged Benjamin Henly £1.10.0 ($5.00). A minor job in 1779 "at the Rope work [*sic*]" of Lewis Billow briefly engaged Job E. Townsend, of Newport, Rhode Island. Many decades later Townsend recorded a job for Daniel Anderson and Company of "four Days Work on their Rope Wolk" at $1.00 per day. Wharf-side countinghouses were relatively common by the second quarter of the nineteenth century, and "through the small-paned windows one could see the firm's new ship being rigged under the owner's eye" (fig.47).[79]

Ship Carvers
Of the substantial amount of ship carving that once existed, little remains today. Period records provide a hint at the variety of options available to the vessel owner. A note dated at New York on November 26, 1799, by Daniel N. Train and Company referencing work completed for merchant

Benjamin Fry of Newport, Rhode Island, was delivered to Fry by Captain Henry Cahoone of Newport. Undertaken in August and September, the work included carving, painting, and boxing figures of *Venilia* and *Hero*, the charge £37.14.0 ($125.67, New England currency). Naming a vessel (and thus its figurehead) for a mythological subject was relatively common. A receipted copy of the bill showing payment dated December 18 also included a job on December 2 for a "Pair [of] trailboards" at £4.8.0 and

Figure 48 Joseph Howard (1780–1857), detail of bow of the frigate U.S.S. *Essex*, Salem, Massachusetts, after 1799. Gouache and watercolor on paper. Overall H. 19¾", W. 27¾". (Courtesy, Peabody Essex Museum, gift of John P. Howard, 1888, acc. M167.) Displayed in this detail are several carved and painted features that customarily were part of the overall design of a large vessel: a figurehead, here in the unusual form of a Native American, and whose left leg is bent at the knee in a "walking attitude"; a trail board, one of a pair, mounted on the sides of a vessel below the figurehead and extending the full or partial length of the vessel; a catface, a whimsical depiction of the facial features of a wild cat on either blunt end of a cathead.

"Brackets" at 16s. (totaling $17.33). Trailboards, narrow carved or otherwise ornamented boards mounted on either side of a vessel, extended fully or partially along the length (see fig. 48). The date of the posting indicates the trailboards were not for the brig *Venilia* and possibly not for the *Hero*. On November 12 the *Newport Mercury* carried an advertisement submitted by Fry soliciting freight or passengers for Baltimore on the "fast-sailing new BRIG VENILIA." Fry owned several other brigs, including the *Favorite*, which left Newport late in 1800 for a voyage to St. Christopher in the West Indies. On the way, she was seized by a French privateer disregarding American neutrality, taken to Guadeloupe, and on January 2, 1801, condemned. This episode was just one instance of the hundreds of violations of American neutrality by the French and the English during the turbulent period of the 1790s and early nineteenth century.[80]

Figure 49   John H. Bellamy (1836–1914), carved lion's head made as a catface for one end of a cathead, Portsmouth, New Hampshire, 1859. Pine. H. 13″, W. 14″. (Courtesy, Old Sturbridge Village.) A note pasted on the back of the image reads: "This piece was carved by John H. Bellamy, at 77 Daniel Street, January 1859."

More insight on the ornamentation of vessels occurs in work completed by Samuel McIntire of Salem, Massachusetts, in 1803 for "Owners of the new Ship Asia," identified as Israel Thorndike of neighboring Beverly and partners. Carving (and probably painting) the figurehead was calculated at 40s. per foot and cost $58.33 for the 8¾-foot figure. The charge relates closely to that paid by Benjamin Fry for each of the figureheads for his new brigs. Slightly more expensive, at $60.00, was the cost of carving the stern of the *Asia*. Four sketches for stern designs in the McIntire papers indicate the general appearance of the work: within an arched framework extending the width of the stern is a row of five window openings below a wide arched band containing carved ornament consisting of fruit, floral, and classical motifs. Another job of carving and installing "Badges," or ornamental "window" surrounds, at the stern cost $20.00. A final item on the bill of work describes "Cat faces" and other finishing at a charge of $3.50. The "cat faces" were carved into either blunt end of the cathead, a large wooden beam located crosswise at deck level behind the bowsprit and used to support the vessel's anchor when raised, lowered, or suspended over the side. A catface is represented in figure 48 by dots forming a face at a beam end projecting behind the sailors at deck level. A rare surviving catface, carved by John H. Bellamy in 1859 at Portsmouth, New Hampshire, for an unknown vessel, is illustrated in figure 49.[81]

Caleb Davis, an entrepreneur who rose from shopkeeper to trader to merchant rather quickly, did business with members of the Skillin family of Boston during the 1770s and 1780s. A bill from Simeon Skillin Jr. to Davis in October 1777 itemizes work completed on the brig *Hazard*. First is "Carve[d] work" for a "Minerva Head 6 feet 9 Inches" at £6 ($20.00), followed by "Brackets & trailbord" at £2 ($6.67) and badges for around the windows of the stern at £4 ($13.33). Given the cost, the work does not appear to have been as decorative as comparable work completed by Daniel N. Train for Benjamin Fry or by Samuel McIntire for Israel Thorndike and partners. Continuing with the bill, there are entries for "Quarter Pieces" £6 and a "Taffrel" (taffrail) £6. The quarter pieces were used in the ship's quarter, possible for a quarter gallery (a small balcony near the stern), with the taffrail forming a railing around it. Davis called upon the Skillin family again in the 1780s for "Repairing Brig Juno's Head," when Simeon and his brother John were in partnership. Priming carved work occurred prior to applying a finish coat of paint. Frequently applied by the carver, priming might be farmed out if the shop was busy, as suggested in a 1790 transaction when John and Simeon Skillin Jr. engaged Daniel Rea Jr., ornamental painter of Boston, to prime a "Figure Head" at 6s. ($1.00). Another member of the Skillin family carried the craft of ship carving into the third generation. In 1797 Simeon Skillin III, son of Samuel (who was brother to Simeon Jr. and John), located in New York, was engaged by merchants Pfister and Macomb from their countinghouse on Front Street near the East River to carve a figurehead at a cost of £10.7.0 ($25.88, New York currency).[82]

Philadelphia merchants looked to William Rush for quality carved work for ship's figureheads and related jobs. Rush, when in his teens, served an apprenticeship with Edward Cutbush, a ship carver from England. Sometime after the Revolution he opened his own shop, at which time he probably also learned wax modeling from Joseph Wright, another Englishman. Rush took as an apprentice Daniel N. Train who, as indicated, later set up a ship-carving business in New York. After the United States Navy established a yard in Philadelphia, Rush was in demand for carving or designing figureheads for military vessels along with his activity in the private sector. In later life Rush's work as a sculptor in wood brought him additional renown. Among his early merchant customers was Stephen Girard, a Frenchman who settled as a young man in Philadelphia, where he became a self-made merchant, banker, and philanthropist. Of particular note is a bill from Rush to Girard dated October 10, 1811: "to Carving Large Indian Figure for Ship North America," the price $100.00. Considering the cost and use of the term "large," the figurehead probably was equal to or larger in size than the 8¾-foot unidentified figure carved for the *Asia* by Samuel McIntire. The Salem, Massachusetts, carver also is credited with a Native American figurehead, carved for the U.S.S. frigate *Essex* some years earlier (see fig. 48). Dressed in a loin cloth and cloak, the figure is depicted in a "walking attitude," the left leg raised and the foot resting on a carved scroll. The introduction of this feature to American ship carving from its origin in Europe is credited to William Rush, probably via Edward Cutbush, with whom he served his apprenticeship.[83]

After installation of the "Large Indian" figurehead on the *North America*, finishing work continued to ready the vessel for sea, although an initial voyage was delayed by war with Great Britain. The vessel's first voyage possibly occurred after August 8, 1815, when Girard purchased four Windsor chairs as part of the furnishings. The voyage apparently was short, possibly to the West Indies and return. The *North America* was ready to sail again shortly after July 9, 1816, the date of a bill of lading for the cargo, including "Ten doz & Eight Fancy chairs" valued at $608.00. Although the route was long, the voyage was planned to include stops at known ports and to seek new markets. Initial stops were made in Continental Europe at Lisbon and Marseilles, but the principal destination was Port Louis on Isle de France (Mauritius) in the Indian Ocean, a French possession found on arrival to be in British hands in consequence of Napoleon's defeat. Nevertheless, the bent-back cane-colored chairs and the painted rosewood chairs with gilt or bronze decoration were deposited with Martin Bickham, Girard's contact on the island. Other stops were made at Saint-Denis on Réunion Island and in India and Java.[84]

Ship Equipment

Discovery of the polarity of the magnet and the subsequent invention of the mariner's compass revolutionized water travel. No longer was it necessary for mariners to keep within sight of land, permitting the substitution of sails for oars. Two principal instruments used by mariners from before the period covered by this study were the mariner's compass and the Hadley quadrant, a hand-held instrument used to determine a vessel's position

Figure 50 Samuel King (1749–1820), *Little Navigator*, Newport, Rhode Island, ca. 1810. Carved and polychromed wood shop sign. H. 24″. The sign hung over the shop door of James Fales, nautical instrument maker of Newport and later over the shop of James Fales Jr. of New Bedford, Massachusetts, ca. 1830–1880. (Courtesy, New Bedford Whaling Museum.)

at sea (fig. 50). Both were sold by instrument makers such as William Hinton of New York, who in 1772 was located at the Sign of Hadley's Quadrant. It was the woodworker's job to provide boxes and cases for these instruments. Nathaniel Knowlton made several compass boxes for a customer at Eliot, Maine, at a total charge of $4.00, whereas George Short of Newburyport, Massachusetts, reported making repairs to a compass box. Some compasses were housed in a binnacle, a box located near the ship's helm. Stephen Collins, a merchant of Philadelphia, paid George Pickering for joinery work in 1781 that included "mending the Benicle" on the "Brig Betsie." Earlier, in 1746, Joseph Lindsey provided "Shutters for a Binacle" for a Massachusetts customer. The quadrant required a case that varied in price between one and two dollars, as noted by craftsmen working at Middletown and Essex, Connecticut. After use at sea, repairs sometimes were necessary. Benjamin Gladding of Providence, Rhode Island, patronized Job Danforth Sr. when a "Quandren case for Son" required mending in 1799, possibly the same son he had furnished with a "Sea Chest" the previous year. Repairs to the quadrant case of a patron of George Short at Newburyport, Massachusetts, were described as "1 pair brass hinges & screws & putting on" for 25¢. The chronometer, an instrument for measuring time, which was improved during the early nineteenth century, was used in determining longitude at sea. Jesse Smith Jr. paid Mark Pitman of Salem $2.25 in 1835 "For a Box for chronometer for Capt Bailey." The telescope, another instrument required for a sea voyage, was built into its own

case. During the 1780s a "Spying Glass" was among acquisitions assembled by Elias Hasket Derby for use on his ship *Grand Turk I*. After Derby's death in 1799, estate records indicate the merchant had kept a "Spy Glass" handy at his "Counting Room" on Derby's Wharf in Salem.[85]

A miscellany of other equipment on shipboard addressed a variety of needs. A speaking trumpet was an essential means of communication with another vessel at sea—a way to learn the status of distant markets and be advised of adverse conditions (fig. 51). In 1789 Joseph Callender, ship chandler, engaged Daniel Rea Jr. of Boston to paint "40 speaking Trumpetts Large & Small" at 9d. each to restock his store. Whereas few individuals on shipboard had real knowledge of medical practice, vessels of any size were furnished with a box or chest fitted with bottles to hold basic medications. Robert Rantoul, a druggist of Beverly, Massachusetts, obtained medical chests for sale at his shop from Ebenezer Smith Jr. A New York newspaper notice of 1759 offered "a large Medicinal Chest fitted with large and small square Bottles, Wanting but very Trifles to make it compleat for Sea." The same equipment was referred to as a "Doctors box for ship." A general collection of tools was indispensable on shipboard. Woodworkers frequently were called upon to make new handles for tools by members of all trades. The Proud brothers, Daniel and Samuel, of Providence, Rhode Island, were engaged by Samuel Butler to make "4 Drawing knief hand[les for his] Brig" in 1787. Another customer required an "adz handle for Brig." Because the Prouds were turning specialists, the handles probably were fashioned on a

Figure 52 Ship Montesquieu off the Harbor of Macao, anonymous, Philadelphia, 1812. Oil on canvas mounted on wood. H. 20¾", W. 27". (Courtesy, Girard College History Collections, Philadelphia, Pa., acc. 0063.) This ship was one of a variety of vessels owned by Stephen Girard (1755–1831); the figurehead of the ship was carved by William Rush (1756–1833).

lathe. Another tool, usually supplied by a blacksmith but very useful in the maritime business, was the branding iron. Stephen Girard bought an iron at Philadelphia in 1794 that weighed nine pounds and contained fifteen letters for the captain of his ship *Good Friends*. In an era of candles and whale oil, the lantern was the shipboard lighting device, and several are identified in craftsmen's records. At Philadelphia, Thomas Passmore, a "manufacturer" of tin and japanned ware, supplied a $14.00 "Magazine Lanthern" for John Slesman's ship *Magnus*. The substantial cost suggests the lantern was large and the "tin" body finished with japan (a colored varnish, frequently medium brown). Another city manufacturer of tinware supplied Stephen Girard with "2 Horn Lantherns" for his ship *Montesquieu*, one of several vessels the merchant named after French philosophers (fig. 52). Horn, cut into thin sheets, was a substitute for glass. Appraisers addressing the estate of Elias Hasket Derby at Salem, Massachusetts, also found in the counting room on the wharf a "Poop [deck] Lanthorn," which they valued at $8.00. On another subject, Samuel Hendrick of Amesbury, Massachusetts, was engaged by Capt. Hooper in 1816 to provide "fifty Banisters for his hen Coops on board his Ship." Fresh food was welcome at sea, and hencoops with their tenants were common. The circumnavigation of the globe from 1794 to 1796 by the sixty-foot, sloop-rigged *Union* sailing from Newport, Rhode Island—with nineteen-year-old John Boit Jr., captain—was an adventurous trading affair. When homeward bound after passing Madagascar in the Indian Ocean, the vessel encountered a "westerly gale [that] stove in part of the . . . bulwarks and swept the hen-coops off her deck."[86]

Ship Furniture

The most common request by owners and masters of vessels for shipboard furniture was for seating and tables, sometimes en suite. Alexander Edwards, a cabinetmaker of Boston, fabricated a "Cabben tabl" in 1772 for £1.1.4 ($3.56) accompanied by six "Cabbn Stools" at £1 ($3.33) for merchant John Erving Jr. The cost, location, and prewar date indicate the stools had woven rush seats. Some years earlier the merchant Jeremiah Lee of neighboring Marblehead purchased six chairs and a table for his ship *Vulture* from Joseph Lindsey. At 4s. (67¢) per chair, the seats again were of woven rush. Continuing use of rush for shipboard seating in the pre-revolutionary period is confirmed in Christopher Champlin's purchase in October 1773 at Newport, Rhode Island, of "3 Cabbing Chairs" and "2 Bunshes of flages" (rush) for his sloop *Adventure*, which sailed four days later for the coast of Africa, Robert Champlin master. By the 1790s Windsor chairs, with their more durable wooden seats, had taken over the market for common shipboard seating. Benjamin Cloutman of Salem, Massachusetts, charged 6s. per chair for Elias Hasket Derby's brig *Exchange*. Additional information on form, feature, and wood is available for tables. Elisha H. Holmes of Essex, Connecticut, made several large ship's tables, as reflected in their cost or dimensions. Captain Day of New York paid him $40.00 in 1826 for "2 Cherry ship tables." Two other ship's tables of long rectangular form from the same shop were $13.00 each, although the woods are unidentified. One table measured 8 feet by 2 feet, 10 inches; the second table was slightly smaller at 7 feet, 6 inches by 2 feet, 7 inches, but it had a drawer. Farther west along the coast, at East Haven, Amos Bradley made a mahogany table for Captain Zebulon Bradley's packet and charged him $20.00. Of more modest cost and size were two "Cabbin" tables fabricated by Daniel Trotter of Philadelphia for Stephen Girard in 1786, each priced at 12s. 6p. ($2.08). One table was identified as pine, although given the similarity of description and cost, both probably were pine. The second table was made specifically for use on Girard's sloop *Two Friends*. A "ship table with four drass [drawers]," made in 1837 for Captain Ivory Lord, was $8.00 in the Kennebunk, Maine, shop of Paul Jenkins. Jenkins frequently priced tables at one dollar per foot and fifty cents per drawer, which could imply a six-foot table with two drawers on each long side. At Hampden, Maine, William H. Reed recorded a specialty table in 1810. The pembroke, or breakfast, table with falling leaves cost $4.50 and was made for use on the *Venus*, a vessel owned by storekeeper Reuben Newcomb Jr. The construction material likely was maple or birch, as suggested by the cost and the stock of material maintained by Reed.[87]

Ship Repairs and Painting

There were always repairs to be made to a wooden vessel, whether a sloop or a ship. At the busy post-revolutionary port of Providence, Rhode Island, Job Danforth Sr. recorded two customers in 1789 for unnamed "work a Board your Sloop," both jobs requiring a day or more and each priced slightly more than six shillings. Minor work at Gloucester, Massachusetts, undertaken by Nathaniel Kinsman in 1757 "on Bord the Schooner Olive Branch" owned by Nathaniel Low cost only 1s. 8d. (28¢). Typical shipboard work, when identified, might include "Turning three Small Banisters" (see fig. 10) for a brig at 25¢ or "Putting up shelf in state room" at 75¢. A substantial job of "Joynering on his Vessil Cabing" was completed in 1785 by Bartholomew Akin at New Bedford, Massachusetts, for William Wood at a cost of £5.8.0 ($18.00). Woodworking craftsmen in Philadelphia were kept as busy as their counterparts in New England serving merchants and vessel owners. In 1781 Patrick McDowell and George Pickering collaborated for work on Stephen Collins's "Brig Betsie." McDowell supplied "turning work" while Pickering completed "joinery work," which included "2 Companion Doors" and "Work Done in the Cabbin." As noted previously, Pickering also repaired the binnacle. Work by Richard Mills in 1768 for an unnamed ship owned in the city by William Barrell contrasted two types of jobs. The first, described as "Turning 12 Pillars & fluting them" at £2.8.0 ($8.00), was ornamental work, possibly for the cabin of the ship's captain. The other job involved securing "2 Chairs in Cabin" to render them immobile in heavy seas. Following a visit with her father in England, Susanna Dillwyn began a letter to him on shipboard to America: "The wind is now quite a fresh breeze & the water is rough [and] the chairs and things begin to ship about so that I cant write much longer" (fig. 53).[88]

Figure 53 John Lewis Krimmel (1786–1821), *Cabin of a Sailing Vessel*, Philadelphia, Pennsylvania, 1812–1813. Ink, ink wash, and pencil on paper. H. 4⅜", W. 6¼". From Krimmel, Sketchbook 2, 1812–1813, p. 11. (Courtesy, Winterthur Library, Joseph Downs Collection of Manuscripts and Printed Ephemera.) The water through which the vessel is sailing has become rough, and it is playing havoc with activity in the cabin.

Weather of all types, and constant exposure to seawater and fresh water alike, took a toll on a vessel's finish. Because large quantities of paint were required to cover the surfaces of even a small sailing vessel, this discussion

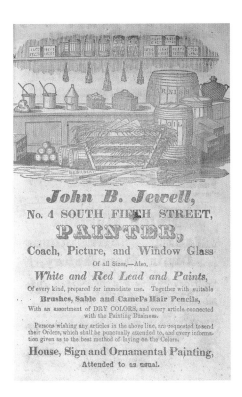

will focus on the jobs that a small or medium-size painting business could handle. A paint stone and hand muller would have been inadequate to grind sufficient material for many jobs (see fig. 2); however, hand-operated paint mills were available even before the Revolution. If the paint mill was inadequate, a painter could patronize a paint dealer, such as John Morgan of New York, who in 1785 installed a large mill "for the sole purpose of grinding Colours." These mills were operated by horse power, waterpower, or, eventually, steam power. Specialty stores of this type sold painting materials in quantity—by the gallon, cask, or even by the ton (fig. 54). Some large stores made it a point to inform ship chandlers that "white lead, Spanish brown, Verdigrease, &c., will be ground for them on the shortest notice." Painters distant from a large center usually could obtain sufficient pigment and other materials from an area merchant or apothecary.[89]

At Southampton, Long Island, John Green spent 3½ days in 1800 painting the sloop *Republican* for David Rose at the rate of 7s. ($1.17) per day. There appears to have been little change in the cost of this work over a period of several decades. In upstate New York at Ogdensburg, on the St. Lawrence River, Frederick K. Coady still charged $2.50 in 1842 for slightly more than two days' work painting a sloop for the partners Tomlinson and Cowen. Materials required for a job that preceded the Revolution was the focus of "one Days worke grinding [pigment] and Painting" the sloop *Speedwell* belonging to Obidiah Brown of Providence, Rhode Island. To the base ingredient of four pounds of white lead was added one pound of yellow and a smaller amount of Venetian red, a ferric oxide having a brownish cast. When mixed with linseed oil, these materials created orange-color paint. The "verde greese" on the list was used for green trim. Orange paint appears to have been appropriate for a sailing vessel. Joseph Stone of East Greenwich charged 12s. ($2.00) for two days' "painting . . . the Sc[h]ooner orrange" in 1794 for William Arnold, a merchant of Narragansett Bay. On the north shore of Cape Cod, Nathaniel Holmes, painting specialist at Barnstable, Massachusetts, had good trade by the early nineteenth century. In May 1807 he recorded a "half Days work on Bord the Liberty," probably a schooner. Additional work in September described the two-part job: "to finding paints fore second Coat for the Cabbin." Five years later Holmes had a job painting the cabin on board the *Romeo*. An extra charge for the paint identifies the type of finish: "for graining wood." The following year Holmes spent time "grinding paints for the Sc[h]ooner thomas," a job he further described as "my Self and Wm B[arnes] one Days painting on the thomas." Based on the several recorded working times and charges, Barnes likely was a journeyman. The overall paint color of the vessel is unknown, but the trim was identified as "green for Caben window Blinds." As recorded by Holmes, a painter occasionally was called upon for specialized work on a vessel. After completing his grain painting of the *Romeo*'s cabin, he charged $1.99 for "putting on the name." William Gray described similar work undertaken for Joseph Parsons at Salem, Massachusetts, as "Marking Sch[oone]r Hannah Name."[90]

Figure 55 John Lewis Krimmel, *Steamboat Travel on the Hudson River*, Philadelphia, Pennsylvania, 1812–13. Watercolor and gouache on white wove paper. H. 10", W. 14½". (Courtesy, Metropolitan Museum of Art, Rogers Fund, 1942, acc. 42.95.7; Art Resource, New York.) While traveling in America from 1811 to 1813, Paul Petrovich Svinin (1787/88–1839) assembled a portfolio of 52 watercolor views of North America, some purchased from Krimmel, including this view of an early steamboat. Carried back to Russia, the portfolio eventually came into the possession of an American following the tumult of the Russian Revolution. By 1930 the portfolio was in the possession of R. T. Haines Halsey, from whom in time it was transferred to the Metropolitan Museum of Art, where Halsey was founder of the American Wing. See also Anneliese Harding, *John Lewis Krimmel: Genre Artist of the Early Republic* (Winterthur, Del.: Winterthur Publications, 1994), pp. 238–49.

Furnishings for Steamboats on Eastern Waters

The need for furnishings on steamboats was immediate. The vessel in figure 55, possibly the *Northern Star*, an early design with a mast for auxiliary sails, describes the substantial deck present from an early date for viewing the landscape. The deck area grew quickly in size and was soon covered with an awning to protect passengers from sun and showers. Vernacular seating was practical on deck; a mixture of vernacular and formal furniture was appropriate below deck. Robert Fulton's *Paragon*, launched in 1811, had separate interior sections for men and women, plus a dining saloon, and everywhere there were "comfortable seats which lure the passengers thither." Whereas early travel centered on the Hudson River, it soon expanded to connect New York City by steamboat with other regional centers. The *Emerald*, *Thistle*, and *Bellona* plied between New York and New Brunswick, New Jersey, located fifteen miles inland on the Raritan River and accessible by steamboat. The *Experiment*, under other ownership, left its dock in Manhattan and steamed along the East River and Long Island Sound to Saybrook Point, where it entered the Connecticut River for the journey upriver to Middletown and Hartford, Connecticut.[91]

For purposes of this study, discussion of steamboat furnishings centers on the 1820s, when the owner(s) of the *Emerald*, *Thistle*, and *Bellona* made purchases from a small group of craftsmen located on Broad Street, New York, between Beaver and Liberty Streets in the vicinity of today's New York Stock Exchange. Below that location Broad Street extends to the East River. The craftsmen included Alexander Welsh, Charles Fredericks, Fredericks and Farrington (Charles and Benjamin, respectively), and Benjamin and Elijah Farrington (working singly or in partnership). Patronage appears to have been dictated by the ability to fill an order quickly or the availability of ready-made stock. Purchases for the *Thistle* were made at two shops in May 1824: from Welsh, thirteen settees (six curled maple at $12.00 each, six Windsor at $5.00 each, and one rush-seated at $5.00), five curled maple chairs at $3.50 each, and eight stools at $3.00 each (probably curled maple), the total cost being $148.50 before a $7.00 discount. The same month the vessel's owner(s) bought six Windsor chairs from Fredericks and Farrington for $1.25 apiece. The reverse of that bill bears the notation "Windsor chairs/ cabin," indicating this seating was for interior use, not on deck. Welsh was patronized again in 1826 by owners of the *Emerald*, who acquired curled maple cane-seat settees, chairs, and stools and "30 wooden bottom Settees" (Windsors), for a total cost of $341.00. At the same time the owner(s) paid Welsh $206.00 for 19½ gallons of varnish and labor to apply it at the following rates: $2.00/day (15 days), $1.50/day (8 days), and $1.00/day (8 days). The furniture would already have had a varnish coat included as part of the original cost; therefore, additional charges for liquid varnish and labor, and the substantial cost, suggest the *Emerald* was taken out of service temporarily for application of a new protective coating, probably of the interior woodwork. A number of painters working at various jobs at the different rates may have been employed at the same time to hasten the process. Owner(s) of the *Bellona* hired Charles Fredericks the same year (1826)

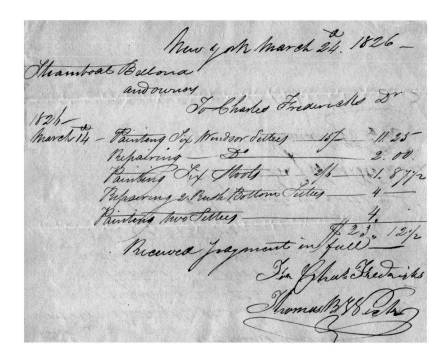

to repair and repaint vernacular seating, consisting of stools, rush-bottom settees, and six Windsor settees (fig. 56). The Windsor settees may have been the same furniture bought from Fredericks and Farrington for that vessel in 1824 for $30.00.[92]

From an early age, Cornelius Vanderbilt (later called the "Commodore") had a vested interest in the ferrying business. Born on Staten Island in 1794, he worked as a boy on his father's sailing ferry, which carried freight and passengers between Staten Island and Manhattan. Before he was out of his teens, Vanderbilt had established a similar business with a small sailing ferry of his own. In 1813, at age nineteen, he married his cousin, and they moved to a boarding house on Broad Street, Manhattan. Thus Vanderbilt had first-hand knowledge of the flourishing chair-making community at the southern tip of Manhattan. His drive and ambition came to the attention of Thomas Gibbons, who in 1817–1818 hired Vanderbilt as captain of his new steamboat *Bellona*. Vanderbilt also became Gibbons's business manager and under his tutelage quickly learned the steamboat business. John D. Brown at 45 Broad Street was engaged in April 1821 by Vanderbilt to refurbish steamboat seating, which included painting four settees and six stools, preceded by stretcher repair. Stretchers on furniture were vulnerable since patrons frequently used them as foot racks. By 1821 Gibbons probably had acquired the steamboats *Thistle*, *Emerald*, and *Swan*. Sometime during this period Vanderbilt and his growing family moved across the bay to New Brunswick, New Jersey. Purchases for the *Swan* from Alexander Welsh in 1827 as replacement or additional curled maple seating included twenty-four stools priced at $2.25 apiece. Stools were popular with children and among young working men. During the same year Vanderbilt acquired a "high stool" from Philip I. Arcularius, probably for use at a desk. At that date both chair makers were located on John Street. Thomas Gibbons died in

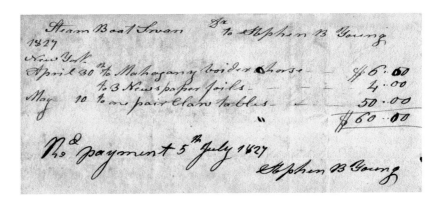

1826, and the business was taken over by his son William. Vanderbilt bought out William in 1829 and expanded the line into Long Island Sound and the lower Hudson River.[93]

Several records describe furniture purchases for other steamboats. The *Experiment* acquired settees, chairs, flag-seat stools and "2 Ball Back Rocking Cheirs" in 1822 from Elizur Barnes of Middletown, Connecticut. Ball-backs featured small turned beads in the structure. Other information focuses on Salem, New Jersey, on the Delaware River south of Philadelphia. There the chair maker-painter William G. Beesley made six stools in 1828 for the owner of the steamboat *Essex*. Another job of the mid-1830s involved "letring the stern of the steamboat Flushing." The acquisition of vernacular furniture for steamboat use describes only part of the furnishings for these vessels. A further survey of purchases for the *Bellona*, *Emerald*, *Swan*, and *Thistle* made during the 1820s reveals the variety of other articles acquired for a steam vessel. A pair of claw tables was purchased for the *Swan* from Stephen B. Young on Broad Street, New York, together with a "Mahogany voider" (tray to clear a dining table), a "horse" to support the voider, and "3 Newspaper foils" (fig. 57). John Voorhis on Maiden Lane supplied large and small cupboards for the same vessel in addition to providing extensive upholstery work, including damask curtains with silk fringe and the hardware for hanging; additional acquisitions included a sofa cushion and bedding consisting of blankets, pillows and cases, and counterpanes. The *Bellona* was furnished with a "Mantle Glass 5 feet 10 by 21 inches" from the looking-glass store of Elias Thomas on Pearl Street. The acquisition of four lanterns and four lamps from the Water Street store of Samuel Nichols, tin and coppersmith, augmented the lighting aboard the same vessel. For the *Emerald*, elegant glassware described as cut tumblers, rich cut wines, knob tumblers, and cut quart and pint decanters was furnished from the Pine Street shop of George Dummer and Company. Possibly for use in the same area was almost ninety yards of Brussels carpeting from the store of Henry Andrews on Broadway. The *Thistle* was the recipient of "2 dz Brittania tea Spoons" acquired from the firm of Wood and Van Wagenen on Greenwich Street. When new, Britannia spoons had a brilliant shine almost like silver, and they were considerably more practical than silver for a public vessel. Steamboats attracted increasing popularity during the 1820s and 1830s. The prominent Philadelphian Samuel Breck, reflecting in 1830 on the rapidity of steamboat travel, was particularly aware of the changes it had brought: "He who goes abroad now-a-days must submit to the hugger-mugger assemblage of a steamboat on the water and a procession of ten or twelve coaches on the land. Our fathers were not in such haste, nor so fond of kicking up a dust. We have acquired much more speed, but lost the old-fashioned security and comfort."[94]

Conclusion

The work that occupied craftsmen in wood when interacting with members of the business community varied and frequently was influenced by location, be it a rural setting, an urban environment, or a site close to the seacoast or a navigable body of water. In urban areas, craftsmen usually were within walking distance of a woodworking shop. Rural customers and craftsmen often required more mobility in their interaction. Geographic location—New England, the Middle Atlantic region, or the South—played a part in where job emphasis might lie, which also was influenced by shop size and the specific skills of a woodworker. The eventful passage of time, including such factors as war and embargoes, sometimes brought adverse changes to conducting business. The aftermath often presented new opportunities but frequently required the woodworker to adjust and adapt to new conditions. Like Samuel Breck, the woodworker likely reflected on changes that occurred during his lifetime and attempted to balance what was gained against what was lost. Some craftsmen were able to navigate these pathways better than others.

1. Jacques-Pierre Brissot de Warville, *New Travels in the United States of America* (Dublin: P. Byrne, 1792), p. 315.

2. Susan P. Schoelwer, ed., *Lions & Eagles & Bulls: Early American Tavern & Inn Signs* (Princeton, N.J.: Princeton University Press for the Connecticut Historical Society, 2000); William Chappel Ledger, Danbury, Connecticut, 1793–ca.1816, account with Hiram Adams, April 8, 1812, Joseph Downs Collection of Manuscripts and Printed Ephemera, Winterthur Museum Library, Winterthur, Delaware (hereafter DCM); Allen Holcomb Account Book, New Lisbon, New York, 1809–ca. 1828, account with Dr. Walter Wing, June 1816, Metropolitan Museum of Art, New York.

3. J. Thomas Scharf and Thompson Westcott, *History of Philadelphia, 1609–1884*, 3 vols. (Philadelphia: L.H. Everts and Co.,1884), 2: 875; Esther Singleton, *Social New York under the Georges, 1714–1776* (New York: D. Appleton and Co., 1902), pp. 21, 366; William Allen Ledger, Providence, Rhode Island, 1774–1797, account with Truman and Company, May 1785, Rhode Island Historical Society, Providence (hereafter RIHS); Daniel Rea Jr. Daybook, Boston, 1789–1793, account with Simon Hall, July 16, 1791, Baker Library, Harvard University, Cambridge, Massachusetts (hereafter BL); George Davidson Waste Book, Boston, 1793–1799, accounts with William Williams, April 30, 1796, and Reuben Sanborn, April 13, 1799, Old Sturbridge Village, Sturbridge, Massachusetts (hereafter OSV).

4. Thomas Boynton Ledger, Windsor, Vermont, 1810–1817, account with Johonnet and Smith, September and December 1815, Account Book Collection, MS-1218, Rauner Special Collections Library, Dartmouth College, Dartmouth, New Hampshire (hereafter DC), film DCM; Daniel and Samuel Proud Daybook and Ledger, Providence, Rhode Island, 1810–1834, account with Phillip Lewis, September 1, 1825, RIHS; William Taylor Inventory, Boston, September 10, 1832, Suffolk County Probate Court, Boston, film DCM; Pifer Washington Case Daybook, Johnstown, New York, 1834–1838, account with Daniel Kennedy, November 24, 1836, DCM; George Ritter Account Book II, Philadelphia, 1829–1838, account with Levick and Jenkins, February 17, 1835, DCM.

5. Robert Donald Crompton, ed., "A Philadelphian Looks at New England—1820," *Old-Time New England 50*, no. 3 (January–March 1960): 60.

6. Thomas Gladding Bill, Albany, New York, February 1, 1831, account with Peter Gansevoort, Peter Gansevoort Papers, Gansevoort-Lansing Collection, ca.1790s–1840s, MssCol 1199, New York Public Library, New York (hereafter NYPL); George Ritter Account Book I, Philadelphia, 1818–1828, account with John Jordan, February 22, 1828, DCM; Ritter Account Book II, account with Dr. George F. Alberti, October 5, 1833; Thomas J. Moyers and Fleming K. Rich Account Book, Wythe Court House, Virginia, 1834–1840, account with Robert Kent, January 4, 1838, DCM.

7. William H. Reed Account Book, Hampden, Maine, 1803–1848, account with Nathaniel Nurse (priming), December 3, 1806, DCM; Boynton Ledger (1810–1817), account with Stephen Conant (painted borders), July 11, 1815; Richard M. Candee, "House Paints in Colonial America: Their Materials, Manufacture, and Application," *Color Engineering* 5, no. 2 (March–April 1967): 37; George Rutter advertisement, *General Advertiser* (Philadelphia), March 3, 1791, as quoted in Alfred Coxe Prime, comp., *The Arts and Crafts in Philadelphia, Maryland, and South Carolina, 1786–1800* (Topsfield, Mass.: Walpole Society, 1932), p. 306; Frédéric Louis Moreau de Saint-Méry, *American Journey*, translated and edited by Kenneth Roberts and Anna M. Roberts (Garden City, N.Y.: Doubleday and Co., 1947), p. 176.

8. William Gray Ledger, Salem, Massachusetts, 1774–1814, accounts with Ephraim Ingalls, January 25, 1774, and Col. Ebenezer Thompson, February 3, 1804, Peabody Essex Museum, Salem, Massachusetts (hereafter PEM); Boynton Ledger (1810–1817), account with Johonnot and Smith, October 30, 1815; William Wilson Account Book, Lowell, Massachusetts, 1837–1838, account with A. W. Burnham, July 26, 1837, DCM; John Doggett Account Book, Roxbury, Massachusetts, 1802–1809, account with Jesse Doggett, July 16, 1808, DCM; Jesse Doggett's place of business is identified in Mabel M. Swan, "The Man Who Made Simon Willard's Clock Cases," *Antiques* 15, no. 3 (March 1929): 200.

9. Schoelwer, ed., *Lions & Eagles & Bulls*; Nancy Goyne Evans, *Windsor Chair-Making in America: From Craft Shop to Consumer* (Hanover, N.H.: University Press of New England, 2006), p. 186; Luke Houghton Ledger A, Barre, Massachusetts, 1816–1827, account with Kendall and Baker, August 1816, Barre Historical Society, Barre, Massachusetts, film DCM.

10. Whitfield J. Bell, ed., "Addenda to Watson's Annals of Philadelphia: Notes by Jacob Mordecai, 1836," *Pennsylvania Magazine of History and Biography* 98, no. 2 (April 1974): 136; Boynton Ledger (1810–1817), account with Frederick Pettes, December 11, 1815; Ezra Ames Account Book, Albany, New York, 1790–1797, account with Mr. Ford? (irons for sign), March 27, 1794, New-York Historical Society, New York (hereafter N-YHS); Schoelwer, ed., *Lions & Eagles & Bulls*, cats. 6 and 7 with original hardware, pp. 118–19; Joseph Bolton Bill, Philadelphia, July–August 1762, account with Stephen Collins, Stephen Collins Papers, ca. 1760s–1810s, Library of Congress, Washington, D.C. (hereafter LC); Job Danforth Sr. Ledger 2, Providence, Rhode Island, 1788–1818, account with Gershom Jones, March 11, 1789, RIHS.

11. Paul Jenkins Daybook, Kennebunk, Maine, 1836–1841, account with Bryent and Worrin (Bryant and Warren?), December 20, 1837, DCM; Moses Parkhurst Account Book, Paxton, Massachusetts, 1814–1839, account with George Day, April 30, 1819, OSV; William Fifield Ledger, Lyme, New Hampshire, 1810–ca. 1826, account with Daniel Smith, Jr., late 1821, DCM; Wilson Account Book, account with W. C. Burrows, November 18, 1837; John Bernard, *Retrospection of America, 1797–1811* (New York, 1887), as quoted in Eleanor H. Gustafson, ed., "Clues and Footnotes," *Antiques* 117, no. 4 (April 1980): 806.

12. Moses Ferrey Ledger, Hartford, Connecticut, 1781–1818, accounts with James Hosmer (moving), October 18, 1796, and John Thomas (shingling and painting), May 5, 1789, DCM; Chappel Ledger, accounts with Rufus Clark (moving), May 1800, and Ebenezer B. White (shop roof), August 7, 1798; Proud Ledger, account with Zachariah Chafee (rollers for building), August 26, 1820; Moses and Samuel Grant Receipt Book, Boston, 1756–1805, account with Thomas Christy, January 1782, Boston Public Library, Boston (hereafter BPL); Nathaniel Kinsman Bill, Gloucester, Massachusetts, May 30, 1757, account with Samuel Whitemore, Nathaniel Kinsman Papers, 1750–1807, PEM; Job E. Townsend Daybook, Newport, Rhode Island, 1778–1803, account with Thomas Borden, July 24, 1795, Newport Historical Society, Newport, Rhode Island (hereafter NHS), film DCM; Anonymous Carpenter's Account Book, Middletown, New Jersey, 1765–1788, account with John Henry, November 10, 1769, N-YHS; Nathaniel Holmes Ledger, Barnstable, Massachusetts, 1805–1841, account with John Munroe (painting steps), June 10, 1817, DCM; Henry Wansey, *An Excursion to the United States of North America in the Summer of 1794* (Salisbury, England: J. Easton, 1798), p. 173.

13. Peter Emerson Daybook, Reading, Massachusetts, 1749–1759, account with Thomas Emerson, July 2, 1753, BPL; Job Townsend Jr. Ledger, Newport, Rhode Island, 1750–1778, account with Abraham Dennis, September 22, 1756, NHS; Ritter Account Book II, account with Abel Wyman, November 21, 1835; David Evans Daybook, Philadelphia, 1784–1806, account with Charles Shoemaker, April 9, 1791, Historical Society of Pennsylvania, Philadelphia (hereafter HSP), film DCM.

14. N. Holmes Ledger, account with John Munroe, June 10, 1817; Thomas Boynton Ledger, Windsor, Vermont, 1817–1847, account with G. W. and C. F. Merrifield, September 16, 1845, DC, film DCM.

15. Frederick K. Coady Ledger, Ogdensburg, New York, 1841–1845, accounts with Charles Sheppard, May 14, 1842, and S. B. Strickland, June 9, 1842, DCM; J. E. Townsend Daybook (1778–1803), account with Phillip Morss [sic], June 5, 1788; Wilson Account Book, account with A. W. Moulton, December 8, 1837; Rutter advertisement, *General Advertiser* (Philadelphia), March 3, 1791, as quoted in Prime, *Arts and Crafts in Philadelphia, 1786–1800*, p. 306.

16. Richard P. Foulke Receipt Book, Philadelphia, 1819–1823, account with Joseph Dives, April 26, 1822, Virginia State Library, Richmond, Virginia; Hatton and Miller Bill, Norfolk, Virginia, November 26, 1783, account with Richard Blow, Richard Blow Papers, 1760–1825, Swem Library, College of William and Mary, Williamsburg, Virginia; Elizur Barnes Account Book, Middletown, Connecticut, 1821–1825, account with Peas and Fowler, July 4, 1823, Middlesex Historical Society, Middletown, Connecticut, film Connecticut Historical Society, Hartford (hereafter CHS); Silas E. Cheney Ledger, Litchfield, Connecticut, 1816–1822, account with Charles L. Webb, November 12, 1819, Litchfield Historical Society, Litchfield, Connecticut (hereafter LHS), film DCM; Harris Beckwith Ledger, Northampton, Massachusetts, 1803–1807, accounts with Levi Shepherd and Sons, April 6, 1805, and Job White, September 19, 1803, Forbes Library, Northampton, Massachusetts.

17. J. E. Townsend Daybook (1778–1803), accounts with John Clark (partition), October 30, 1801, and Edward Stanhope (hole for pipe), January 20, 1800; Job E. Townsend Ledger, Newport, Rhode Island, 1794–1802, account with William Potter (moving partition), November 13, 1800, NHS, film DCM; Danforth Ledger 2, account with Robert Adam, October 22, 1792; Beckwith Ledger, account with Charles Chapman, February 15, 1805.

18. Hatton and Miller Bill, account with Richard Blow, November 26, 1783; Boynton Ledger (1817–1847), accounts with Samuel Patrick, December 20, 1837, February 28, 1838, and July 24, 1841, and Windsor Tavern Company, May 25 to June 20, 1840; Coady Ledger, accounts with G. N. Seymour, September 20, 1842, and S. B. Strickland, June 10, 1842.

19. George G. Channing, *Early Recollections of Newport, R.I.* (Newport, R.I.: A. J. Ward, 1868), p. 151.

20. Samuel Williams advertisement, *Pennsylvania Journal* (Philadelphia), June 2, 1773, as quoted in Alfred Coxe Prime, comp., *The Arts and Crafts in Philadelphia, Maryland, and South Carolina, 1721–1785* (Philadelphia: Walpole Society, 1929), p. 186; Nathan Lucas Ledger, Kingston, Massachusetts, 1800–1853, account with William Washburn, August 1824–1827, DCM; Jeduthern Avery Ledger, Coventry, Connecticut, 1811–1855, account with Ela [sic] Lyman, April 1819, CHS; Samuel Durand Daybook, Milford, Connecticut, 1806–1838, account with Richard Fenn, October 21, 1815, Milford Historical Society, Milford, Connecticut, film DCM; Amos D. Allen, Memorandum Book, Windham, Connecticut, 1796–1803, accounts with Thomas Tilestone, March 18 and May 1800, CHS; Jenkins Daybook, account with William Safford, October 27, 1838.

21. Edward Hazen, "The Hatter," *Popular Technology, or, Professions and Trades*, 2 vols. (1846; reprint, Albany, N.Y.: Early American Industries Association, 1981), 1: 84–87; Samuel Wing Bill, Sandwich, Massachusetts, December 1803, account with John Elles (hatter's bows), Samuel Wing Papers, 1800–1808, OSV; Abner Taylor Account Book, Lee, Massachusetts, 1806–1832, account with Amos Burchard (hatter's bow, brush blocks), September 4, 1812, and December 7, 1815, DCM; Daniel and Samuel Proud Ledger, Providence, Rhode Island, 1770–ca. 1825, account with William Peabody, March 25, 1812, RIHS; Job Townsend Jr. Daybook, Newport, Rhode Island, 1762–1778, account with William Roberson, April 13, 1774, NHS; Daniel Trotter Bill, Philadelphia, 1782–1795, accounts with Samuel Bispham, Daniel Trotter Family Papers, late eighteenth century, DCM.

22. Hazen, "The Milliner," *Popular Technology*, 1: 100–102.

23. Barnes Account Book, accounts with Ebenezer Roberts (bonnet blocks), August 24, 1822, and Miss Johnson (bleaching box), April 16, 1822; Holcomb Account Book, account with Deborah Chamberlain, April 2, 1827; George Landon Daybook and Ledger, Erie, Pennsylvania,

1813–1832, account with Ebenezer D. Gunnison, April 21, 1824, DCM; John Cate Daybook, Wolfeboro, New Hampshire, 1833–1842, account with George W. Warren, February 26, 1836, DCM; Solomon Cole Account Book, Glastonbury, Connecticut, 1794–1809, accounts with Israel Holeston, July 12, 1804, and Abram Kilborn, July 30 and September 20, 1804, CHS; Abner Haven Account Book, Framingham, Massachusetts, 1809–1830, account with Capt. John J. Clark, February 1825, DCM; Elisha Blossom Jr. Account Book, New York, 1811–1818, account with Zebiah Richards (milliner), October 23, 1813, N-YHS; Hazen, "The Milliner," *Popular Technology*, 1: 101; A. Taylor Account Book, account with Amos Burchard, December 7, 1815.

24. Perez Austin Account Book, Canterbury, Connecticut, 1811–1832, accounts with Joseph Simms, March 26, 1820, and July 1821, CHS; Ritter Account Book I, account with Joseph Cake, May 27, 1824; Nathan Cleaveland Ledger, Franklin, Massachusetts, 1810–1828, account with Davis Thayer and Company, May 1822 to November 1824, OSV; Wilson Account Book, accounts with E. D. Gordon, August 17, 1837, and J. Skinner, May 9, 1837.

25. Robert Whitelaw Ledger, Ryegate, Vermont, 1804–1831, account with Robert Scott (shoemaker's bench at $1.00), November 16, 1810, Vermont Historical Society, Montpelier, Vermont (hereafter VtHS); Samuel Davidson Ledger, Plainfield, Massachusetts, 1795–1824, account with Eliphas Parish (shoemaker's seat at 7s. 6p. [$1.25]), August 1797, Pocumtuck Valley Memorial Association, Deerfield, Massachusetts; Titus Preston Ledger, Wallingford, Connecticut, 1795–1817, account with Phineas Pond, January 23, 1807, Sterling Memorial Library, Yale University, New Haven, Connecticut; Hazen, "The Shoe and Boot Maker," *Popular Technology*, 1: 118; David Pritchard Jr. Account Book, Waterbury, Connecticut, 1827–1838, account with James Harrison, n.d., Mattatuck Museum, Waterbury, Connecticut.

26. Hazen, "The Shoe and Boot Maker," *Popular Technology*, 1: 118–120; Charles Tomlinson, "The Shoemaker," *Illustrations of Trades* (1860; reprint, Ambridge, Pa.: Early American Industries Association, 1972), pp. 44–45; Philip Deland Account Book, West Brookfield, Massachusetts, 1812–1846, accounts with Cephas Lawrence, January 1829, and Vernon Lawrence (helves), December 31, 1829, OSV; J. E. Townsend Daybook (1778–1803), account with Benjamin Whitman, March 15, 1799; Lemuel Tobey Ledger, Dartmouth, Massachusetts, 1797–1806, accounts with Edward Wing, June 6 (boot trees) and July 28, 1797 (shoemaker's bench), OSV; Whitelaw Ledger, account with William Whitelaw, November 20, 1808.

27. Wait Stoddart Ledger, Windham Center, Connecticut, 1798–1810, accounts with Amos D. Allen, December 16, 1799, to January 20, 1803, when account "Reconed and Settled," Windham Historical Society, Willimantic, Connecticut; Florence M. Montgomery, *Textiles in America, 1650–1870* (New York: W. W. Norton and Co., 1983), pp. 328–29, definition of prunella; François Alexandre Frédéric duc de La Rochefoucauld Liancourt, *Travels through the United States of North America . . . in the Years 1795, 1796, and 1797*, 2 vols. (London: R. Phillips, 1799), 1: 478, 546.

28. Ritter Account Book II, account with Nicholas Kohlencamp, June 15, 1837; J. Danforth Sr. Ledger 2, accounts with Amos Throop, July 8, 1790, and November 28, 1793; Fifield Ledger, accounts with James Proctor, June 5 and 17, 1812; John Hayward, *The New England Gazetteer*, 8th ed. (Boston: John Hayward, 1839), s.v. ; James and Drinker Receipt Book, Philadelphia, 1767–1786, account with John Folwell, November 5, 1774, Drinker Papers, HSP; Daniel Trotter Bill, Philadelphia, 3rd month 4th, 1786, account with Henry Drinker, Henry Drinker Papers, Journal, 1776–1791, HSP, as quoted in Anne Castrodale Golovin, "Daniel Trotter: Eighteenth-Century Philadelphia Cabinetmaker," in *Winterthur Portfolio* 6, edited by Richard K. Doud and Ian M. G. Quimby (Charlottesville, Va.: University Press of Virginia, 1970), p. 163.

29. Timothy Dwight, *Travels in New England and New York*, 4 vols., edited by Barbara Miller Solomon (Cambridge, Mass.: Belknap Press, 1969), 2: 255; *Journal* advertisement for runaway Irish servant, as quoted in Rita S. Gottesman, comp., *The Arts and Crafts in New York, 1726–1776* (1938; reprint, New York: Da Capo Press, 1970), p. 338; drugget defined in Montgomery, *Textiles in America*, pp. 226–27; Thomas Pratt Account Book, Malden, Massachusetts, 1730–1768, account with Timothy Wait, May 8, 1755, DCM; Daniel Ross Ledger, Ipswich, Massachusetts, 1781–1804, accounts with Benjamin Ross, November 21, 1781, to August 9, 1783, and November 27, 1782 (buttonhole board), PEM.

30. Landon Daybook and Ledger, account with John C. Wallace (barber chair), August 18, 1821, and credit for Rufus Clough (irons for chair), August 13, 1831; David Alling Daybook, Newark, New Jersey, 1836–1854, accounts with Smith and Lippins, April 19, 1837, and Peter Ennis, December 13, 1838, New Jersey Historical Society, Newark, film DCM; Ritter Account Book I, account with McElheney and Van Pelt, September 20, 1827; Ritter Account Book II, accounts with Doctor Roper, December 15, 1830, and Samuel C. Bunting, April 5 1830.

31. Carl and Jessica Bridenbaugh, *Rebels and Gentlemen: Philadelphia in the Age of Franklin* (New York: Oxford University Press, 1962), pp. 263–303; Hazen, "The Druggist and Apothecary," *Popular Technology*, 1: 236–38.

32. Lunt Family Account Book, Newbury, Massachusetts, 1736–1772, account with Dr. John Newman, May 4, 1759, PEM; Barnes Account Book, account with Dr. Charles Dyer, March 27, 1824; Amos Darlington Jr. Ledger 3, Westtown, Pennsylvania, 1824–1852, account with Wilmer Worthington, April 14, 1826, Chester County Historical Society, West Chester, Pennsylvania; Rea Jr. Daybook (1789–1793), account with Dr. William Jackson, January 3, 1792; Daniel Rea Jr. Account Book, Boston, 1796–1802, account with Samuel Miller, November 1797, BL; W. Allen Ledger, account with Truman and Company, January 1784; Samuel Blythe Bill, probably Boston, Massachusetts, July 1784, account with Dr. William Sterns, William Sterns Manuscripts, 1744–1839, PEM; Joshua Delaplaine Account Book, New York, 1720s–1770s, account with Doctor Brownjohn (drug boxes), 1742, N-YHS, film DCM; Rea Jr. Daybook (1789–1793), account with Dr. William Jackson (painting four pill boxes), January 30, 1792; Samuel Silliman Account Book, Duanesburgh, New York, 1804–1807, account with Dr. Richard Ely (making boxes for salts), May 20, 1807, New York State Historical Association, Cooperstown, New York; Ebenezer Smith Jr. Bill, Beverly, Massachusetts, June 11, 1812, account with Robert Rantoul, Robert Rantoul Papers, ca. 1796–ca. 1830s, Beverly Historical Society, Beverly, Massachusetts; Margaret B. Schiffer, *Chester County, Pennsylvania, Inventories, 1684–1850* (Exton, Pa.: Schiffer Publishing, 1974), excerpt from inventory of David Eaton, 1813, p. 118.

33. Barnes Account Book, accounts with Dr. Charles Dyer, April 22 and March 27, 1824; Jenkins Daybook, accounts with Dr. Burley Smart, December 22, 1836, and June 6, 1840; J. E. Townsend Daybook (1778–1803), account with Dr. Jonathan Easton, February 1798; Schiffer, *Chester County Inventories*, excerpt from inventory of Dr. Jacob Ehrenzeller, 1838, p. 352; Evans Daybook (1784–1806), account with Dr. John H. Gibbons, March 19, 1790.

34. Taylor and Bayard Receipt Book, New York, 1778–1779, account with Peter Marselis, January 13, 1779, N-YHS; John Hall Bill, Philadelphia, October 1772, account with William Barrell, Stephen Collins Papers, Accounts, Box 11, LC; Job E. Townsend Daybook, Newport, Rhode Island, 1803–1828, account with Joseph Cozzens, August 17, 1818, NHS; Ritter Account Book I, account with Jacob Ritter Jr., March 31, 1825; Silas E. Cheney Daybook, Litchfield, Connecticut, 1807–1813, account with Isaac Thompson, August 14, 1810, LHS; William Rawson Account Book, Killingly, Connecticut, 1835–1841, account with Leonard Bowen (cherry counter), April 5, 1838, OSV; Boynton Ledger (1817–1847), account with Forbes and Smith, May 3, 1817; Cate Daybook, accounts with Joseph Farmer, February 14, 1837, and William Rose, March 17, 1838; Wilson Account Book, account with Peter Eaton, October 7, 1837.

35. Philemon Robbins Account Book, Hartford, Connecticut, 1833–1836, account with Colton and Robbins, April 1, 1834, CHS; Barnes Account Book, account with Charles Brewer, July 14, 1823; Coady Ledger, accounts with Hecock and Curry, November 7, 1841, and Miss Gardner (staining showcase), November 19, 1842; J. E. Townsend Daybook (1803–1828), account with Harvey Sessions, September 30, 1822; Rea Jr. Daybook (1789–1793), account with "Howard the Barber" (painting mahogany color), March 31, 1792; Boynton Account Book (1810–1817), account with Stephen Conant (varnishing), July 11, 1815.

36. Hall Bill, October 1772, account with William Barrell, Collins Papers; George T. Cornell Bill, Newport, Rhode Island, November 8, 1769, account with Christopher Champlin, Christopher Champlin Papers, RIHS; Avery Ledger, account with Christopher H. Talcott, June 1826; Elisha H. Holmes Daybook, Essex, Connecticut, 1825–1830, account with Elias Redfield, May 21, 1826, Connecticut State Library, Hartford (hereafter CSL); Christopher Clark, "The Diary of an Apprentice Cabinetmaker: Edward Jenner Carpenter's 'Journal,' 1844–45," *Proceedings of the American Antiquarian Society* 98, pt. 2 (1989): 369; Ames Account Book, account with unknown storekeeper, January 1796; William Ripley Ledger, Washington County, Vermont, ca. 1809–1856, account with Day and Pollard, July 24, 1819, DCM; Silas E. Cheney Daybook, Litchfield, Connecticut, 1813–1821, account with Sophia Jones, June 20, 1815, LHS, film DCM; J. E. Townsend Daybook (1803–1828), accounts with Harvey Sessions, October 31 and December 3, 1821, August 16, 1822, and April 26, 1823.

37. Robbins Account Book, accounts with Messrs. S. and W. Kellogg (locust desk, repairing lock), July 7, 1834, and Messrs. D. Burgess and Company (cherry desk), August 18, 1835; James Gere Ledger, Groton, Connecticut, 1822–1852, account with Jesse Chapman (pine desk), September 25, 1828, CSL; Barnes Account Book, accounts with S. Spalding (desk fall), and A. M. Williams (table for store), January 15, 1822; David Evans Daybook, Philadelphia, 1774–1782,

account with Tench Cox (two stools for store), July 31, 1781, HSP, film DCM; Samuel Hall Ledger, Middletown, Connecticut, 1754–1795, account with David Sage, February 7, 1778, CHS; A. Taylor Account Book, account with Major Nathan Dillingham, October 2, 1815 (cupboard), and November 15, 1813 (drawer and cleats); Amos Bradley Ledger, East Haven, Connecticut, 1802–1815, account with Abram and Jared Bradley, April 1807, DCM; Alling Daybook (1836–1854), account with Smith and Wright, August 24, 1838.

38. Allen Memorandum Book, account with Benjamin Dyer, February 2, 1802; Ritter Account Book II, account with Mr. Clark, September 8, 1834; Elisha H. Holmes Ledger, Essex, Connecticut, 1825–1830, account with Alvin F. Wittemore, March 5, 1827, CHS (also listed earlier in E. H. Holmes Daybook with enhanced description, January 23, 1826, CSL); Evans Daybook (1784–1806), accounts with James Thompson, July 31, 1790, and Charles Shoemaker (ladder), April 9, 1791; E. H. Holmes Ledger, account with Alvin F. Wittemore (candlesticks), February 1, 1829; William Chambers, *Things as They Are in America* (Philadelphia: Lippincott Grambo, 1854), p. 307.

39. Hazen, "The Merchant" and "Attorney at Law," *Popular Technology*, 1: 181–89 and 215–16, 220.

40. J. Townsend Jr. Ledger (1750–1778), account with John Wanton, April 1754; John Eastmond (commission merchant) Account Book, New York, 1803–1806, "Cash pd for a Mahogany Writing desk &c" $8.25, July 27, 1804, NYPL; Robbins Account Book, account with Hutchinson and D___ (?) for a "mahogany Counting room Desk" $30.00, May 13, 1835; John Sager Daybook, Bordentown, New Jersey, 1805–1817, account with Doctor Hunter for Mr. Jonson for "one Cherry Counting Desk" $7.00, December 20, 1809, HSP; A. Darlington Jr. Ledger, accounts with Owen Stover, Esq., for a "Cherry Counting Desk" $7.00, June 7, 1830, and Jesse Good for "A Counting hous Desk Walnut" $4.50, January 19, 1825; David Evans Daybook, Philadelphia, 1796–1812, account with Wheelen and Miller for "a Cherry Tree Wrighting Desk 2 Draws in frame," February 8, 1796, HSP; Ritter Account Book II, account with William Boller for pine desk, February 18, 1837; Evans Daybook (1784–1806), account with Joseph Miller for a "Large Pine wrighting Desk" £4.10.0 ($15.00), February 1791; William Webb 4th Bill, Salem, Massachusetts, August 29, 1833, account with Joseph G. Waters, Esq., for "a pine Writting Desk" $6.00, Waters Family Papers, PEM; Rea Jr. Daybook (1789–1793), account with Head and Amory (mahogany color), November 12, 1791; Daniel Rea Jr. Daybook, Boston, 1772–1800, account with John Codman, Esq., August 1, 1797, BL.

41. Blossom Account Book, account with David Loring, February 20, 1813; details of Blossom's training as a cabinetmaker and his working relationship with David Loring are related in Peter M. Kenny, "From New Bedford to New York to Rio and Back: The Life and Times of Elisha Blossom, Jr., Artisan of the New Republic," in *American Furniture*, edited by Luke Beckerdite, (Milwaukee, Wis.: Chipstone Foundation, 2003), pp. 250–51; Blossom's desk construction is a simplified version of that described for "A Counting-House Desk" in *The New-York Revised Prices for Manufacturing Cabinet and Chair Work* (New York: Printed by Southwick and Pelsue, 1810), pp. 35–37; although the Price Book identifies only six turned gallery pillars, Blossom's desk had fourteen pillars—probably one at each end corner, the others along the length at one-foot increments, and numbers 13 and 14 reinforcing the center of each end.

42. Ritter Account Book II, accounts with Isaac Smyth and William Boller, February 18, 1837.

43. Henry Connelly Bill, Philadelphia, November 9, 1811, account with Stephen Girard, Girard Papers, American Philosophical Society, Philadelphia (hereafter APS), film: Series II, Reel 210; Abel Allen Bill, Providence, Rhode Island, December 1798, account with Almy and Brown, Almy and Brown Papers, 1789–1800, RIHS; Montgomery, *Textiles in America*, p. 152; John Mifflin, Esq., Inventory, Philadelphia, April 5, 1759, Register of Wills, Philadelphia; Eastmond Account Book, item in list of office furnishings acquired by gift from J. Hobson, July 27, 1804; Barnes Account Book, account with Josiah Williams and Company, June 12, 1823; Evans Daybook (1784–1806), accounts with Charles Shoemaker, April 9, 1791, and Joseph Miller, February 1791.

44. Ritter Account Book II, account with William Boller, March 4, 1837; the long drawers in Boller's counter were arranged in two tiers of three drawers each; Isaac Greene Ledger, Windsor, Vermont, 1788–1800, credit for Hezekiah Healy, June 15, 1790, Nathan Stone Collection, VtHS; Hatton and Miller Bill, November 26, 1783, and Bonner and Lindsey Bill, November 5, 1791, accounts with Richard Blow, Richard Blow Papers.

45. Hatton and Miller Bill, November 26, 1783, account with Richard Blow, Richard Blow Papers; Rea Jr. Daybook (1772–1800), account with John Codman, August 1, 1797; John Treadwell Bill, Boston, April 14, 1829, and Eben Jackson Bill, April 15, 1829, accounts with

Andrew Dunlap, Esq., Andrew Dunlap Papers, PEM; Darlington Ledger 1, account with Owen Stover, Esq., June 7, 1830; William Cragg Bill, Philadelphia, November 30, 1835, account with John Cadwalader, Esq., Cadwalader Papers, Judge John Cadwalader, HSP.

46. Greene Ledger, credit for Hezakiah Healy, June 28,1790; Rea Jr. Account Book (1796–1802), accounts with John Codman, Esq., November 20, 1801, and January 1802.

47. Ritter Account Book II, account with William Boller, February 25, 1837; John Gillingham Bill, Philadelphia, March 1750, account with Nicholas Scull, Penn-Physick Papers, vol. 4, p. 215, HSP; Thomas Burling and Son Bill, New York, February 4, 1795, account with Robert R. Livingston, Robert R. Livingston Papers, N-YHS; Nicholas Silberg Bill, Charleston, South Carolina, August 9 to November 26, 1799, account with William Wragg, Esq., as quoted in Bradford L. Rauschenberg and John Bivins Jr., *The Furniture of Charleston, 1680–1820*, 3 vols. (Winston-Salem, N.C.: Museum of Early Southern Decorative Arts, 2003), 3: 1217; Jnoban Boskerck Bill, New York, September 27, 1838, account with Arthur Bronson, Bronson Family Papers, Papers of Arthur Bronson, NYPL.

48. Boskerck Bill, September 27, 1838, account with Arthur Bronson, Papers of Arthur Bronson; Joseph Nancrede Bill, Boston, March 1, 1798, account with Thomas Hancock (letter racks), Hancock Collection, BL; Treadwell Bill, May 24, 1829, account with Andrew Dunlap, Esq. (desk rack), Andrew Dunlap Papers; W. Webb 4th Bill, August 29, 1833, account with Joseph G. Waters (book rack for safe), Waters Family Papers; Ritter Account Book I, account with William Biddle, June 28, 1828; John Slesman Receipt Book, Philadelphia, 1799–1802, account with John Rea, March 3, 1800, HSP; Evans Daybook (1796–1812), accounts with Baker and Commeges, June 20, 1800, and Simon Gratz, August 22, 1808; Daniel Rea Jr. Daybook, Boston, 1794–1797, account with John Codman, May 15, 1794, BL; Amos Darlington Ledger 2, West Chester, Pennsylvania, 1819–1836, account with Joseph Peirce, Esq., April 30, 1825, CCHS.

49. Samuel Eliot Morison and Henry Steele Commager, *The Growth of the American Republic*, 4th ed., 2 vols. (New York: Oxford University Press, 1950), 1: 208; Evans Daybook (1784–1806), accounts with Bank of North America (blinds), July 6, 1790, and Bank of the United States (clock case), December 12, 1791; "Excerpts from the Day-Books of David Evans, Cabinet-Maker, Philadelphia, 1774–1811," *Pennsylvania Magazine of History and Biography* 27 (1903): 53; Doggett Daybook, account with Boston Bank via Simon Willard, June 7, 1804; Cheney Daybook (1813–1821), account with Lucius Smith and Company for local bank, December 21, 1814; Robbins Account Book, account with Exchange Bank, June 11, 1835; Darlington Ledger 2, accounts with a local bank, July 25 and August 10, 1824, and Ledger 3, accounts with a local bank, March 24 and May 1, 1830; Henry Wilder Miller Account Book, Worcester, Massachusetts, 1827–1831, account with Central Bank, January 2, 1830, Worcester Historical Museum, Worcester, Massachusetts.

50. William Bentley, *The Diary of William Bentley, D.D.*, 4 vols. (Salem, Mass.: Essex Institute, 1905–1914), 2: 55; John Lambert, *Travels through Canada and the United States of North America in the Years 1806, 1807, & 1808*, 2 vols. (London: C. Cradock and W. Joy, 1813), 2: 29; Dwight, *Travels*, 1: 309.

51. Margaret Van Horn Dwight, *A Journey to Ohio in 1810, As Recorded in the Journal of Margaret Van Horn Dwight*, edited by Max Ferrand (New Haven: Yale University Press, 1913); James M. Miller, *The Genesis of Western Culture: The Upper Ohio Valley, 1800–1825* (1938; reprint, New York: Da Capo Press, 1969), pp. 17–18; duc de La Rochefoucauld Liancourt, *Travels*, 1: 458; François Jean, marquis de Chastellux, *Travels in North-America in the Years 1780, 1781, and 1782*, 2 vols. (London: G. G. and J. and J. Robinson, 1787), 1: 144, 2: 217.

52. Hayward, *New England Gazetteer*, s.v. "Windsor, Vt."; William N. Hosley Jr., "Architecture and Society of the Urban Frontier: Windsor, Vermont, in 1800," in *The Bay and the River: 1600–1900*, The Dublin Seminar for New England Folklife: Annual Proceedings, 1981, edited by Peter Benes (Boston: Boston University, 1982), pp. 76–77; Boynton Ledger (1810–1817), accounts with Frederick Pettes, October 8, 1813, and July 18, 1814, to August 11, 1815.

53. Hayward, *New England Gazetteer*, s.v. "Litchfield, Ct."; Dwight, *Travels*, 2: 259; Silas E. Cheney Ledger, Litchfield, Connecticut, 1799–1817, boarding with Grove Catlin, 1801, LHS; Cheney Daybook (1807–1813), accounts with Grove Catlin, 1809 (fireboards), 1811 (mending rocker; replacing backs, painting, and ornamenting fifteen chairs, and painting and ornamenting fourteen other chairs), 1812 (purchasing one dozen fancy chairs); Cheney Daybook (1813–1821), account with Grove Catlin, June 24, 1813 (spitting boxes); Grove Catlin Inventory, Litchfield, Connecticut, October 2, 1829, Probate records, CSL.

54. Wansey, *Excursion*, pp. 57–58; Tontine Coffee House Ledger, New York, 1791–1816, accounts with craftsmen named in text, 1793–1794, N-YHS; Thomas P. Cope, *Philadelphia Merchant: The Diary of Thomas P. Cope, 1800–1851*, edited by Eliza Cope Harrison (South Bend, Ind.: Gateway Editions, 1978), p. 67.

55. Vernon H. Nelson, "The Sun Inn at Bethlehem, Pennsylvania" (excerpts from a lecture presented in 1971 at the Central Moravian Church, Bethlehem, including appended elevations and floor plans, an inventory of furnishings from 1772, and comments of travelers from abroad, as follows): Johann David Schöpf, *Travels in the Confederation, (1783–1784)*, translated and edited by Alfred J. Morrison (Philadelphia: W. J. Campbell, 1911), and Isaac Weld, *Travels through the States of North America and the Provinces of Upper and Lower Canada . . . 1795, 1796, and 1797*, 2 vols. (London: John Stockdale, 1800), with Inventories-Sun Inn, 1772–1822 (boxed documents), all in Archives of the Moravian Church, Moravian College, Bethlehem, Pennsylvania; William J. Murtagh, *Moravian Architecture and Town Planning* (Chapel Hill: University of North Carolina Press, 1967), pp. 79–82.

56. Moreau de Saint-Méry, *American Journey*, p. 354 (City Tavern); Francisco de Miranda, *The New Democracy in America: Travels of Francisco de Miranda in the United States, 1783–84*, translated by Judson P. Wood and edited by John S. Ezell (Norman: University of Oklahoma Press, 1963), p. 41; Kym S. Rice, *Early American Taverns* (Chicago: Regnery Gateway, 1983), pp. 132–33, 148; *Dictionary of American Biography*, s.v. "Fraunces, Samuel"; Samuel Fraunces Will and Inventory, Register of Wills, Philadelphia, October 1795.

57. Fraunces Inventory, October 24, 1795.

58. Fraunces Inventory, October 24, 1795; color illustration of shell, waxwork, and paper tableau of Hector and Andromache gifted to Martha Washington by Samuel Fraunces of New York, in *Decorative Arts Trust Newsletter* 21, no. 1 (Spring 2012); Grant Quertermous, "New Research on the Tudor Place Tableau," *Decorative Arts Trust Newsletter* (winter 2016–2017).

59. Oscar Theodore Barck Jr. and Hugh Talmage Lefler, *Colonial America* (New York: Macmillan Co., 1958), pp. 337–40.

60. Dwight, *Travels*, 1: 266 and 2: 306; *Travels of Francisco de Miranda*, p. 100; Wansey, *Excursion*, p. 93.

61. Charles Carroll Journal, Carrollton, Maryland, 1776, as quoted in Roland Van Zandt, ed., *Chronicles of the Hudson* (New Brunswick, N.J.: Rutgers University Press, 1971), p. 84; Dwight, *Travels*, 3: 150–51; Lambert, *Travels*, 2: 508; John W. Barber and Henry Howe, *Historical Collections of the State of New York* (New York: S. Tuttle, 1841), p. 267.

62. Chappel Ledger, account with John McLean, March 17, 1794; Charles F. Hummel, *With Hammer in Hand: The Dominy Craftsmen of East Hampton, New York* (Charlottesville: University Press of Virginia, 1968), p. 252 (Rysam background); Nathaniel Dominy V Daybook and Ledger, East Hampton, New York, 1798–1847, accounts with William J. Rysam, June 18, 1798, Jesse Hedges and John White, August 24, 1801 (fulling mill), Timothy Miller, January 9, 1815, and Elisha Miller, January 23, 1817 (sawing), DCM; Nathaniel F. Martin Account Book, Windham, Connecticut, 1784–1833, accounts with William Fuller, March and November 1795, March 1800, and credit by sawmill use, April 1804, CHS; Lewis C. Hunter, *A History of Industrial Power in the United States, 1780–1930*, vol. 1, *Waterpower in the Century of the Steam Engine* (Charlottesville: University Press of Virginia, 1979), pp. 53–54, 64–68.

63. Lucas Ledger, account with William Simmons, October 14, 1825; Chapman Lee Ledger, Charlton, Massachusetts, 1799–1850, account with Asa Clemens, March 24, 1813, OSV; Fifield Ledger, accounts with Daniel Smith, Esq., November 8 and 26, 1813; note on Ebenezer Allen in Brock Jobe et al., *Harbor and Home: Furniture of Southeastern Massachusetts, 1710–1850* (Hanover, N.H.: University Press of New England, 2009), p. 35; Hunter, *Waterpower*, pp. 54, 80.

64. Hunter, *Waterpower*, pp. 130–31; Carl Bridenbaugh, *Cities in Revolt: Urban Life in America, 1746–1776* (New York: Alfred A. Knopf, 1955), p. 268; Carl Bridenbaugh, *The Colonial Craftsman* (Chicago: Phoenix Books, 1961), pp. 18–20, 58–60; Morison and Commager, *Growth of the American Republic*, 1: 100–101; Marshall B. Davidson, *Life in America*, 2 vols. (Boston: Houghton Mifflin Co., 1951), 1: 405; Barber and How, *Historical Collections*, p. 267.

65. Hunter, *Waterpower*, p. 84; Lemuel Tobey Daybook, Dartmouth, Massachusetts, 1786–1792, account with Stephen Table, November 10, 1792, OSV; James Gere Ledger, Groton, Connecticut, 1809–1829, account with Peleg Rose, July 4, 1821, CSL; Chappel Ledger, account with Red Mill owner, September 1, 1808; Lucas Ledger, account with Stephen Bradford, September and October 1820 and August 1838; Martin Account Book, account with William Fuller, March 1805.

66. Hunter, *Waterpower*, pp. 95, 107; Lloyd Payne, *The Miller in Eighteenth-Century Virginia*, Williamsburg Craft Series (Williamsburg, Va.: Colonial Williamsburg, 1958), pp. 12, 29–30; Hazen, "The Miller," *Popular Technology*, 1: 35–37; Dr. James Tilton, in *The American Museum, or, Repository of Ancient & Modern Fugitive Pieces, etc.* 5 (1789): 380–81, as quoted in Jonathan L. Fairbanks, "The House of Thomas Shipley 'Miller at the Tide' on the Brandywine Creek," in *Winterthur Portfolio* 2, edited by Milo M. Naeve (Winterthur, Del.: Winterthur Museum, 1965), p. 157; Davidson, *Life in America*, 1: 484, 492–93.

67. Jedidiah Morse, *The American Gazetteer* (Boston: S. Hall, and Thomas and Andrews, 1797), s.v. "East Greenwich"; Lambert, *Travels*, 2: 305; William Strickland, *Journal of a Tour in the United States of America, 1794–1795*, edited by J. E. Strickland (New York: New-York Historical Society, 1971), p. 67; Thomas Anbury, *Travels through the Interior Parts of America*, 2 vols. (Boston: Houghton Mifflin Co., 1923), 2: 165; *Lewis Miller: Sketches and Chronicles* (York, Pa.: Historical Society of York County, 1966), p. 84.

68. Insights into the built structure and operation of the cider mill are found in Alice Morse Earle, *Home Life in Colonial Days*, American Classics Series (Lee, Mass.: Berkshire House Publications, 1993), pp. 161–62; another description of the cider-making process and images of the equipment are given in Tomlinson, *Illustrations of Trades*, pp. 9–10; Bangs Account Book, account with Lt. Jeffe Peirce, October 1800; Stephen Tracy Ledger, Lisbon, Connecticut, and Plainfield, New Hampshire, 1804–1827, account with Simon Smith of Cornish, New Hampshire, August 28, 1826, and later, document privately owned, film CHS; Dominy Daybook and Ledger, account with David Scoy, September 30, 1807; Lucas Ledger, account with Nathan Chandler, August 1825.

69. Barck and Lefler, *Colonial America*, pp. 338–39; Bridenbaugh, *Colonial Craftsman*, p. 93; Jedidiah Morse, *The American Geography* (Elizabethtown, N.J.: Shepard Kollock for the author, 1789), p. 2.

70. Samuel Eliot Morison, *The Maritime History of Massachusetts, 1783–1860* (London: William Heinemann, 1923), p. 156; Chastellux, *Travels*, 1: 326; Morse, *American Geography*, p. 353; Liancourt, *Travels*, 2: 129–30; Davidson, *Life in America*, 1: 385; Strickland, *Tour*, p. 43; Weld, *Travels*, 1: 264; Lambert, *Travels*, p. 54; Wansey, *Excursion*, pp. 27–28; Miranda, *New Democracy*, p. 158; S. E. Morison, *Maritime History*, p. 124.

71. Morison and Commager, *Growth of the American Republic*, 1: 269–70; Davidson, *Life in America*, 1: 301; Marcus Cunliffe, *The Nation Takes Shape: 1789–1837*, Chicago History of American Civilization (Chicago: University of Chicago Press, 1959), p. 98.

72. Morison and Commager, *Growth of the American Republic*, 1: 400–406; S. E. Morison, *Maritime History*, pp. 173–75, 187–93.

73. Morison and Commager, *Growth of the American Republic*, 1: 409–10, 419–30; S. E. Morison, *Maritime History*, pp. 192–99, 205–207, 212–15.

74. Liancourt, *Travels*, 2: 273; Dwight, *Travels*, 3: 330; Warville, *New Travels*, pp. 150–51; S. E. Morison, *Maritime History*, p. 231; Watson, *Annals*, 1: 242; Cunliffe, *Nation Takes Shape*, p. 100; Cope, *Philadelphia Merchant*, p. ix; Morison and Commager, *Growth of the American Republic*, 1: 499.

75. Davidson, *Life in America*, 2: 224-26, 232; Dwight, *Travels*, 3: 330; Carl David Arfwedson, *The United States and Canada*, 2 vols. (1834; reprint, New York: Johnson Reprint Corp., 1969) 1: 225, 295–96; Cunliffe, *Nation Takes Shape*, p. 104.

76. Jobe, *Harbor and Home*, pp. 167–68; Jean Lipman and Alice Winchester, *The Flowering of American Folk Art, 1776–1876* (New York: Viking Press, 1974), fig. 316; A. D. Allen Memorandum Book, account with Gidion Hoxey, July 5, 1799; sea chests were also made and sold in Providence, Rhode Island, in 1798, by Job Danforth Sr. and the Proud brothers; E. H. Holmes Daybook, account with David W. Williams, June 11, 1828.

77. Bridenbaugh, *Colonial Craftsman*, p. 110; Liancourt, *Travels*, 1: 477; Montgomery, *Textiles in America*, p. 191 (canvas, no. 4); D. Trotter Estate Bill, January 28, 1790, account with John Dowers, Trotter Family Papers; E. H. Holmes Ledger, account with Henry Bradick, September 27, 1825; Harry Brober, *Jan Van Vliet's Book of Crafts and Trades* (Albany, N.Y.: Early American Industries Association, 1981), plate 11; Hazen, "The Rope-Maker," *Popular Technology*, 1: 91–93, 177.

78. Bridenbaugh, *Colonial Craftsman*, p. 94; Watson, *Annals*, 1: 228; Philip Padelford, ed., *Colonial Panorama, 1775: Dr. Robert Honyman's Journal for March and April* (San Marino, Ca.: Huntington Library, 1939), p. 46; Moreau de St. Méry, *American Journey*, p. 169; Lambert, *Travels*, 2: 212.

79. Hazen, "The Rope-Maker," *Popular Technology*, 1: 91–95; Joseph Lindsey Ledger, Marblehead, Massachusetts, 1739–1764, account with Benjamin Henley, November 30, 1758, DMC; J. E. Townsend Daybook (1778–1803), account with Lewis Billow, July 30, 1779, and Daybook (1803–1828), account with Daniel Anderson and Company, October 8, 1825; S. E. Morison, *Maritime History*, p. 230.

80. Daniel Train and Company Bill, New York, November 26 and December 18, 1799, work completed for Benjamin Fry, Benjamin Fry Correspondence and Papers, John Hay Library, Brown University, Providence, Rhode Island; Fry Advertisement, *Newport Mercury* (Newport, R.I.), November 12, 1799; information on the brig *Favorite* from searches on google.com, <https://www.google.com/>; in Roman mythology Venilia was a nymph associated with the wind and sea; Hero was a young woman whose lover, Leander, nightly swam the Hellespont (Dardanelles), a narrow strait between Asia Minor and Europe, to be with Hero, until one stormy night he drowned, whereupon Hero threw herself into the sea and perished.

81. Samuel McIntire Bill, Salem, Massachusetts, October 12, 1803, account with owners of ship *Asia*, Benjamin Pickman Jr. Papers, PEM; McIntire's sketches for stern designs are illustrated in Dean T. Lahikainen, *Samuel McIntire: Carving an American Style* (Salem, Mass.: Peabody Essex Museum, 2007), pp. 89–90.

82. Simeon Skillin Jr. Bill, Boston, account with Caleb Davis, October 10, 1777, Caleb Davis Papers, Massachusetts Historical Society, Boston (hereafter MHS); Simeon Skillen Jr. and John Skillen Bill, Boston, March 21, 1786, account with Caleb Davis, Davis Papers, MHS; Daniel Rea Jr. Ledger, Boston, 1789–1797, account with John and Simeon Skillin Jr., March 18, 1790, BL; Simeon Skillin III Receipt, New York, May 13, 1797, account with Pfister and Macomb, Pfister and Macomb Receipt Book, New York, 1796–1798, Constable-Pierrepont Papers, NYPL; Minerva, also known by the name Athena, was goddess of wisdom, war, and the liberal arts; Juno, a daughter of Saturn and wife of Jupiter, competed for the famous golden apple but lost to Venus.

83. Pennsylvania Academy of the Fine Arts, *William Rush: American Sculptor* (Philadelphia: Pennsylvania Academy of the Fine Arts, 1982), pp. 9, 47; William MacPherson Hornor Jr., *Blue Book: Philadelphia Furniture* (1935; reprint, Washington, D.C.: Highland House, 1977), pp. 119–20; William Rush Bill, Philadelphia, October 10, 1811, account with Stephen Girard, Girard Papers, film: Series II, Reel 154, APS; Lahikainen, *Samuel McIntire*, pp. 35, 79, 92–93, 95.

84. Thomas Ashton Bill, Philadelphia, August, 8, 1815, account with Stephen Girard for ship *North America*, Girard Papers, film: Series II, Reel 154, APS; Stephen Girard Invoice Book, Philadelphia, 1811–1824, invoice of cargo, bill of lading, and miscellaneous papers for ship *North America*, July 9, 1816, film: Series II, Reels 155–56, and Series III, Reel 38, APS.

85. Hazen, "The Mariner," *Popular Technology*, 1: 179, 181–83; William Hinton advertisement, *New-York Gazette and the Weekly Mercury*, May 4, 1772, as quoted in Gottesman, comp., *Arts and Crafts in New York, 1726–1776*, pp. 307–308; Nathaniel Knowlton Account Book, Eliot, Maine, 1812–1831, account with Benjamin Lamson, July 5, 1814, Maine Historical Society, Portland; George Short Account Book, Newburyport, Massachusetts, ca. 1807–1821, account with Thomas H. Balch, March 1815 (repairs to compass box and quadrant case), PEM; George Pickering Bill, Philadelphia, 1781, account with Stephen Collins, Collins Papers, LC; Lindsey Ledger, account with Robert Swan, August 23, 1746; Barnes Account Book, account with Sage and Russell (quadrant case), August 12, 1824; E. H. Holmes Daybook, account with C. U. Hayden (quadrant case), July 1826; J. Danforth Sr. Ledger, account with Benjamin Gladding, September 3, 1799; Mark Pitman Bill, Salem, Massachusetts, September 1835, account with Jesse Smith Jr., PEM; "A List of Stores for Ship Grand Turk," including a "Spying Glass," Salem, Massachusetts, n. d., Derby Family Papers, PEM; Elias Hasket Derby Estate Inventory, Salem, Massachusetts, March 31, 1800, Essex Probate and Family Court, Salem, Massachusetts.

86. Rea Jr. Daybook (1789–1793), account with Joseph Callender, September 13, 1789; E. Smith Jr. Bill, items October 1, 1796, February 4, 1797, and July 2, 1812, account with Robert Rantoul, Rantoul Papers; anonymous advertisement, *New-York Mercury*, July 16, 1759, as quoted in Gottesman, comp., *Arts and Crafts in New York, 1726–1776*, pp. 316–17; J. Danforth Sr. Ledger, account with Thomas Jackson, January 2, 1801; Proud Brothers Ledger (1770–1825), accounts with Samuel Butler, December 21, ca. 1787, and Zephaniah Brown, November 13, 1792; Benjamin Price Bill, Philadelphia, October 10, 1794, account with Stephen Girard via Capt. Henry Skinner for ship *Good Friends*, Girard Papers, film: Series II, Reel 140, APS; Slesman Receipt Book, account with Thomas Passmore, December 28, 1799; Samuel H. Williams Bill, Philadelphia, December 24, 1819, account with Stephen Girard for ship *Montesquieu*,

Girard Papers, film: Series II, Reel 200, APS; Derby Inventory, March 31, 1800; Samuel Hendrick Daybook, Amesbury, Massachusetts, 1816–1825, account with Capt. Hooper, November 24, 1816, DCM; S. E. Morison, *Maritime History*, pp. 74–76.

87. Alexander Edwards Bill, Boston, January 6, 1772, account with Grant Webster for John Erving Jr., Greenough Papers, MHS; Lindsey Ledger, accounts with Jeremiah Lee, June 2, 1759, and January 16, 1760; Joseph Vickary Bill, Newport, Rhode Island, October 18, 1773, account with Christopher Champlin, and sailing of sloop *Adventure*, October 22, 1773, Shepley Papers, RIHS; Benjamin Cloutman Bill, Salem, Massachusetts, October 23, 1796, account with Elias Hasket Derby, Derby Family Papers, PEM; E. H. Holmes Daybook, accounts with Capt. Day, December 11, 1826, Calvin Williams, October 7, 1829, and Capt. D. Cal___(?) November 26, 1828; Bradley Ledger, account with Capt. Zebulon Bradley, June 18, 1806; Daniel Trotter Bill, Philadelphia, August 28, 1786, account with Stephen Girard for pine table, Girard Papers, film: Series II, Reel 210, APS; Daniel Trotter Bill, Philadelphia, August 25, 1786, account with Stephen Girard for table for sloop *Two Friends*, Girard Papers, film: Series II, Reel 165, APS ; Jenkins Daybook, account with Capt. Ivory Lord, January 11, 1837; Reed Account Book, account with Reuben Newcome Jr., June 8, 1810.

88. J. Danforth Sr. Ledger, accounts with Mason and Lanard, June 8, 1789, and Amos Throop, September 16, 1789; Kinsman Bill, September 12, 1757, account with Nathaniel Low, Kinsman Papers; Hendrick Daybook, account with Capt. Batchelor for brig, September 10, 1817; E. H. Holmes Daybook, account (for shelf) with Capt. D. Cal___(?), November 26, 1828; Bartholomew Akin Account Book, New Bedford, Massachusetts, 1774–1829, account with William Wood, April 10, 1785, DCM; Patrick McDowell and George Pickering Bills, Philadelphia, 1781, accounts with Stephen Collins, Collins Accounts, Box 14, LC; Richard Mills Bill, Philadelphia, November 30, 1768, account with William Barrell, Collins Accounts, Box 5, LC; Susanna Dillwyn Letter to William Dillwyn, August 14, 1788, Dillwyn Correspondence, 1770–1818, HSP.

89. John Morgan advertisement, *Independent Journal, or, The General Advertiser* (New York), April 20, 1785, as quoted in Rita Susswein Gottesman, comp., *The Arts and Crafts in New York, 1777–1799*, (New York: New-York Historical Society, 1954), p. 343; J. Cholwell advertisement, *American Citizen and General Advertiser* (New York), September 23, 1801, as quoted in Rita Susswein Gottesman, comp., *The Arts and Crafts in New York, 1800–1804* (New York: New-York Historical Society, 1965), p. 272.

90. John Green Account Book, Southampton, New York, 1790–1803, account with David Rose, September 1800, DCM; Coady Ledger, account with Tomlinson and Cowan, April 11, 1842; Joshua Brown Bill, Providence, Rhode Island, April 14, 1758, account with Capt. Urian Davis, master of sloop *Speedwell*, Obadiah Brown Papers, RIHS; Joseph Stone Bill, East Greenwich, Rhode Island, item December 13, 1794, account with William Arnold, 1793–1795, A. C. and R. W. Greene Collection, RIHS; N. Holmes Ledger, accounts with Ezekiel Crocker, May 20 and September 29, 1807, for the *Liberty*, and with Barnabas Hinckley, July 28, 1812, for the *Romeo*, and with Capt. Silvester Baker, July 29–31, 1813, for the *Thomas*; Gray Ledger, account with Josiah Parsons, July 4, 1794.

91. Anneliese Harding, *John Lewis Krimmel: Genre Artist of the Early Republic* (Winterthur, Del.: Winterthur Museum, 1994), p. 52; Arrahm Yarmolinsky, *Picturesque United States of America: A Memoir on Paul Svinin* (New York: William Edwin Rudge, 1930), pp. 9–10; Davidson, *Life in America*, 2: 224–26; on July 21, 1826, Samuel Breck, a prominent Philadelphian, traveled via the steamboat *Emerald* from New Brunswick, New Jersey, to New York: "The Diary of Samuel Breck, 1823–1827," *Pennsylvania Magazine of History and Biography* 103, no. 1 (January 1979): 100; *Lippincott's Gazetteer* of 1888 indicates that New Brunswick, New Jersey, and Middletown, Connecticut, were still accessible by steamboat at that publication date.

92. Alexander Welsh Bill, New York, May 24, 1824, account with steamboat *Thistle* owner(s), DCM; Fredericks and Farrington Bill, New York, May 10, 1824, account with steamboat *Thistle* owner(s), DCM; Alexander Welsh Bill, New York, February 12, 1827, account with steamboat *Thistle* owner(s), DCM; Alexander Welsh Bill, New York, May 6, 1826, account with steamboat *Emerald* owner(s), DCM; Charles Fredericks Bill, New York, March 24, 1826, account with steamboat *Bellona* owner(s) DCM; Fredericks and Farrington Bill, New York, August 30, 1824, account with steamboat *Bellona* owner(s), DCM.

93. Profiles of Vanderbilt and the Gibbons family are from Wikipedia <https://www.wikipedia.org/>; the name Bellona was that of a Roman goddess of war; John D. Brown Bill, New York, April 1821, account with Capt. Vanderbilt, DCM; Alexander Welsh Bill, New York, April

27, 1827, account with steamboat *Swan*, DCM; Philip R. Arcularius Bill, New York, April 19, 1827, account with steamboat *Swan*, DCM.

94. Barnes Account Book, accounts with steamboat *Experiment*, July 2, 16, 30 and August 8, 1822; William G. Beesley Daybook, Salem, New Jersey, 1828–1841, accounts with steamboat *Essex*, August 21, 1828, and steamboat *Flushing*, September 7, 1835, Salem County Historical Society, Salem, New Jersey; Stephen B. Young Bill, New York, April 30 and May 10, 1827, account with steamboat *Swan*, DCM; John Voorhis Bill, New York, May 7, 1827, account with steamboat *Swan*, DCM; Elias Thomas Bill, New York, March 11, 1822, account with steamboat *Bellona*, DCM; Samuel Nichols Bill, New York, October 23, 1828, account with steamboat *Bellona*, DCM; George Dummer and Company Bill, New York, April 24, 1826, account with steamboat *Emerald*, DCM; Henry Andrews Bill, New York, April 13, 1826, account with steamboat *Emerald*, DCM; Wood and Van Wagenen Bill, New York, July 4, 1825, account with steamboat *Thistle*, DCM; H. E. Scudder, ed., *Recollections of Samuel Breck, . . . 1771–1862* (Philadelphia: Porter and Coates, 1877), p. 181.

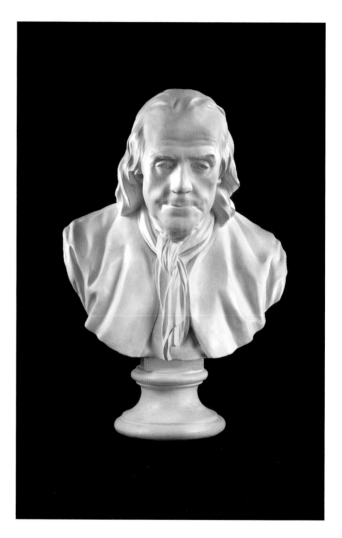

Figure 1 Bust of Benjamin Franklin, attributed
to Martin Jugiez, Philadelphia, Pennsylvania,
1779–1790. White pine; iron. H. 35". (Chipstone
Foundation; photo, Gavin Ashworth.)

Figure 2 Jean Jacques Caffieri, *Benjamin
Franklin*, Paris, France, 1779–1805. Plaster.
H. 28". (Courtesy, New-York Historical Society.)

Luke Beckerdite

The Concept of Copying in the Eighteenth-Century Carving Trade

Among the engravings in the [Harvard] library, was one from a painting by . . . [Charles Antoine] Coypel, — Rebecca at the well . . . . This I admired and copied in oil, the same size as the engraving; the forms, expressions, characters, and light and shadow were before me; the colors I imagined as well as I could from my own imagination. This received so much approbation from the officers and students in college, that I ventured to show it to Mr. Copley, and had the pleasure to hear it commended by him also.

John Trumbull, 1773

▼ FOR CENTURIES, PAINTERS, engravers, and sculptors have produced copies of earlier works. This practice was typically performed to refine one's skills or satisfy the demands of a patron who wanted an object renowned for its beauty, historical importance, or technical achievement (figs. 1, 2). In the decorative arts, copying was much less common. A chair maker might have produced seating that resembled a fashionable import, or a cabinetmaker might have made a case piece to augment an object produced by another craftsman, but few eighteenth-century artisans attempted to totally replicate the work of others. This essay will examine the concept of "copying" in the carving trade, both from a functional standpoint and as interpreted by modern scholars. It will also show why the production of exact replicas in that medium, as well as many others, was usually impractical in terms of cost and labor.[1]

Copying had a role in the carving trade, but it typically occurred on the drawing table rather than at the bench. Drawing was an essential skill that apprentices developed by copying the conceptual and working designs of their masters. During his tenure in the shop of London carver James Whittle, Thomas Johnson copied the drawings of fellow journeyman Mathias Lock, whom he, and many others, considered "the best Ornament draughts-man in Europe." Copying designs and drawings on paper also helped apprentices develop working styles that aligned with their masters'. This is clearly seen in the carving of Hercules Courtenay, who served his apprenticeship with Thomas Johnson before immigrating to Philadelphia. The outlining and modeling of Courtenay's leaves, which often have multiple overlaps and complex twists and turns, bear a striking resemblance to Johnson's published etchings that, along with a few watercolors, are the only documented examples of the latter's work (figs. 3–5).[2]

Furniture scholars often refer to cabinetmakers and carvers "copying" designs like those published by Johnson and Thomas Chippendale, but that was rarely the case. Unlike full-size shop drawings, which were supple-

Figure 3 Pier table with carving attributed to Hercules Courtenay, Philadelphia, Pennsylvania, ca. 1770. H. 32", W. 54", D. 27". (Courtesy, Rhode Island School of Design, bequest of Charles Pendleton.)

mented by models, patterns, and procedures to regulate production, etchings in design books lacked sufficient detail for true copying. The latter were intended to illustrate objects or ornaments that reflected current tastes, provide craftsmen with designs that could be adapted or altered to conform to their working styles and tool kits, and promote their publisher. As the preface to Thomas Chippendale's *The Gentleman and Cabinetmaker's Director* (first distributed as loose sheets in 1753 and then as a complete volume in

Figure 4   Design for a chimneypiece frieze illustrated on plate 12 in Thomas Johnson's *A New Book of Ornaments, by Thos. Johnson Carver, Design'd for Tables & Friezes; Useful for Youth to Draw After* (London, 1762). (Courtesy, © Victoria & Albert Museum.)

Figure 5   Detail of the knee carving on the table illustrated in fig. 3.

1754) notes, his publication was "calculated to assist the . . . [gentleman] in the Choice, and the [cabinetmaker] in the Execution of the Designs; which are so contrived, that if no one Drawing should singly answer the Gentleman's Taste, there will be found a Variety of Hints, sufficient to construct a new one."

A side chair attributed to Philadelphia carver Martin Jugiez shows how artisans used published designs as guides rather than patterns to be copied literally (fig. 6). The maker of that object was clearly inspired by a chair design illustrated on plate 12 in the first and second editions of Chippendale's *The Gentleman and Cabinet Maker's Director* (fig. 7), but Jugiez's chair differs from the etching in having gadrooning below the seat rails; simple, rounded rear legs; and front legs with a shallower curve. His carving departs even further from Chippendale's design, incorporating a flower with a stippled reserve on the knees and different leaves both there and on the knee blocks. Those details were part of Jugiez's design vocabulary, and they occur on many other examples of furniture and architectural carving attributed to him.

The degree to which carvers and furniture makers adhered to published designs was largely determined by their patron's tastes and budget, at least for highly skilled craftsmen like Jugiez and his contemporary, John Pollard, both of whom were capable of performing the most technically demanding work. When Germantown, Pennsylvania, merchant David Deshler commissioned the set of side chairs represented by the example illustrated in figure 8, he could have instructed the maker and carver to follow one of the

Figure 6 Side chair with carving attributed to Martin Jugiez, Philadelphia, Pennsylvania, ca. 1765. Mahogany. H. 39", W. 25½", D. 23½". (Chipstone Foundation; photo, Gavin Ashworth.) This chair is from a set of at least six.

Figure 7 Design for a side chair shown on pl. 12 of the first and second editions of Thomas Chippendale's *The Gentleman and Cabinet-Maker's Director* (1754; 1755). (Courtesy, Winterthur Library.) This design appears on pl. 14 in the third edition (issued in loose sheets in 1762 and as a complete volume in 1763).

engravings in Chippendale's *Director* precisely. Instead, he approved a design that incorporated just three details from the chair on the left of plate 13: the husk in the center of the crest, the trefoil at the base of the splat, and the leafage directly above (fig. 9). Philadelphia carvers like Pollard, to whom the Deshler ornament is attributed, routinely adapted London carved designs to suit local tastes for seating and other furniture forms, which in side chairs typically included stump legs at the rear and cabriole legs with claw-and-ball feet in the front.[3]

Figure 8 Side chair with carving attributed to John Pollard, Philadelphia, Pennsylvania, ca. 1769. Mahogany with white cedar and yellow pine. H. 37½". (Private collection; photo, Christie's.) This example, which has the period ink inscription "Deshler" on its slip-seat frame, is from a suite comprising at least six side chairs, two card tables, and an easy chair.

Figure 9 Designs for side chairs shown on pl. 13 in the first and second editions of Thomas Chippendale's *The Gentleman and Cabinet-Maker's Director* (1754; 1755). (Courtesy, Winterthur Library.) This design appears on pl. 10 in the third edition (issued in loose sheets in 1762 and as a complete volume in 1763).

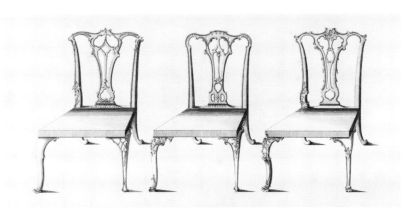

Figure 10 High chest of drawers, Philadelphia, Pennsylvania, 1750–1760. Mahogany with white cedar and tulip poplar. H. 102½", W. 46⅛", D. 21¾". (Courtesy, Winterthur Museum.)

Figure 11 Dressing table, Philadelphia, Pennsylvania, 1765–1775. Mahogany with white cedar and tulip poplar. H. 28⅜", W. 37", D. 18¾". (Courtesy, Winterthur Museum.)

Even when consumers commissioned objects to fill out sets or suites, they did not expect "copies" in the literal sense of the word. A high chest and dressing table that descended in the family of Philadelphia merchant Michael Gratz illustrate the point (figs. 10, 11). Although these objects are visually similar and were once thought to be contemporaneous, the dressing table is probably a five to ten years later than the high chest. The chest has original plate brasses, whereas the dressing table was originally fitted with bail and rosette brasses. Comparison of the appliques and shells on the center drawer in the base of the high chest and in the dressing table reveals the work of two carvers (fig. 12). Although the designs are similar, the carvers used different tools and different techniques in performing their work. For example, when the carver of the high chest modeled and shaded his leaves, he stopped his cuts short of the leaf ends; the carver of the dressing table did not. There was no effort by the later hand to mimic precisely the carving of the earlier craftsman, nor any expectation on the part of the patron that the work on the high chest and dressing table would be identical.[4]

Figure 12 Details showing the carving on the lower center drawer in the base of the high chest illustrated in fig. 10 (left) and in the dressing table illustrated in fig. 11 (right). (Photo, Gavin Ashworth.)

As the Gratz high chest and dressing table suggest, some carvers had access to objects their patrons wanted "copied." The Boston side chair illustrated in figure 13 is part of a large group of seating, the design of which was likely derived from a set of English chairs that reputedly belonged to merchant William Phillips Sr. (fig. 14). As might be expected, the appearance and construction of the earliest chairs in the Boston group are the closest to the imported model, having hairy paw feet and veneered rear seat rails. Later examples from this Boston group typically have solid mahogany rear rails and either paw or claw-and-ball feet. (fig. 15).[5]

Figure 13 Side chair, Boston, Massachusetts, ca. 1765. Mahogany with maple and oak. H. 38¼", W. 25½", D. 18¼". (Courtesy, Wadsworth Atheneum; photo, Gavin Ashworth.)

Figure 14 Side chair, England, ca. 1765. Mahogany with beech. H. 37¼", W. 23¼", D. 19¼". (Courtesy, Museum of Fine Arts, Boston; gift of Mrs. Joshua Crane in memory of her husband.)

Figure 15 Side chair, Boston, Massachusetts, ca. 1765. Mahogany with maple. H. 37⅞", W. 25", D. 22". (Chipstone Foundation; photo, Gavin Ashworth.)

Figure 16 Details showing the crests of chairs identical to the examples illustrated in fig. 15 (left) and fig. 14 (right).

The carver of the Boston chairs appears to have taken rubbings of the ornament on the crest, splat, and knees of Phillips's chairs, but he changed the designs to accommodate his tools and techniques. This is most discernable in the gouge cuts used to set in the leaves on the crests and knees (see figs. 16, 17). Small wrought nail holes in the knee acanthus of all the chairs

Figure 17 Details showing the knee carving of the side chair illustrated in fig. 15 (left) and a chair identical to those in the Phillips set (fig. 14) (right).

Figure 18 Detail showing the nail holes from pattern attachment on the side chair illustrated in fig. 15. (Photo, Gavin Ashworth.)

in the Boston group indicate that their carver created patterns, which he used to transfer his designs from piece to piece (fig. 18). Two settees and more than thirty chairs from several different sets have similar knee carving, and in almost every instance the nail holes are in the same locations. The angular shape of New England cabriole legs was particularly suited to that type of design transfer. In contrast, the British chairs do not have nail holes. If the patterns for their carving were attached with nails, the holes were most likely in the adjacent ground, which would have been removed in the relieving process.[6]

Few eighteenth-century carving patterns survive, probably because most were made of paper and either wore out or were discarded when styles changed. An example from the portfolio of London carver Gideon Saint is typical in being made of paper and in delineating the outline of a design that required frequent replication, in this instance a leaf motif most likely used for the sides, top, and bottom of a picture frame (fig. 19). To produce the pattern, Saint folded a sheet of paper in two, drew half of the motif on the right side, refolded the paper, then used a pin to prick through the drawing and create a symmetrical design. By pricking through the pattern into his work-piece or dusting the pattern with pounce, Saint or one of his workmen could transfer the basic outline of the design and use a pencil to fill in missing or pertinent information. Patterns of this type could also be shared with, or duplicated for use by, subcontractors. They were used to regulate, standardize, and expedite production but did not include enough detail to permit the production of exact copies.[7]

Figure 19 Carving pattern from the shop of Gideon Saint, London, ca. 1760. (Courtesy, Metropolitan Museum of Art; photo, Art Resource.)

Hercules Courtenay and an anonymous competitor appear to have used the same or duplicate patterns to lay out the carving on the crests and splats of several rococo side chairs (see figs. 20, 21) and armchairs, all produced in the same cabinetmaking or chair making shop. Although visually similar, the ornament on the two groups of chairs is divergent because Courte-

Figure 20   Side chair with carving attributed to Hercules Courtenay, Philadelphia, Pennsylvania, ca. 1770. Mahogany. H. 41½", W. 21½", D. 17". (Private collection; photo, Gavin Ashworth.)

Figure 21   Side chair, Philadelphia, Pennsylvania, ca. 1770. Mahogany. H. 41 ¼", W. 23", D. 21 ¼". (Chipstone Foundation; photo, Gavin Ashworth.)

nay and his competitor had different tool kits and carving styles, which were ingrained during their apprenticeships and work as journeymen. The most obvious areas of divergence are in the ribbon and knee carving (figs. 22, 23). On Courtenay's knees, the convex surfaces of the leaves are broader and more rounded, and the concave surfaces have finer shading. In addition to spotlighting differences in these carvers' techniques, the knee carving suggests that Courtenay produced the original pattern for that design. As his documented trusses in the Samuel Powel House reveal, Courtenay's leaves typically have small lobes that flip over and convex surfaces (occasionally articulated with chip cuts) leading up to that point (fig. 24). The carver responsible for the other group of chairs attempted to mimic the flipped lobes, but not the modeling preceding them. Numerous instances of different carvers working from the same or similar patterns as well as influencing each other's work are known, as the appendix to this article reveals.[8]

In *The London Tradesman* (1747), Robert Campbell wrote that many carvers, particularly those involved in chair work, "are generally Paid by the Piece, according to the Pattern of the Work." This system of production

Figure 22 Details of the splats of the side chairs illustrated in figs. 20 (left) and 21 (right). (Photos, Gavin Ashworth.)

Figure 23 Details of the knee carving on the side chairs illustrated in figs. 20 (left) and 21 (right). (Photos, Gavin Ashworth.)

Figure 24 Detail of the right truss on the chimneypiece from the parlor of the Samuel Powel House, Philadelphia, 1770. (Courtesy, Philadelphia Museum of Art; photo, Gavin Ashworth.)

Figure 25 Armchair with carving attributed
to Hercules Courtenay and an anonymous
competitor, Philadelphia, Pennsylvania, ca. 1770.
H. 40¼", W. 25¼", D. 21¾". (Private collection;
photo, Gavin Ashworth.)

allowed chair makers and cabinetmakers to subcontract work as needed
rather than have one or more carvers in their workforce. The carved components of the side chairs illustrated in figures 20 and 21 may represent piecework, although Courtenay and his competitor appear to have collaborated
occasionally. Both hands are present in architectural carving from the Black-
well parlor (Winterthur Museum) and on contemporaneous furniture. The
tassel-back armchair illustrated in figure 26 has arm carving attributed to
Courtenay, but the remainder of the work is by the hand responsible for the
side chair shown in figure 21. Two very similar armchairs from the same shop
are attributed to Courtenay alone (see figs. 26–29). This shop most certainly
used piece work components in the production of seating. Arm supports
were typically cut to seat neatly into notches in the side seat rails, like those

Figure 26 Armchair with carving attributed to Hercules Courtenay, Philadelphia, Pennsylvania, ca. 1770. H. 40¼", W. 25½", D. 22". (Chipstone Foundation; photo, Gavin Ashworth.) The mate to this armchair is in the collection of the Philadelphia Museum of Art.

Figure 27 Details showing the backs of the armchairs illustrated in figs. 25 (left) and 26 (right). (Photos, Gavin Ashworth.)

Figure 28 Details showing the knees of the armchairs illustrated in figs. 25 (left) and 26 (right). (Photos, Gavin Ashworth.)

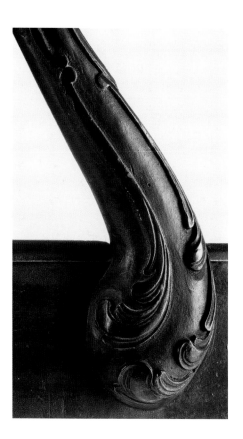

Figure 29 Details showing the arm supports of the armchairs illustrated in figs. 25 (left) and 26 (right). (Photos, Gavin Ashworth.)

on the armchair illustrated in figure 25, yet on the examples represented by the armchair shown in figure 26, the arm supports were coped. The notches in the side rails of the latter armchair had to be patched to accommodate the shaping on the underside of the arms, which strongly suggests that those rails, and likely the arm supports and other components were piecework.[9]

In some shops, master carvers produced models to guide the work of their apprentices and journeymen and, in certain instances, record details for future use. In his autobiography, London carver and designer Thomas Johnson recalled:

> I told . . . [James] Whittle he had given me nothing worth doing with my own hands, and informed him I had carved a girandole ['in a taste never before thought on'], if he pleased to see it I believed it would convince him there was no work in his shop that I was not capable of doing. I shewed him my girandole, which he purchased immediately . . . and bespoke a fellow to it; and so great was it esteemed, that many of his men took molds from the heads of the figures.

The section on sculpture in Robert Campbell's *The London Tradesman* refers to the "Master-Statuary" drawing his design on paper, then "forming a model in Clay or Wax, from whence the Workman Blocks out the Figure in Stone." Carving masters undoubtedly followed similar procedures, although they may also have made models in wood. No colonial models are known to survive, but they were most likely used in the production of components made repetitively. Examples would be claw, paw, and scroll feet; the flame sections of finials; and pediment ornaments like the cartouche variant common on case furniture attributed to Philadelphia carver Nicholas Bernard. For a frame made for "His Royal Highness the Prince of Wales's picture," Thomas Johnson "made the model, and executed the principal." In this instance the model was most likely done to work out problems and finalize the design before beginning work on the frame. It is also possible that the model was smaller in size.[10]

In large carving shops, procedures like boasting were used to turn out consistent work, increase production, and optimize each craftsman's abilities. According to Thomas Sheraton's 1803 *The Cabinet Dictionary* (London: W. Smith),

> Boasting, amongst carvers and statuaries . . . . is the great ground work of the finer parts of relief, and requires the skill of a master in carving . . . . Those carvers which are the ablest in drawing, are for the most part employed in boasting, as they are the best acquainted with the necessary projecture to be given to the respective parts. Hence it becomes the province of the boaster, after making out the sketch, to shape the outline by gouges or saws, and then make out the prominences of each part, by glueing on pieces of wood for that purpose. These rude pieces are glued to a board, and paper inserted between to make the carving come off easier when finished. When the work is sufficiently dry, the boaster proceeds to place his gouges by a judicious choice of such kind as will suit the turn of the parts . . . ; for to have more would only hinder him. Lastly, he proceeds to give the principal strokes of the whole piece . . . . This being a sufficient guide, the work is put into the hands of the carver, who is in the habit of giving the finishing strokes. In small factories, it is common for one carver to begin and finish the whole of carving. But where there are a number of hands employed, and in pieces that require much skill, the other is the most preferable way.

As Sheraton's definition suggests, boasting was typically done on large
appliques and high relief or three-dimensional work. Two pages of sketches
and notations by Matthias Lock record his work boasting for chimneypieces,
a figural keystone, a sconce, and profile busts during the 1740s, probably
while working in James Whittle's shop (fig. 30).

Figure 32 Side chair, Philadelphia, Pennsylvania, ca. 1769. Mahogany with white cedar. H. 36¾", W. 23", D. 21". (Chipstone Foundation; photo, Gavin Ashworth.)

There is abundant period evidence that carving shops used patterns and procedures to produce visually similar objects, particularly for large sets and suites that mandated the work of several hands. However, the efforts of craftsmen involved did not entail adopting another's working style, which would have been required for literal copying. This is clearly seen in the celebrated suite of furniture made for the Philadelphia townhouse of John and Elizabeth (Lloyd) Cadwalader. The genesis of the suite was an elaborate set of commode-front side chairs, probably purchased in 1769 or 1770. One is depicted in Charles Willson Peale's portrait of Cadwalader's brother Lambert, likely completed before September 1, 1770 (fig. 31). The chair illustrated in figure 32 is marked "I" on the underside of the shoe and may be the example in Lambert's portrait. The carving on the back and seat rails is more detailed and rendered more precisely than that on the other surviving chairs, which suggests that it may have been submitted for approval before work began on the remainder of the set. During the fall of 1769 Lambert acted as John and Elizabeth's agent while the couple cared for her ailing father in Maryland. In September of that year John reimbursed Lambert

£94.15 for "B. Randolph[s] acct for Furniture" and £30 for "2 marble Slabs etc. had of C. Coxe." Although it is impossible to attribute the chairs to Philadelphia cabinetmaker Randolph's shop based solely on that entry, £94.15 would have been sufficient for a large set.[11]

Figure 33 Easy chair attributed to the shop of Thomas Affleck with carving attributed to Bernard and Jugiez, Philadelphia, Pennsylvania, 1771. Mahogany with yellow pine, white oak, white cedar, black walnut, and tulip poplar. H. 46", W. 36½", D. 34". (Courtesy, Philadelphia Museum of Art, 125th Anniversary Acquisition, gift of H. Richard Deitrich, Jr., 2001; photo, Gavin Ashworth.)

Several pieces of furniture made by Thomas Affleck and carved by James Reynolds and the firm Bernard and Jugiez were designed to be *en suite* with the aforementioned chairs. Between October 13, 1770, and January 14, 1771, Affleck's shop made over eighteen pieces of furniture, including two mahogany commode sofas "for the Recesses" valued at £16, "one Large ditto" valued at £10, "an Easy Chair to Sute ditto" valued at £4.10, and two commode card tables valued at £10. Although all of these examples probably had corresponding rail, knee, and foot carving, only the easy chair and card tables are known to survive (figs. 33–35). The ornament on the easy chair is attributed to Bernard and Jugiez based on similarities to architectural carving documented to their firm (see figs. 36, 37), whereas the carving on the card tables relates to that on pier glasses documented and attributed to Reynolds's shop, including a surviving example made for the Cadwaladers (see figs. 38–40). Although the carving on the card tables was almost

Figure 34 Card table attributed to the shop of Thomas Affleck with carving attributed to the shop of James Reynolds, Philadelphia, Pennsylvania, 1771. Mahogany with yellow pine, white oak, and tulip poplar. H. 28¾", W. 39¾", D. 19¾". (Courtesy, Dietrich American Foundation; photo, Gavin Ashworth.)

Figure 35 Card table attributed to the shop of Thomas Affleck with carving attributed to the shop of James Reynolds, Philadelphia, Pennsylvania, 1771. Mahogany with yellow pine, white oak, and tulip poplar. H. 28½", W. 39½", D. 19¾". (Courtesy, Philadelphia Museum of Art; photo, Gavin Ashworth.)

Figure 36 Detail of the carving on the leg of the easy chair illustrated in fig. 33.

Figure 37 Bernard and Jugiez, truss over a door in Cliveden, Philadelphia, Pennsylvania, 1766. (Courtesy, Cliveden; photo, Luke Beckerdite.)

Figure 38 Details of the carving at the center of the front rail of the card table illustrated in fig. 34 (top) and fig. 35 (bottom). (Photos, Gavin Ashworth.)

Figure 39 Pier glass attributed to the shop of James Reynolds, Philadelphia, Pennsylvania, 1771. White pine; gesso, gold leaf. 55½" x 28½". (Courtesy, Winterthur Museum.)

Figure 40 Details of the carving on the pier glass illustrated in (fig. 39).

certainly laid out with the same, or identical, patterns, the feet of the tables are different and variations in the outlining cuts and modeling of the leafage indicate the involvement of two hands (figs. 41, 42). To the eighteenth-century eye, a measure of disparity was acceptable, even in the production of pairs and sets.[12]

Figure 41 Details of the carving on the front rails of the card table illustrated in fig. 34 (top) and the card table illustrated in fig. 35 (bottom). (Photos, Gavin Ashworth.)

Figure 42 Details of the carving on the legs of the card table illustrated in fig. 34 (left) and the card table illustrated in fig. 35 (right). (Photos, Gavin Ashworth.)

Figure 43 Charles Willson Peale, *Martha Cadwalader*, 1771. Oil on canvas. 50¾" x 37⁹⁄₁₆". (Courtesy, Philadelphia Museum of Art.)

Figure 44 Details of the carving on the frames of Charles Willson Peale's portraits of (right) Lambert Cadwalader and (left) Martha Cadwalader. (Photos, Gavin Ashworth.)

Consumers like the Cadwaladers did not presume that similar forms would be identical in every detail, but they did expect those objects to be uniform and, in some instances, echo details in their architectural settings. While acting as subcontractors for Affleck, Reynolds and Bernard and Jugiez worked directly for the Cadwaladers. In October 1770 Bernard and Jugiez billed John £28.10.7 1/2 for architectural carving, and in December Reynolds charged him £140.18.1 for several large carved and gilt looking glasses, three half-length picture frames "in Burnish gold," and 539 yards of papier-mâché borders described as "Palmyra Scrowl" and "Leaf & Reed." Although the Cadwaladers' townhouse does not survive, it is easy to imagine how details in the furniture and architectural carving might have resonated.[13]

Reynolds's picture frames, which cost £18 each, were for Charles Willson Peale's portraits of Lambert (fig. 31), Thomas, and Hannah Cadwalader. Entries in John's Waste Book note payments of £50 to "Mr. Peal in part for Paint^{g}" in August 1770 and £60 for "2 miniatures & 3 portrait Paintings in full" the following month. In the summer of 1771 Peale painted two additional portraits: a family group depicting John, Elizabeth, and their daughter Anne; and a likeness of John's sister Martha (fig. 43). The frames on these portraits have been attributed to Hercules Courtenay and described as "exact copies" of those furnished by Reynolds (see figs. 31, 43). Scholars advancing that attribution have cited an entry in the accounts of John Cadwalader's secretary, William Gouge, noting payment to Courtenay in full "for 2 Picture Frames @£14" each on March 22, 1774.[14]

Figure 45 Details of the carving on the frames of Charles Willson Peale's portraits of (right) Lambert Cadwalader and (left) Martha Cadwalader. (Photos, Gavin Ashworth.)

Figure 46 Details of the carving on the frames of Charles Willson Peale's portraits of (top) Lambert Cadwalader and (bottom) Martha Cadwalader. (Photos, Gavin Ashworth.)

Figure 47 Details of the carving on the frames of Charles Willson Peale's portraits of (left) Lambert Cadwalader and (right) Martha Cadwalader. (Photos, Gavin Ashworth.)

The inference that Courtenay copied Reynolds's frames can be challenged on several points. The three-year gap between the completion of the second group of portraits and Gouge's payment to Courtenay suggests that the latter's frames were for two other paintings—possibly the British "pieces" mentioned in Peale's letter of March 22, 1771. Cadwalader had commissioned the artist to paint landscapes the year before, but Peale failed to do so: "I hope you will pardon my neglect . . . for really too much difidence prevented my attempts after nature had lost her green mantle, the pieces you get

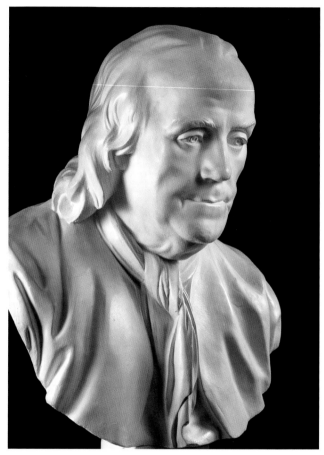

Figure 48 Details of the busts illustrated in figs. 1 and 2.

from England I hope will be very clever." Landscapes were often displayed in overmantle architraves, so it would have been desirable and consistent with eighteenth-century furnishing practices to have their frames resemble the adjacent architectural carving. On September 17, 1770, Courtenay charged Cadwalader £81.2.11 for "27 Books of Gold laid on Cornice" and carving that included components—moldings, trusses, a tablet, frieze appliques, and a "Lyons Head"—for chimneypieces in his patron's townhouse.[15]

The cost of the frames mentioned in Gouge's accounts also argues against their having been "exact copies," as they were £4 less than those furnished by Reynolds. To replicate Reynolds's work precisely, Courtenay would have needed to make a pattern (or, more likely, patterns) of one of the "original" frames and meticulously duplicate his competitor's outlining, modeling, and shading cuts using similar tools. In short, it would have taken Courtenay considerably more time to mimic Reynolds's carving than to work in his own style. If Cadwalader wanted the frames for his family portrait and that of his sister to match those furnished by Reynolds, the most expedient and cost-effective solution would have been to order them from that carver's shop. Cadwalader's subsequent patronage of Reynolds indicates that their business relationship was sound.[16]

Lastly, the carving on the frame of Martha Cadwalader's portrait looks nothing like that associated with Courtenay (see figs. 3, 5), whose work and career are the subject of an article in the 2016 volume of *American Furniture*. The ornament is much more akin to carving documented and attributed to Reynold's shop. as the pier glass and the card tables suggest (figs. 34. 35, 39–42). Indeed the variations in cutting, moldeling, and shading of the leafage on the frames of Martha and Lamert's portraits are consistent with those observed on the card tables (figs. 38–42, 44–47). Like most craftsmen of his stature, Reynold's took apprentices and almost certainly employed journeymen. He also appears to have been associated with Richard Watson, a London carver who immigrated to Philadelphia before 1774, when the latter's name appeared on the Provincial Tax List. Reynolds witnessed Watson's will, probated on April 27, 1775. William Macpherson Hornor alluded to a business connection between the two men in his *Blue Book: Philadelphia Furniture* (1935). Although he did not cite his source, Hornor noted that Watson made "1 Pair Mahoganey brackets" and "1 Pair Paint'd Do."[17]

In the fine arts of the eighteenth century, the production of exact replicas was an act of respect and admiration, primarily by the patron but also occasionally by the copier. It was not until the nineteenth century that notions of proprietary authorship and plagiarism began to emerge, even in the field of writing. For craftsmen like Martin Jugiez, whose bust of Benjamin Franklin was based on a plaster cast by Jean-Jacques Caffieri, copying was less about paying homage to an acclaimed artist or work than producing an object that was similar enough to satisfy his patron's expectations. Arguably America's first sculptor, Jugiez had the ability to copy Caffieri's likeness in every detail, but as variations in the sculpting of the eyes and modeling of the hair indicate, he chose not to do so (fig. 48). For his patron, and for many like him, close was good enough.[18]

1. John Trumbull, "Sketch of the Life of John Trumbull, Written by Himself, 1835," in *Autobiography, Reminiscences and Letters of John Trumbull, from 1756 to 1841* (New York & London: Wiley and Putnam, 1841), p. 13, <https://play.google.com/books/reader?id=ojQGAAAAQAAJ &printsec=frontcover&output=reader&hl=en&pg=GBS.PA13>. Luke Beckerdite and Alan Miller, "A Philadelphia-Carved Bust of Benjamin Franklin," in *American Furniture*, edited by Luke Beckerdite (Hanover, N.H.: University Press of New England, 2016), pp. 2–22.

2. Jacob Simon, "Thomas Johnson's *The Life of the Author*," *Furniture History* 39 (2003): 3. Luke Beckerdite, "Thomas Johnson, Hercules Courtenay, and the Dissemination of London Rococo Design," in *American Furniture*, edited by Luke Beckerdite (Hanover, N.H.: University Press of New England for the Chipstone Foundation, 2016), p. 24.

3. Beckerdite, "Thomas Johnson, Hercules Courtenay, and the Dissemination of London Rococo Design," pp. 55–59. Martha Willoughby, "The Deshler Family Chippendale Carved Mahogany Card Table," in Christie's, *Philadelphia Splendor: The Collection of Mr. and Mrs. Max R. Zatiz*, New York, January 22, 2016, lot 172, <https://www.christies.com/lotfinder/Lot/the-deshler-family-chippendale-carved-mahogany-card-5970199-details.aspx>.

4. Charles F. Hummel, *A Winterthur Guide to American Chippendale Furniture* (New York: Crown Publishers for the Winterthur Museum, 1976), p. 91.

5. For the Phillips chair, see Walter Meir Whitehill et. al., *Paul Revere's Boston: 1735:–1818* (Boston: Museum of Fine Arts, 1975), p. 50. Luke Beckerdite, "Carving Practices in Eighteenth-Century Boston," in *Old-Time New England: Essays in Memory of Benno Forman*, edited by Brock Jobe (Boston: Society for the Preservation of New England Antiquities, 1987), pp. 123–39.

6. Beckerdite, "Carving Practices," pp. 132–33.

7. Morrison H. Heckscher, "Copley's Picture Frames," in Carrie Rebora Barratt, et al., *John Singleton Copley in America* (New York: Harry Abrams for the Metropolitan Museum of Art, 1995), pp. 146–47.

8. Between August and October 1770, Powel paid Courtenay £60 for carving in his "dwelling house" (Samuel Powel Ledger, 1760–1793, Historical Society of Pennsylvania, Philadelphia).

9. Robert Campbell, *The London Tradesman* (1747, reprinted; Devon, Eng.: Latimer & Trend Company for David & Charles, Ltd., 1969), p. 172.

10. Simon, "Thomas Johnson's *The Life of the Author*," pp. 7–8. Beckerdite, "Thomas Johnson, Hercules Courtenay, and the Dissemination of London Rococo Design," p. 29. Campbell, *London Tradesman*, pp. 138–39. Simon, "Thomas Johnson's *The Life of the Author*," p. 47.

11. John Cadwalader Waste Book, p. 53, box 8, Series 2: General John Cadwalader Papers (hereafter cited GJCP), Cadwalader Family Papers, Historical Society of Pennsylvania, Philadelphia. Nicholas B. Wainwright, *Colonial Grandeur in Philadelphia: The House and Furniture of General John Cadwalader* (Philadelphia: Historical Society of Pennsylvania, 1964), p. 22. For more on these chairs, see Leroy Graves and Luke Beckerdite, "New Insights on John Cadwalader's Commode-Seat Side Chairs," in *American Furniture*, edited by Luke Beckerdite (Hanover, N.H.: University Press of New England for the Chipstone Foundation, 2000), pp. 132–68. See also Samuel W. Woodhouse Jr., "Benjamin Randolph of Philadelphia," *Antiques* 11, no. 5, (May 1927): 366–71; Samuel W. Woodhouse Jr., "More About Benjamin Randolph," *Antiques* 17, no. 1 (January 1930): 21–25; *Philadelphia: Three Centuries of American Art* (Philadelphia: Philadelphia Museum of Art, 1976), pp. 113–15; Philip D. Zimmerman, "A Methodological Study in the Identification of Some Important Philadelphia Chippendale Furniture," in *American Furniture and Its Makers*, edited by Ian M. G. Quimby (Chicago: University of Chicago Press for the Winterthur Museum, 1978), pp. 193–208; and, Mark J. Anderson, Gregory J. Landrey, and Philip D. Zimmerman, *Cadwalader Study* (Winterthur, Del.: Winterthur Museum), pp. 8–13.

12. Thomas Affleck to John Cadwalader, April 18, 1771, box 2, folder 18, GJCP. Affleck's bill includes eighteen pieces of furniture, two knife trays, bed and window cornices, and services from October 13, 1770, to January 14, 1771. Notations at the bottom of the bill indicate that Affleck subcontracted the carving on these pieces to James Reynolds and Bernard and Jugiez. Affleck's bill, which totaled £119.8, is reproduced in Wainwright, *Colonial Grandeur*, p. 44.

13. Bernard and Jugiez's receipted bill, dated February 13, 1771, is in box 2, folder 18, GJCP. Reynolds's receipted bill, dated June 29, 1771, is in box 2, folder 20, GJCP. The bills from both carving firms are reproduced in Wainwright, *Colonial Grandeur*, pp. 29, 46.

14. Wainwright, *Colonial Grandeur*, p. 45. John Cadwalader Waste Book, p. 53, box 8, GJCP. The payment to Peale was for "2 minature & 3 portrait Paintings in full." For more on the sitters, see Wainwright, *Colonial Grandeur*, pp. 108–11, 114–15.

15. For the Peale quote and Cadwalader's ordering English landscapes, see Wainwright, *Colonial Grandeur*, p. 47. Incoming Correspondence, Bills, and Receipts, 1770, box 2, folder 17, GJCP; reproduced in Wainwright, *Colonial Grandeur*, p. 12.

16. On November 25, 1771, Reynolds received £14 for a looking glass "in a Carv'd white frame" (£11.15.0), "putting up [papier-mâché] Borders in the Chamber" (£1.10), and two pounds of brass nails used to install those borders (15*s.*) (Incoming Correspondence, Bills, and Receipts, 1771–1772, box 3, folder 14, GJCP; reproduced in Wainwright, *Colonial Grandeur*, p. 124.

17. <http://files.usgwarchives.net/pa/philadelphia/taxlist/northward1774.txt>. Will of Richard Watson, probated April 27, 1775, Philadelphia Wills, 1775, no. 115, p. 134, City Hall, Philadelphia. William Macpherson Hornor, *Blue Book: Philadelphia Furniture, William Penn to George Washington* (Philadelphia: by the author, 1935), p. 284.

18. Beckerdite and Miller, "A Philadelphia-Carved Bust of Benjamin Franklin," pp. 9–12.

Figure 1 Detail of J. Stevens, *A View of the Landing the New England Forces in ye Expedition against Cape Breton*, printed by John Bowles, London. 14" x 19¼". Colored line engraving. This engraving shows a ship with carved ornaments of the type produced by Anthony and Brian Wilkinson. (Chipstone Foundation; photo, Gavin Ashworth.)

Figure 2 Anthony Wilkinson's bill for ship carving for Thomas Penn's barge, Philadelphia, August 28, 1734. (Courtesy, RAAB Collection)

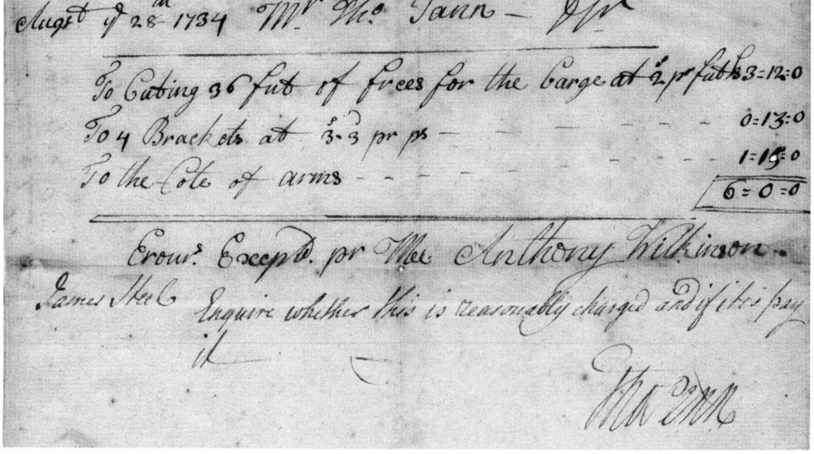

Luke Beckerdite

Brian Wilkinson, Samuel Harding, and Philadelphia Carving in the Early Georgian Style

▼ B R I A N (B R Y A N) W I L K I N S O N and Samuel Harding have long been associated with Philadelphia carving from the mid-eigh-teenth-century. Although references to these men can be found in various publications on that city's architecture and decorative art, their careers and work have not been thoroughly explored. This article will address that shortcoming by presenting new biographies of both craftsmen and by using their documented work to attribute other examples of architectural and furniture carving to their shops. Because Brian likely trained in the shop of his father Anthony, the elder Wilkinson will also be included in this study.

Anthony Wilkinson
Anthony Wilkinson was born in Philadelphia in 1698. Although his mother has not been identified, his father Gabriel, a baker, was present in the city by 1686. The earliest reference to Anthony working in the carving trade is in a 1724 deed, wherein his father conveyed part of a lot that extended from Front Street to Water Street to him. Many tradesmen involved in the ship-building industry were located nearby. On January 6, 1729, Quaker mer-chant John Reynell (Reynel, Reynolds) paid Wilkinson £4.6.6 for carving a "Lyon [figurehead] &c." for the ship *Torrington*, a fifty-ton vessel built by Philadelphia shipwright Aaron Goforth. Anthony carved ornaments for sev-eral ships during the 1730s and 1740s (fig. 1). He charged £4.4 for a six-foot lion figurehead for the ship *Tryal* in July 1730; £3.12 for 36 feet of frieze, 13s. for four brackets, and £1.15 for a coat of arms for Thomas Penn's barge in 1734 (fig. 2); and £19 for unspecified work for the ship *Mary* in 1742.[1]

There are few clues as to the size and composition of Wilkinson's shop, but presumably he took apprentices and employed journeymen. Although there is no record of Brian Wilkinson's apprenticeship, it is likely that he trained in his father's shop. The only reference to a journeyman working there is Anthony's June 27, 1734 advertisement in the *Pennsylvania Gazette*, offering a £3 reward for John Nicholson, a runaway servant carver "about 27 Years of Age." Wilkinson noted that Nicholson "pretends to be a Chair carver, and can speak a little Indian, having lived a Twelve month among those People." Although there is no conclusive evidence that Anthony's shop produced furniture carving, it would not have been unusual for the period. Moreover, the Wilkinsons were connected to at least one fam-ily of Philadelphia joiners through the marriage of Anthony's niece Mary to Joseph Claypoole. Joseph's father George was one of the most prolific cabinetmakers in the city, with a career that extended from the mid-1730s into the early 1780s.[2]

In addition to carving, Wilkinson worked as a mason and stone cutter. On November 2, 1727, he offered four shillings reward for a runaway stonecutter named Richard Peckford, and on March 8, 1734, Philadelphia joiner John Head credited Wilkinson £1.11.16 for a "marvel harth." Head's hearth was probably made of Pennsylvania clouded limestone, commonly referred to today as "King of Prussia marble." As decorative arts scholar R. Curt Chinnici noted, the earliest quarries were located near Harmanville in Whitemarsh Township and are mentioned in a deed for 150 acres of land David Henry sold Thomas Coldee in 1714. Wilkinson purchased 85 acres of that tract from Coldee in 1731 and acquired the remaining 65 acres by 1739. The former may have furnished stone for his Philadelphia neighbor, William Holland, who described himself as a mason "lately from London" and advertised "Chimney Pieces, Grave Stones, Mortars, Tables, Monuments and Steps, Pavements of all Kinds, [and] Hearths." While in New York in 1739, Holland directed all "Gentlemen and others [requiring his services], to apply to Mr. Anthony Wilkinson, Ship Carver in Philadelphia, until he return." Wilkinson continued to advertise masonry work and ship carving, and in 1741 he reported finding "a vein of [stone] much better than has been formerly us'd." His son Brian later described the stone from his father's quarry as "perhaps . . . the best yet discovered in America."[3]

Wilkinson was referred to as a "stone cutter" more often than a "ship carver" from the mid-1750s until his death, suggesting that most of his business was in the former trade. He was held in high esteem by Benjamin Franklin, who in January 1758 wrote:

> I find Marble Work in great Vogue here, and done in great Perfection at present. I think it would much improve Cousin Josey, if he was to come over and work in some of the best Shops for a Year or two. If he can be spar'd without Prejudice to Cousin Wilkinson, to whom my Love, send him to me by the first Ships, and I will get him into Employ here: As he seems an ingenious sober Lad, it must certainly be a great Advantage to him in his Business hereafter, when he returns to follow it in America.

Wilkinson died in 1765 and was buried at Christ Church in Philadelphia in February of that year. On July 17, 1766, the *Pennsylvania Gazette* reported:

> To be SOLD or LETT . . . several Lots of Ground in the Northern Liberties, on Second and Green-streets, opposite the Barricks; a Plan of which may be seen, and Terms known, by Applying to Brian Wilkinson, the upper End of Water-street. Also to be Lett by the Year, or for a Term of Years, the Wharff and Stores where said Wilkinson Lives. A Mason or Stone-cutter, that understands working in Marble, may meet with Encouragement, by applying to said Wilkinson, he being possessed of the Marble Quarry, late his Father, Anthony Wilkinson's.[4]

Brian Wilkinson
Brian Wilkinson was born in Philadelphia in 1718 and married Hester Leech in 1745. The following year he purchased a lot on the east side of Front Street between Sasafrass and Vine Streets that became the location of his

shop. If Brian trained with his father, as seems likely, and completed his apprenticeship at the customary age of 21, he may have worked as a journeyman in Anthony's shop from the late 1730s until the mid-1740s. That was the period when Anthony consolidated his quarrying business and turned his attention increasingly to masonry and stone cutting.[5]

In the December 1, 1748 issue of the *Pennsylvania Gazette*, Brian advertised twenty-one months remaining on the indenture of "a servant [man] . . . a carver by trade." Subsequent advertisements by him were largely for runaways. On April 5, 1749, he offered fifteen shillings reward for the return of an "Irish servant man, named William Mooney, a little fellow, about twenty years of age, much mark'd with the smallpox, by trade a carver" and expressed willingness to increase the bounty to "Three Pounds, and reasonable charges" if the runaway was captured outside the Philadelphia environs. Two indentured servants who absconded from Wilkinson's shop were described as "Dutch": Lawrence Perkley, "by trade a Carver in wood and stone," was "40 years of age" and reputedly spoke no English, although Wilkinson acknowledged that he was fluent in "several other languages, such as French and Turkish"; the trade of "Matthew or Matthias Luyker" was not specified, but he was only sixteen and may have been an apprentice. The same may have been true of London-born John Forder, a seventeen-year-old who ran away from Wilkinson in May 1750. Wilkinson had at least one enslaved craftsman working in his shop. In the July 9, 1752 issue of the *Pennsylvania Gazette*, he offered a reward for "A Negro Man, named Charles, about 21 years of age . . . used to the carving business."[6]

Documentation regarding Wilkinson's work is scarce. On August 20, 1756, he submitted an account for "carved Work, done for the State-House" totaling £85.8.10. Wilkinson received £35 the following January but did not collect the remainder until September 1769. Like his father, Brian carved ornaments for ships. On April 25, 1762, he charged £20.14.10 for a "Lyon head" [figurehead], two pairs of brackets, frieze work, a tailboard, four scrolls, "quarterpieces," and frieze work for the ship *Delaware* (fig. 3).[7]

Figure 3 Brian Wilkinson's bill for carving for the ship *Delaware*, Philadelphia, April 25, 1762. (Courtesy, Ten Pound Island Book Company).

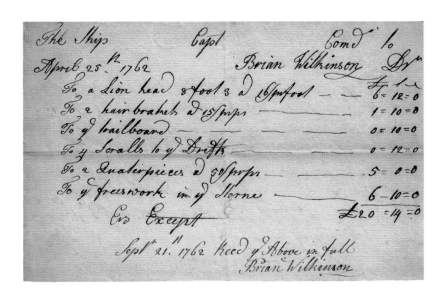

In February 1765, Brian and his brothers-in-law Peter Knight and John Knowles assumed management of Anthony Wilkinson's estate, which included the latter's masonry and stone cutting business. When the Orphan's Court approved land distributions among Anthony's heirs the following spring, Brian received 75 acres that included his father's marble quarry. Brian had earlier begun to acquire land in Whitemarsh Township north of that tract. Although Brian advertised for a craftsman who "understands working in Marble" in 1766, he was described as a "stone cutter" in a deed in 1770 and a tax list in 1772. On December 19, 1774, the *Pennsylvania Packet* reported:

> Brian Wilkinson and son . . . carry on the Marble Stone cutting business, in all its branches, at their shop in Water St. . . . where may be had chimneypieces of all kinds and grave stones neatly lettered, as cheap as any on the Continent of America; They having the best marble quarry of their own.

Brian subsequently moved from Philadelphia to Oxford Township, where he continued to be described as a stone cutter and carver. He died in 1794 and was buried at Christ Church in Philadelphia, as were his father and grandfather.[8]

Samuel Harding

Aside from surviving bills and records of payment for work, little is known about Samuel Harding's life and career. The earliest reference to him is in the cash book of Governor James Hamilton, who, on June 11, 1751, paid Harding for unspecified carving in Bush Hill. Hamilton inherited that house from his father Andrew and began remodeling it during the 1740s. The builder responsible for that project was Robert Smith, who was born in Dalkeith Parish, Midlothian, Scotland and immigrated to Philadelphia in late 1748. James Hamilton's accounts document substantial construction in that year. In March 1750, the Reverend Peter Richards wrote "the Governor has made a double house of Bush Hill & removes his family into it in October next." Although work at Bush Hill was largely completed by the summer of 1751, when Hamilton made his final payment to Smith, a February 2, 1753 entry in James' cash book records payment to Harding for "Carving a Shield."

Hamilton and Smith must have been pleased with Harding's work at Bush Hill, since the latter was commissioned to provide carving for the steeple of Christ Church, a construction project underwritten in part by Hamilton and supervised by Smith (fig. 4). Work on the steeple probably began in late 1751 or early 1752 and appears to have been completed in 1754. Harding received £12 for carving eight trusses with masks, or "faces" in 1753 (fig. 5).

Harding's most important commission extended from January 29, 1753 to January 7, 1757, when his shop provided carved ornaments valued at £195.13.11 for the Pennsylvania State House (fig. 6). Construction of the State House began many years earlier. Andrew Hamilton, Speaker of the Assembly, "produced a Draught of the State-House, containing the Plan and Elevation of that Building" in 1732, but it is unlikely that substantive work started before 1735, when master builder Edmund Wooley submitted a bill for "drawing the elevation of the Frount one End of the Roof Balcomey Chimneys and Torret. . . . With the fronts and Plans of the Two offices

Figure 4   James Peller Malcolm, *Christ Church, Philadelphia*, 1814. 12¼" x 14¼". (Courtesy, Arader Galleries).

Figure 5 Truss on the steeple of Christ Church, attributed to the shop of Samuel Harding, Philadelphia, 1753.

Figure 6 Elevation of the North façade of the Pennsylvania State House shown on Matther A. Lotter's *A PLAN of the City and Environs of PHILADELPHIA,* Pennsylvania, 1777. (Courtesy, Winterthur Museum.)

And Oiazzas Allso the Plans of the first and Second floors." The Assembly Room, Hall, and Supreme Court Chamber appear to have been serviceable by the early 1740s, but work on the stair tower, where much of Harding's carving was installed, and the final outfitting of the second-floor rooms did not begin before January 1749/50 when authorization "to carry up a Building on the South-side . . . to contain the Stair-case, with a suitable Place thereon for hanging a Bell" occurred. During the period of the stair tower's construction Harding worked under the supervision of Thomas Leech, one of the superintendents of the State House and father of Hester Wilkinson, Brian's wife.

In addition to architectural carving, Harding's shop produced ornaments for a variety of furniture forms. He is documented working for George Claypoole between 1755 and 1757 (see fig. 55), and carving attributed to him also occurs on furniture from other, contemporaneous Philadelphia cabinet shops. As furniture scholar Andrew Brunk has shown, Claypoole was active from the late 1730s until the 1780s and enjoyed the patronage of prominent merchants including Edward Shippen, Jr. and John Reynell.[9]

Harding signed his will on June 2, 1758 and probably died before August 23, 1758, when his executor Elizabeth Downey received the final payment for his carving for the State House. His will, proven on September 28, 1758, noted that she was his executor and listed witnesses John Downey (Elizabeth's husband), Robert Black (cabinetmaker), and Alice Drumbrell.

The Pennsylvania State House
The carving in the Pennsylvania State House is the rosetta stone for attributing work to Samuel Harding and Brian Wilkinson. Harding's account is unusually descriptive both in terms of the ornament and its architectural context (fig. 7). His shop furnished all of the carving for the exterior of the building and interior of the stair tower. Additional work included four

Historical Society of Pennsylvania, Norris Papers,
General Loan Office Account Books, 1750 – 1768.
(Bound, unpaged MS)
Samuel Harding Accounts.

29th   1753   Carved Work Done for the State house

Jan[y]   by Samuel Harding for the out Side of the Stepel [Steeple]

	£	s	d
To 8 blases [blases or flames] for the balconey hurns [urns] at 10[s] p[r] blase	4	0	0
the out Side of the back door to 5 flowers at 4[s] p[r] peice	1	0	0
to all flowers for dito door at 2[s]6[d] p[r] peice	1	7	6
to 6 flowers & 6 fishes for the pillars of ditto door	0	6	0
to 4 Compositta Capittals 2 plasters [pilasters] & 2 quarter plasters in them five fronts at 1[£]15[s]0[d] p[r] front these Capittals for the green room	10	10	0
to 21 brackits for the uper Stairs at 5[s] p[r] peice	5	5	0

1754   to 53 Mundulyouns [modillions] with the Stepel at 8[s] p[r]

	£	s	d
peice	21	4	0

Jan[y] 1   to 4 truses for the 2 winders within y[e] Stepel at 1[£]10[s]0[d]

	£	s	d
	6	0	0
to 44 flowers betwen y[e] Mundulyouns at 1[s]3[d] p[r] peice	2	15	0

The Carven [carving] of 2 tabernackels [tabernacles] frames
one of each

Side of the Venneshon Winder [Venetian window]

	£	s	d
to 4 Small truses for ditto frames at 5[s] p[r] trus	1	0	0
to 2 freses [freizes] for ditto frames at 1[£]0[s]0[d] p[r] frame	2	0	0
to 8 flowers for ditto frames at 2[s] p[r] flower	0	16	0
to 4 bottom truses for ditto frames at 16[s] p[r] truses	3	4	0
to 4 Ionick Capittals for the Out Side of the Venneshon Winders in them 7 frunts at 1[£]2[s]6[d] p[r] front	7	17	6
to 6 ditto Capittals for y[e] inside of ditto Winder in them 12 fronts at 1[£]2[s]6[d] p[r] front	13	10	0
to 6 draps[drops?] of husks for the open plasters y[e] Side of the ditto Winders at 12[s] p[r] drap	3	12	0

Jany 1 to 4 draps of husks in the open plasters oposite the

Venneshon Winder at 10^s p^r drap   2   0   0

to 146 Banasters & 6 posts for ye grand Sare Case   7   12   0

at 1^s p^r peice to Nine plasters for ditto   0   9   0

to 4 dubel plasters for ditto Sair Case   0   8   0

to 37 Brackits at 5^s p^r peice for ditto Stair Case   9   0   0

to 2 freses 37 foot at 4^s p^r foot for ditto Stair Case   7   10   0

to 72 foot of 7 Lefe [leaf?] Grass for ye Capings of 16 Capittals
in the doorick order in the passage 9^d pence p^r foot   2   14   0

to 12 Capittals ye oulo [ovolo] Carved egg & in ye fasca
[fascia] 3 fishes
and 3 flowers the 12 Capittals at 12^s p^r Capittals)   7   4   0

to 4 Lesser Capittals at 7^s p^r Capittals   1   8   0

to 53 Mundulyouns in y^e pasage Carved With three Leaf)
grass 3 foot in each at 4^d p^r foot   2   13   0

two pedements frames in y^e Pasage one on each Side of
the door to two kestones [keystones] for ditto frames With   1   10   0

_____

Carryd over to the other Side £ 126   15   0

(p^a. l.)

          £   s   d

1756   to 4 truses for y^e ditto frames at one pound p^r truss   4   0   0

Jany 7th to 28 foot of arakittrive [architrave] Carved 3 members at

1^s 3^d p^r foot   1   18   0

to 32 foot of 3 Leaf Grass in y^e Open plaster at 4^d p^r foot   0   10   8

to 18 foot of eggs for ye pedement of ditto frames at 9^d p^r foot   0   13   6

to 27 foot of 3 Leaf grass for ditto at 4^d p^r foot   0   9   0

to 5 foot of Riblan [ribbon?] & flower for ditto frames at 9^d

p^r foot   0   3   9

Carved Work Don about ye dial at ye East end

to 6 truses that Supports ye pedement at 1^£ 2^s 6^d p^r peice   6   15   0 to 12 fishes for ditto truses at 1^{s} p^{r} fish — 0 12 0

to 25 foot of Large Oulo Carved with eggs at one shilling

3^{d} p^{r} p^{c} [?] — 1 11 0

A Large beed Carved With flower Coap [?] 18 foot at 1^{s} p^{r} foot — 0 18 0

A beed With Riben & flower 14 foot & 1/2 at 1^{s} p^{r} foot — 0 14 6

to 38 foot of 5 Leaf grass at 6^{d} p^{r} foot — 0 19 0

to 33 foot of 3 Leaf grass at 4^{d} p^{r} foot — 0 11 0

to 2 Ornaments hands Cutthr [?] on y^{e} hour & Minit hand — 1 17 6

to 4 truses at 7^{s} p^{r} truse for y^{e} Bottom — 1 8 0

to 2 Cuttusees at y^{e} bottom at 1$^{£}$2^{s}6^{d} p^{r} peice — 2 5 0

to 4 flowers for y^{e} Serfets [soffits?] at 1^{s}6^{d} p^{r} peice — 0 6 0

to 6 draps under y^{e} upper truses at 15^{s} p^{r} peice — 4 10 0

to y^{e} [k]not & Sags [swags] in the pedement — 3 15 0

to y^{e} 2 angel peices at the bottom of y^{e} dial Swep — 0 10 0

the dial at ye West End to 6 truses that Suports ye pedement — 6 15 0

to 6 Cuttuses for ye bottom at one pound p^{r} peice — 6 0 0

to 2 Side ditto at 5^{s} p^{r} peice — 0 10 0

to 38 foot of 5 Leaf grass for ye pedement at 6^{d} p^{r} foot — 0 19 0

to 33 foot of 3 Leaf gras for ditto at 4^{d} p^{r} foot — 0 11 0

to 25 foot of oulo Carved With eggs at 1^{s}3^{d} p^{r} foot — 1 11 0

to 14 foot & 1/2 of riben & flower on a beed at 1^{s} p^{r} foot — 0 14 6

to 18 foot of flower Cope on a Large beed at 1^{s} p foot — 0 18 0

to 6 flowers for ye Serfets at 1^{s}-3^{d} p^{r} peice — 0 7 6

to 12 fishes for ye truses that Supports ye Pedement — 0 12 0

to 5 draps that is betwen ye Cuttuses at 4^{s} p^{r} drap — 1 0 0

to ye 6 draps Under ye upper truses at 15^{s} p^{r} drap — 4 10 0

to 2 Ornemant hand hour & Minit Cut throu — 1 17 6

to not and Sags in ye pedement — 3 15 0

to 2 angels peices in ye bottom of ye dial Swep — 0 10 0

Memorandom of a frese for ye upper Landing of ye grand Stair
Case it Was got out too broad at first So I Carved Three
Insted of two ye odd peice 20 foot 6 inches at 4^s p^r foot   }   4   2   0

	Sum Totall of page 2	68 18 11
Erros Excepted	Brought from the Other Side	126 15 0
		195 13 11

(p^a. 2.)

Composite capitals and pilasters for the "green room" (presumably the Assembly Room) and all of the carving in the "passage" or hall except for the Indian heads—possibly representing America, pediment scrolls, and egg-and-dart moldings, trailing husks, and scroll-framed shields on the pediments of the doors at the North and South ends, which are not mentioned in his bill and may have been installed earlier (figs. 8, 9).

Harding's carving in the passage consisted of "seven leaf grass" and egg and dart moldings, "fishes," and "flowers" for sixteen capitals in the Doric order, 53 modillions carved with "three leaf grass," and "two pediments

Figure 8 First floor, central hall in the Pennsylvania State House. (Courtesy, Historic American Buildings Survey, Library of Congress; photo, Jack E. Boucher, 1959).

Figure 9 Door pediment in the first floor, central hall in the Pennsylvania State House. (Courtesy, Historic American Buildings Survey, Library of Congress; photo, Jack E. Boucher, 1959).

Figure 10   Pediment and upper section of an architrave on the north wall of the first floor, central hall in the Pennsylvania State House. (Courtesy, Historic American Buildings Survey, Library of Congress; photo, Jack E. Boucher, 1959).

Figure 11   Keystone of a pedimented architrave in the first floor, central hall of the Pennsylvania State House. (Courtesy, Historic American Buildings Survey, Library of Congress; photo, Jack E. Boucher, 1959).

frames [with] . . . kestones . . . With fases (figs. 10, 11)." The pediments surmounted architraves, each with two trusses and three-leaf grass, egg-and-dart, and ribbon-and-flower moldings. The faces on Harding's keystones are flatter and less sculptural versions of those on the trusses his shop furnished for Christ Church (fig. 12), and their modeling differs significantly from that of the Indian heads over the passage doors (fig. 13).

The most extensive work listed in Harding's bill was for the stair tower. His shop furnished 146 bannisters, 58 brackets (fig. 14), 4 friezes (fig. 15), 53 modillions, 44 "flowers between ye Mundulyouns," and two tabernacle frames to flank the "Venneshon Winder" (fig. 16). Each frame had a frieze with a flower and leaf applique (fig. 17), two upper trusses (fig. 18), four flower

Figure 12   Frontal view of a truss on the steeple of Christ Church.

Figure 13   Indian head, door pediment in the first floor, central hall of the Pennsylvania State House. (Courtesy, Historic American Buildings Survey, Library of Congress; photo, Jack E. Boucher, 1959).

Figure 14   Brackets and balusters in the stair tower of the Pennsylvania State House. (Courtesy, Historic American Buildings Survey, Library of Congress; photo, Jack E. Boucher, 1959).

Figure 15　Frieze of a landing in the stair tower of the Pennsylvania State House. (Courtesy, Historic American Buildings Survey, Library of Congress; photo, Jack E. Boucher, 1959).

Figure 16　Venetian window and flanking pilasters and architraves in the stair tower of the Pennsylvania State House. (Courtesy, Historic American Buildings Survey, Library of Congress; photo, Jack E. Boucher, 1959).

Figure 17　Frieze applique on one of the pedimented architraves flanking the Venetian window of the stair tower of the Pennsylvania State House. (Courtesy, Historic American Buildings Survey, Library of Congress; photo, Jack E. Boucher, 1959).

appliques (one in each ear of the architrave), two "bottom trusses" (figs. 19), and long "draps of husks" on either side (fig. 20). For the Venetian window, Harding provided capitals, charging by the "front."

Exterior carving supplied by Harding included eight "balcony urns" with "blases" (flames), "flowers" and "fishes" for the door architraves, and a variety of ornaments for the clock on the west side (fig. 21). Harding's bill was very specific about the location of the major components, which were the, "[k]not & S[w]ags in the pedement," "6 trusses that Supports ye pediment,"

Figure 18　Side view of an upper truss on one of the architraves in the stair tower of the Pennsylvania State House. (Courtesy, Historic American Buildings Survey, Library of Congress; photo, Jack E. Boucher, 1959).

Figure 19　Lower truss on one of the architraves in the stair tower of the Pennsylvania State House. (Courtesy, Historic American Buildings Survey, Library of Congress; photo, Jack E. Boucher, 1959).

Figure 20　Pilaster capital and drops framing one of the architraves in the stair tower of the Pennsylvania State House. (Courtesy, Historic American Buildings Survey, Library of Congress; photo, Jack E. Boucher, 1959).

Figure 21 Exterior clock on the Pennsylvania State House.

Figure 22 Max Rosenthall, *Interior View of Independence Hall*, Philadelphia, 1856. (Courtesy the Library Company of Philadelphia.)

"12 fishes" above and "6 draps Under ye upper trusses," the hour and minute hands "cut thru," two "angel pieces (leafy husks) at the bottom of ye dial swe[e]p," "4 flowers for ye Serfets," and eight "Cuttuses" (buttresses) with drops between for "ye bottom." The clock was further ornamented with a variety of moldings: 50 feet of egg-and-dart, 76 feet of "5 Leaf grass," 66 feet of "3 Leaf grass," 14½ feet of "riben & flower," and 18 feet of "flower."

The account that Brian Wilkinson submitted for architectural carving for the State House has not been located, but the £85.8.10 total indicates that his shop furnished a significant amount of work. Presumably that comprised all of the original carving not listed on Harding's bill, including the large shell-and-leaf applique on the large architrave in the Assembly Room and the ornaments over the north and south doors in the first-floor hall (figs. 8, 9, and 22–25). His shop almost certainly did other work that no longer survives, which likely including additional components, appliques, and moldings for the architrave. The ones currently installed are comprised of salvaged Philadelphia architectural carving dating circa 1770 (inner architrave and upper portion of trusses below) and twentieth-century elements (pediment trusses, flower appliques in the ears below).

For the State House carving, Wilkinson received £35 in January 1757. A notation made at the time notes that the £50.8.10 remaining due "does not

Figure 23   Frieze applique in the Assembly Room of the Pennsylvania State House attributed to the shop of Brian Wilkinson, Philadelphia, 1750–1755. (Courtesy, Historic American Buildings Survey, Library of Congress; photo, Jack E. Boucher, 1959).

Figure 24   Detail of the applique illustrated in fig. 23.

Figure 25   Detail of the applique illustrated in fig. 23.

appear, on the Accounts of the Trustees of the Loan Office, to have been paid by them, or any other Person." It is unclear when or if Brian was paid in full or when his carving was completed and installed. The Assembly Room appears to have been plastered initially and paneled later, although the date when the latter was installed is unknown. Thomas Leech's order for screens and curtains in 1748, suggests that the Superintendents expected work in the Assembly Room to be completed soon. If so, Wilkinson's carving there and in the passage may predate the work provided by Harding's shop.

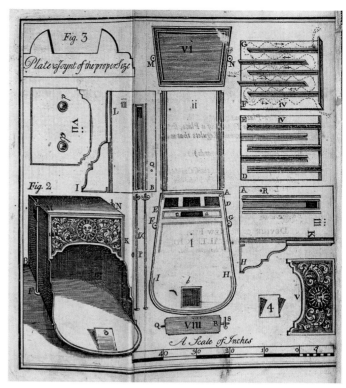

Figure 26 Franklin stove attributed to Warwick or Mount Pleasant Furnace, Chester or Berks County, Pennsylvania, c. 1742–1748. Cast iron. H. 31½", W. 27½", D. 35¾". (Courtesy, Mercer Museum of the Doylestown Historical Society; photo, Philadelphia Museum of Art.)

Figure 27 James Turner (w. 1744–1759) after Lewis Evans, design for *Franklin's Stove*, illustrated in *An Account of the New Invented Pennsylvanian Fire-places*. (Courtesy, Library Company of Philadelphia.)

In addition to being a virtual catalog of Harding's stylistic vocabulary, the carving in the State House provides insights into work methods and idiosyncrasies useful in identifying his undocumented carving. Harding's leaf carving, exemplified by that on the stair friezes and appliques over the Venetian windows, is distinctive, typically featuring long, slender lobes terminating in pointed tips, occasionally articulated with short parallel shading cuts. The larger leaflets typically have convex centers with a raised central spine, whereas the smaller leaflets, as well as larger examples that flip over, tend to have concave centers and lobes. As the applique in the Assembly Room reveals, Wilkinson's leaves are almost invariably convex in the center and typically articulated with fine shading cuts. The tips of his larger leaflets end in points and often have a raised edge suggesting a curl, whereas smaller trailing lobes typically have rounded ends. Like Harding, Wilkinson occasionally shaded the ends of leaves with short parallel gouge cuts made more or less perpendicular to the flow of the design. Although both carvers worked in a similar Anglo-baroque style and sometimes employed like techniques, their work can be separated with adequate scrutiny (see appendix A).

Carving from the Wilkinson Shops
Iron stoves of the type cast at Mount Pleasant Furnace in Berks County, Pennsylvania, and Warwick Furnace in Chester County are potentially the earliest objects linked to the Wilkinson shops, although the precise date when production began is uncertain (fig. 26). A September 23, 1742 entry in a ledger for Coventry Forge, which served Mount Pleasant, recorded

Figure 28   Detail of the front plate of the stove
illustrated in fig. 26.

a charge of £23.3.2 for "seven small new-fashioned fireplaces." Two years
later, Benjamin Franklin published *An Account of the New Invented Pennsylvania Fire-places*, which included an engraving of his hearth stove and
instructions for its manufacture (fig. 27). That design was clearly the inspi-
ration for the stove illustrated in figure 26, but the carver who produced
the pattern for the front plate inverted the banner and incorporated his
own style of leafage (fig. 28). The leaves are remarkably similar to those on
the Assembly Room applique, particularly in their shape and the manner
in which they flip and reverse direction.[10]

A tall case clock with a movement by Peter Stretch and carving attributed
to the Wilkinson shops dates 1745 or earlier (figs. 29–31). The movement

Figure 29 Tall case clock with movement by Peter Stretch and carving attributed to the Wilkinson shops, Philadelphia, 1735–1745. Mahogany with tulip poplar, and yellow pine. H. 110", W. 18½", D. 9". Courtesy, Winterthur Museum: purchase with funds provided by the Henry Francis du Pont Collectors Circle, Winterthur Centenary Fund, Mrs. C. Lalor Burdick, Mr. and Mrs. Richard Chilton, Mrs. Robert N. Downs III, Mr. William K.

du Pont, Mr. and Mrs. Frederick C. Fiechter III, Mr. and Mrs. John A. Herdeg, the Hohmann Foundation, Family of Mr and Mrs. Walter M. Jeffords, Jr., Kaufman Americana Foundation, Mrs. George M. Kaufman, Mr. and Mrs. Barron V. Kidd, Charles Pollak, Peter A. Pollak, Suzanne W. Pollak, Mr. and Mrs. P. Coleman Townsend, and anonymous donors and friends.

Figure 30 Detail showing the hood of the tall case clock illustrated in fig. 29.

bears the coat of arms of Philadelphia merchant Clement Plumstead, who died in that year. The leaves on the sarcophagus section were set in relief, modeled, and shaded much like those of the applique in the Assembly Room in the State House. Their exaggerated features and the termines anti quem of the clock raises the possibility that the carving was done in Anthony Wilkinson's shop. The earliest suggestions that Brian was working independently are his marriage in 1745 and acquisition of property the following year.[11]

A chimney back marked Oxford Furnace and dated 1747 has mantling that also relates closely to the leafage of the Assembly Room applique (fig. 32).

Figure 31   Detail showing the carving on the hood of the tall case clock illustrated in fig. 29.

Built in 1741 by Jonathan Robeston, an ironmaster from Philadelphia, and his partner and financier merchant, Joseph Shippen, Jr., Oxford was the third furnace established in that colony and the first located near a major source of iron ore. According to an 1881 history of Sussex and Warren Coun-

Figure 32   Chimney back, Oxford Furnace, Warren County, New Jersey, 1747. Cast iron. 32¼" x 29¼". (Courtesy, Winterthur Museum.)

ties, the first pigs were cast by March 9, 1743. Two different chimney backs—both depicting the arms of George II—were cast at Oxford Furnace.[12]

Carving attributable to Brian Wilkinson's shop occurs on a wide range of furniture forms including tea tables, desk-and-bookcases, high chests, and dressing tables. Two rectangular tea tables have histories of descent in prominent Philadelphia families. The example shown in figure 33 descended in the Dickinson, Logan, and Norris families and, according to William MacPherson Hornor, may have originally belonged to Charles Norris. Among Philadel-

Figure 33 Tea table with carving attributed to the shop of Brian Wilkinson, Philadelphia, 1745–1755. Mahogany with yellow pine H. 26½", W. 31½", D. 21½". (Courtesy, Library Company of Philadelphia.)

Figure 34 Detail showing the carving on one of the long rails of the tea table illustrated in fig. 33.

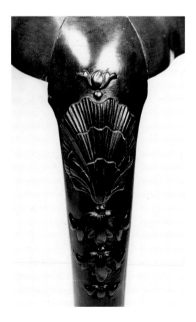

Figure 35 Detail showing the carving on a leg of the tea table illustrated in fig. 33.

phia tables, this example is unique in having rails with cyma-shaped faces, mirroring the contours of the rim molding. The center of each long rail is punctuated with a scallop shell and leafage similar to those on the Assembly Room applique (fig. 34). As in other work associated with Wilkinson, the leaflets are modeled so they appear ready to curl at the tips. Each leg of the table has similar shells with graduated husks below and small claw feet with prominent webbing and a center toe with widely spaced upper and middle knuckles (fig. 35). Closely related carving occurs on contemporaneous pillar-and claw tea tables (figs. 36, 37) and dressing tables.[13]

The rectangular tea table illustrated in figure 38 reputedly belonged to Thomas Graeme, a Scottish physician who immigrated to Philadelphia with

Figure 36 Tea table with carving attributed to the shop of Brian Wilkinson, Philadelphia, 1745–1755. H. 29", Diam. of top: 30" (Private collection; photo, Joseph P. Gromacki.)

Figure 37 Detail of the carving on a leg of the tea table illustrated in fig. 36.

Sir William Keith and his family in 1717 and subsequently married Keith's step-daughter Anne Diggs. When Keith returned to England in 1727, he sold part of his estate "Fountain Low" to Graeme. In 1737, Graeme purchased 835 acres that had been placed in trust for Lady Anne Keith, and renamed the estate "Graeme Park." Although the precise date when Graeme began renovating Keith's house is unknown, it probably occurred during the late 1740s or early 1750s. Presumably the doctor acquired this table around the same time. The leaves and shells on Graeme's table have nearly exact counterparts

Figure 38 Tea table, with carving attributed to
the shop of Brian Wilkinson, Philadelphia, 1745–
1755. Mahogany with white cedar. H. 27½", W.
34⅝", D. 21⅛". (Courtesy, Winterthur Museum.)

Figure 39 Detail showing the carving on a long
rail and leg of the tea table illustrated in fig. 38.

Figure 40 Pier table, England, c., 1740.
H. 31¹³/16", W. 35⅝", D. 24¹/2". Mahogany
with mahogany veneer and larch.
(Courtesy, Drayton Hall.)

on the Assembly Room applique (figs. 25, 39). Despite this relationship and
the table's white cedar secondary wood, furniture scholar Desmond Fitzgerald attributed it to Ireland. While it is possible that elements of the table's
design were introduced by an Irish craftsman like William Mooney, who
worked for Wilkinson in 1749, the style and composition of the carving

Figure 41   Desk-and-bookcase, London, c. 1735.
H. 93³/4", W. 51¹/8", D. 23⁵/8". Oak and rosewood
with unidentified conifer. (Courtesy, Mackinnon
Fine Furniture.)

Figure 42 Pier table with carving attributed to the shop of Brian Wilkinson, Philadelphia, c. 1750. Mahogany with yellow pine and white cedar; clouded limestone. H. 31", W. 42", D. 24⁵/₈". (Private collection; photo, Levy Gallery.)

originated decades earlier. Antecedents can be found in London gessoed and gilded furniture from the 1720–1730 period (figs. 40, 41).[14]

A monumental pier table recently brought to light by furniture scholar Frank Levy shares numerous details with the Graeme table (fig. 38, 42). Both objects have long rails with scallop shells matching the small convex one in the center of the Assembly Room applique as well as baroque strap-work and leafage set in, modeled, and shaded in the same manner (figs. 24, 25, 39, 43, 44). The feet are also distinctive in having flanges between the side and rear toes and long, abruptly sloped center toes.

The top of the pier table is highly-figured, clouded limestone that may be a product of Anthony Wilkinson's quarry (fig. 45). The underside of the stone is tabled where it abuts the frame and was originally indexed with two wooden pins, fragments of which remain in holes drilled into the top and each side rail (fig. 46). A contemporaneous pier table likely made in the shop of cabinetmakers Henry Clifton and Thomas Carteret has a marble top indexed in a similar manner. On the pier table with carving attributed to Brian Wilkinson, the top molding stops short of the back at each side (fig. 47). This suggests that the table may have had a companion pier glass

Figure 43 Detail of the carving on the front rail of the pier table illustrated in fig. 42.

Figure 44 Detail of the carving on the front rail and a leg of the pier table illustrated in fig. 42.

Figure 45 Top of the pier table illustrated in fig. 42.

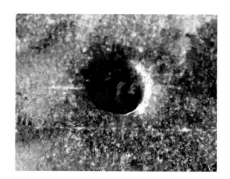

Figure 46 Details showing holes for and remnants of the indexing pins of the pier table illustrated in fig. 42.

Figure 47 Detail showing the back edge of the top of the pier table illustrated in fig. 42.

that rested on the back edge, an arrangement occasionally shown in late seventeenth- and eighteenth-century engravings.[15]

Variations in the design and construction of case furniture with carving from Wilkinson's shop indicates that he provided ornaments for several of the city's cabinetmakers. The chest-on-chest illustrated in figures 48 and 49 is one of several examples attributed to George Claypoole, Sr. or Jr. based on stylistic and structural affinities with an example the younger man signed circa 1755. The carving on the upper center drawer consists of a shell and scroll volutes in deep relief and leaf appliques that emanate below and flow to either side. With their long curling tips and convex centers, the leaflets bear an unmistakable resemblance to other work associated with Wilkinson's shop. One of the Claypooles may been responsible for the basic design, since other chest-on-chests attributed to them have similar drawers with carving from Samuel Harding's shop. One of the largest versions of this design from Wilkinson's shop is the applique on the desk-and-bookcase illustrated in figures 50 and 51. On that ornament, which is cut from a single board laminated for thickness, the leaves are similar in scale to those on the hood of the Plumstead clock (fig. 31).[16]

Figure 48 Chest-on-chest attributed to George Claypoole Sr. or Jr. with carving attributed to the shop of Brian Wilkinson, Philadelphia, c. 1750. Mahogany with tulip poplar, and white cedar. H. 85½", W. 43½", D. 22¾". (Private collection; photo, Sotheby's.)

Figure 49 Detail showing the carving on the upper center drawer of the chest-on-chest illustrated in fig. 48.

Figure 50 Desk-and-bookcase with carving attributed to the shop of Brian Wilkinson, Philadelphia, c. 1750. Mahogany with unrecorded secondary woods. H. 84", W. 42", D. 25". (Private collection; photo, Morphy's.)

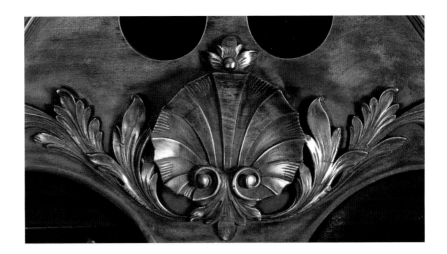

Figure 51   Detail of the applique on the desk-and-bookcase illustrated in fig. 50.

Figure 52   Chimney back, Oxford Furnace, Warren County, New Jersey, 1746. Cast iron. 34¼" x 34". (Private collection; photo, Vine Cassaro.)

Figure 53   Detail of the chimney back illustrated in fig. 52.

Carving from Samuel Harding's Shop

Samuel Harding's documented dates in Philadelphia only extend from 1751 to 1758, but evidence suggests that he may have been there earlier. The pattern used for the largest armorial chimney back cast at Oxford Furnace may have been carved by Harding (fig. 52). The elongated leaflets of the mantling relate closely to those on the front of the upper trusses Harding furnished for the architraves in the State House stair tower (figs. 53, 54), and the modeling of the mane of the lion is similar to that of the beards on the steeple trusses of Christ Church (fig. 12). It is likely that Jonathan Robeston or Joseph Shippen commissioned that pattern as well as the one represented by the smaller Oxford armorial chimneyback (fig. 32) simulta-

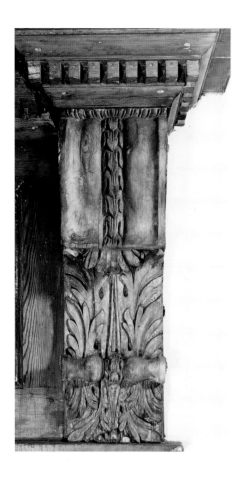

Figure 54 Frontal view of an upper truss on one of the architraves in the stair tower of the Pennsylvania State House. (Courtesy, Historic American Buildings Survey, Library of Congress; photo, Jack E. Boucher, 1959).

May ye 19 1755 Mr Georg Clapole
Dr To Samuel Harding to 4 Claws = 9 = 0
July ye 26 to a Shel & Leves Cut throw for a Book Case — 0 = 15 = 0
To 2 flowers for Dito — 0 = 4 = 0
To 3 blases for Dito — 0 5 0
To a Shel & Leves on a drow for Chest = 7 = 6
Of drows to 3 blases for Dito 0 = 5 = 0
To 2 Flowers for Dito 0 = 4 = 0
Disbr ye 30 to a Card Table 0 = 17 = 0
Febry ye 30 1756 to 3 Legs for a piller table 15 = 0
~~may ye 6 to Dito~~
Augst ye 25 to 8 Claws for 2 tables 1 = 0 = 0
to two florers — 0 = 4 = 0
to 3 Legs for a piller Table 0 = 18 = 0
Febry ye 22 1757 to Dito 0 = 18 = 0
7 = 16 = 6

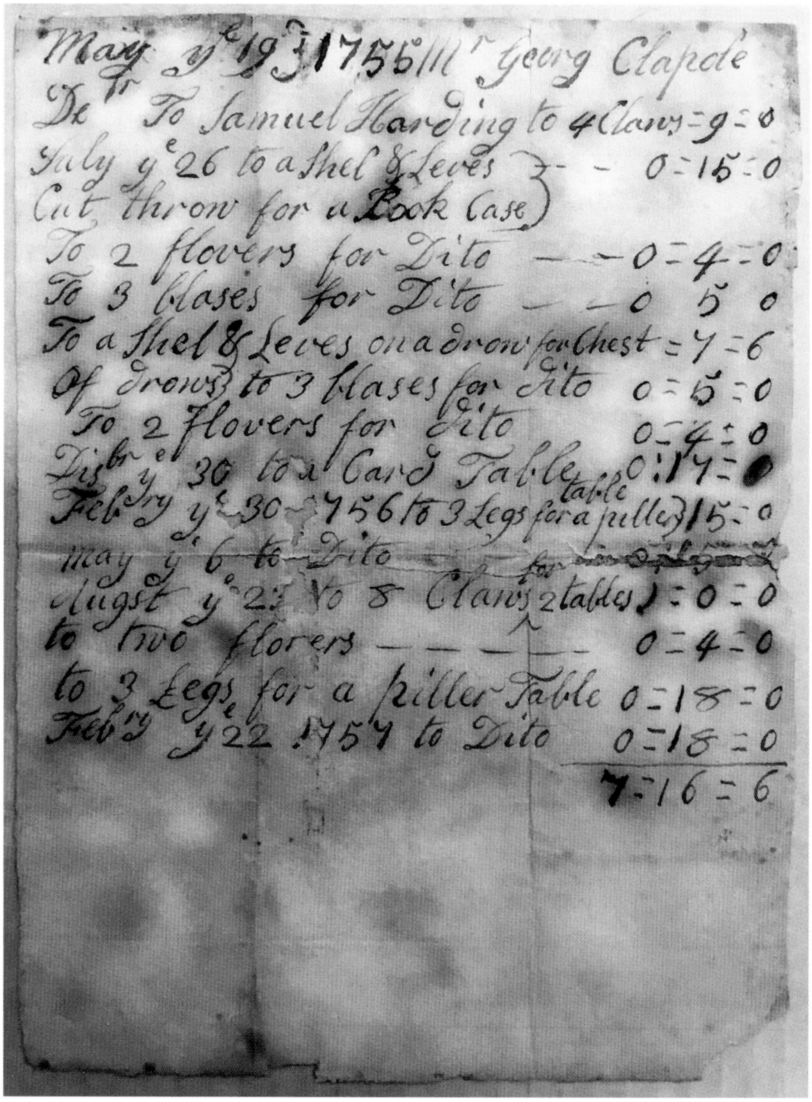

Figure 55 Samuel Harding bill to George Claypoole Sr. or Jr. for carving done between May 19, 1755 and February 22, 1757. (Courtesy, Marion Carson Papers, Library of Congress; photo, Don Fennimore.)

neously, in order to provide options for their customers. If Harding was working as a journeyman for Anthony or Brian then, it would help explain the close correspondence in some of their work.

Most of the surviving carving attributed to Harding is on furniture. A bill from him to "Mr. George Claypoole" lists a variety of components carved between May 19, 1755 and February 22, 1757 (fig. 55). Included were two rosettes, three flame finials and a shell and leaf applique for a desk-and-bookcase; two rosettes, three flame finials, and a relief carved shell with leaf appliques for a chest-on-chest or high chest of drawers; sets of legs for three pillar-and-claw tea tables; claw feet for three tables of unspecified form; and unspecified carving for a card table.

Figure 56 Desk-and-bookcase with carving attributed to the shop of Samuel Harding, Philadelphia, c. 1755. Walnut with tulip poplar, yellow pine, and white cedar. H. 100", W. 40¾", D. 23¾". (Chipstone Foundation; photo, Gavin Ashworth.)

Several desk-and-bookcases with carving attributed to Harding's shop survive, the most elaborate of which is illustrated in figure 56. The pediment is ornamented with a "Shel & Leaves cut throw," two "flowers," and three "blases" and a shield (fig. 57). The primary leaflets on the shield and applique have raised central spines, pointed tips, and turns that echo details on the architrave appliques, sides of the lower trusses, and friezes Harding carved for the stair tower in the State House. The shells at the center of the bookcase applique are stylistically similar to those on the Assembly Room applique attributed to Wilkinson, but the outlining, modeling, and articulation of the large linen-fold elements differ significantly.

No other case pieces with shield ornaments attributed to Harding are known, but several objects have pediments with urn-and-flame finials in the same location, as the desk-and-bookcase illustrated in figures 58 and 59 reveals. The applique on that piece differs from the one on the preceding desk-and-bookcase in the arrangement of the leaves and modeling and articulation of the shells, but both components are by the same hand. Consid-

Figure 58 Desk-and-bookcase with carving attributed to the shop of Samuel Harding, Philadelphia, c. 1755. Mahogany with tulip poplar, yellow pine, and white cedar. H. 104", W. 41", D. 24". (Private collection; photo, Robb Quinn.)

Figure 59 Detail showing the pediment of the desk-and-bookcase illustrated in fig. 59.

Figure 60 Desk-and-bookcase with carving attributed to the shop of Samuel Harding, Philadelphia, c. 1755. Mahogany with tulip poplar, yellow pine, and white cedar. H. 105", W. 41⅛", D. 24¾". (Courtesy, Philadelphia Museum of Art; gift of Daniel Blain, Jr.)

Figure 61 Detail showing the pediment of the desk-and-bookcase illustrated in fig. 60.

Figure 62   Tall clock case with movement by John Wood Sr. or Jr. and carving attributed to the shop of Samuel Harding, Philadelphia, c. 1755. Walnut with tulip poplar. H. 107½", W. 23½", D. 11⅜". (Courtesy, © Metropolitan Museum of Art; bequest of W. Gedney Beatty, 1941.)

Figure 63   Detail showing the pediment of the tall case clock illustrated in fig. 62.

erable variation also occurs in the design of Harding's rosettes and in the modeling of the flame sections of finials.

With its paneled doors and central "blase," a desk-and-bookcase that may have been commissioned by William Logan (fig. 60) is a slightly more modest version of the one shown in figure 56. The composition and components of the applique are simpler, particularly the shell, which has flat lobes with minimal articulation (fig. 61). William Logan was the eldest son of merchant James Logan and worked with his father until the latter's death in 1751. If William was the original owner of the desk-and-bookcase, as family tradition suggests, he likely acquired it after taking up residence in James' house Stenton circa 1751.[17]

Only one clock with carving attributed to Harding is known (figs. 62, 63), and it has a shell and leaf applique very similar to that on the desk-and-bookcase illustrated in figures 58 and 59. The bottom edge of the clock movement's chapter ring is engraved "Jno. Wood Philadelphia," thus it could

Figure 64 High chest of drawers with carving attributed to the shop of Samuel Harding, Philadelphia, c. 1755. Mahogany with white cedar, tulip poplar, and pine. H. 93", W. 40", D. 20". (Courtesy, James Kilvington Antiques.)

Figure 65 Detail showing the carving on the upper center drawer of the high chest illustrated in fig. 64.

Figure 66 Chimneypiece in Woodford Mansion, Philadelphia, c. 1755. (Courtesy, Historic American Buildings Survey, Library of Congress; photo, Jack E. Boucher.)

have been made by John Wood Sr. or Jr. The younger Wood, who was born in 1736, probably completed his apprenticeship by 1751, and his father died in 1760. The finials on the clock differ significantly from others attributed to Harding, and, if original, probably had plinth blocks like those on the desk-and-bookcases illustrated in figures 56–61 and contemporaneous chest-on-chests and high chests of drawers (figs. 64, 65).[18]

The shield Harding carved for James Hamilton's "Bush Hill," does not survive, but it probably resembled the one on the dining room overmantle of Woodford, a late-Georgian house built circa 1756 by Philadelphia merchant and Supreme Court Justice William Coleman (fig. 66). The upper leaves of the Woodford shield are larger versions of those capping the shield of the desk-and-bookcase illustrated in figures 56 and 57, but the scrollwork and central ornament of the two objects differs. Again, the design sources for Philadelphia ornaments of this type were most likely the shields on imported looking glasses.[19]

Much of the surviving furniture and architectural carving executed in Philadelphia from the 1740s to late 1750s is either from the Wilkinson and Harding shops or influenced by them. Although the work illustrated and discussed here is separated into shop groups, a great deal of related, contemporaneous work is more difficult to categorize and is best described as being from the "Wilkinson/Harding School" (see appendix B). Although far more numerous than the objects that can be attributed to Brian Wilkinson and Samuel Harding, the seating, tables, and case pieces comprising this school attest to the importance of those two craftsmen and their respective shops.

ACKNOWLEDGEMENTS For assistance with this article, the author thanks Alan Miller, Jonathan Prown, and Martha Willoughby.

1. Eunice Story Eaton Ullman, "The Gabriel Wilkinson Family," in *Genealogies of Pennsylvania Families from the Pennsylvania Genealogical Magazine* (Baltimore, MD: Genealogical Pulishing Co., 1982), pp. 281–313; See also *Pennsylvania Genealogical Magazine*, 26, no. 2 (1969): 61–93. At least two of Wilkinson's siblings were involved in the shipbuilding trade; his brother Gabriel was a shipwright, and his half-brother Thomas was a ship carver. For the *Torrington*, see Harrold E. Gillingham, "Some Colonial Ships Built in Philadelphia," https://journals.psu.edu/pmhb/article/viewFile/28246/28002, p. 160. The *Tryal* was owned by Samuel Powell and Clement Plumstead (Powell Family Business Papers, Joseph Downs Library, Winterthur Museum, as cited in R. Curt Chinnici, "Pennsylvania Clouded Limestone: Its Quarrying, Processing, and Use in the Stone Cutting, Furniture, and Architectural Trades," in *American Furniture*, edited by Luke Beckerdite [University Press of New England for the Chipstone Foundation, 2002], p. 122, nt. 140). For Penn's barge, see https://www.raabcollection.com/american-history-autographs/thomas-penn-barge. For the *Mary*, see Louis F. Middlebrook, "The Ship Mary of Philadelphia, 1740," https://journals.psu.edu/index.php/pmhb/article/view/28311.

2. Martha Willoughby, Wilkinson family tree, author's possession. Andrew Brunk, "The Claypoole Family Joiners of Philadelphia: Their Legacy and the Context of Their Work," in *American Furniture*, edited by Luke Beckerdite (Hanover, N.H.: University Press of New England, 2002), pp. 147–73.

3. Jay Robert Stiefel, "Philadelphia Cabinetmaking and Commerce, 1718–1753: The Account Book of John Head, Joiner" (Philadelphia: American Philosophical Society, 2001) as cited in Chinnici, "Pennsylvania Clouded Limestone," p. 122, nt. 14. *Pennsylvania Gazette*, August 13, 1741. For Brian's description of the stone quarried by his father, see *Pennsylvania Gazette*, July 17, 1766.

4. For Franklin's letter, see https://founders.archives.gov/documents/Franklin/01-07-02-0157. *Pennsylvania Gazette*, February 28, 1765. https://www.findagrave.com/memorial/11193024/anthony-wilkinson.

5. For Wilkinson's marriage, see https://www.ancestry.com/interactive/2451/40355_267311-00121?pid=4005526&backurl=https://search.ancestry.com/cgi-bin/sse.dll?indiv%3D1%26dbid%3D2451%26h%3D4005526%26tid%3D%26pid%3D%26usePUB%3Dtrue%26_phsrc%3Dlhg2%26_phstart%3DsuccessSource&treeid=&personid=&hintid=&usePUB=true&_phsrc=lhg2&_phstart=successSource&usePUBJs=true.

6. *Pennsylvania Gazette*, December 1, 1748; April 5, 1749; May 3, 1750; July 9, 1752; March 26, 1754; December 25, 1755, September 8, 1757.

7. *Pennsylvania Archives*, Eighth Series, 7:6429. https://tenpound.com/bookmans-log/book/receipt-for-work-performed-on-the-ship-delaware-by-figurehead-carver-brian-wilkinson-philadelphia-1762.

8. Ullman, "Gabriel Wilkinson Family," p. 306. *Pennsylvania Gazette*, July 17, 1766. Ullman, "Gabriel Wilkinson Family," pp. 306–7.

9. Decorative arts scholar Donald Fennimore discovered the bill from Harding to Claypoole. The author is indebted to him for sharing that information.

10. Henry C. Mercer, *The Bible in Iron: Pictured Stoves and Stoveplates of the Pennsylvania Germans* (1914; revised, corrected, and enlarged by Horace M. Mann, Doylestown, Pa.: Bucks County Historical Society, 1961), pp. 110, 241–43, nos. 336–8. See also Jack L. Lindsey, *Worldly*

Goods: The Arts of Early Pennsylvania, 1680–1758 (Philadelphia: Philadelphia Museum of Art, 1999), pp. 41–2.

11. http://www.afanews.com/articles/item/1974-stretch-americas-first-family-of-clockmakers #.XpBZBm57k6U. A dome-top desk-and bookcase that appears to be contemporaneous with or earlier than the Plumstead clock has a shield ornament that may also be a product of Anthony Wilkinson's shop. The leafage on the ornament relates to that attributed to Brian but is perfunctory in comparison. Ornaments of this type were probably derived from those on early Georgian looking glasses. The early history of the desk-and-bookcase is not known, but it descended from Judge Joel Jones of Philadelphia to his son the Rev. John Sparhawk Jones. Judge Jones moved to Philadelphia from Coventry, Connecticut, in 1834 and subsequently married Eliza P. Sparhawk.

12. Mercer, *Bible in Iron*, pp. 96, 103, 130. John Bezís-Selfa, *Forging America: Ironworkers, Adventurers, and the Industrial Revolution* (Ithica, N.Y.: Cornell University Press, 2004).

13. William Macpherson Hornor, Jr., *Blue Book: Philadelphia Furniture* (Philadelphia: by the author, 1935), p. 65, pl. 74; Lindsey, et al, *Worldly Goods*, p. 154, no. 87.

14. https://horshamhistory.org/history/people/dr-thomas-graeme. An elegant but much simpler table with carving from Wilkinson's shop has also been incorrectly attributed to Ireland. That object is illustrated and discussed in Lindsey, et al, *Worldly Goods*, pp. 154–55, no. 89. Lindsey attributed the table to Philadelphia, whereas Desmond Fitzgerald described it as Irish.

15. For the other table, see Chinnici, "Pennsylvania Clouded Limestone," figs. 30–32. The top of that table was probably indexed with metal pins.

16. Brunk, "Claypoole Family Joiners," p. 167, fig. 26; http://www.sothebys.com/en/auctions/ ecatalogue/lot.284.html/2009/important-americana-no8512.

17. Lindsey, et al., *Worldly Goods*, p. 148, no. 75. Luke Beckerdite, "An Identity Crisis: Philadelphia and Baltimore Furniture Styles of the Mid-Eighteenth Century," in *Shaping a National Culture: The Philadelphia Experience, 1750–1800*, edited by Catherine Hutchins (Winterthur, Del.: Winterthur Museum, 1990), pp. 274–75, figs. 35, 36.

18. Morrison H. Heckscher, *American Furniture in the Metropolitan Museum of Art, II., Late Colonial Period: The Queen Anne and Chippendale Styles* (N.Y.: Random House for the Metropolitan Museum of Art, 1985), pp. 306–7, no. 198.

19. https://en.wikipedia.org/wiki/Woodford_(mansion).

Appendix A

Figure 1 Details showing carved linen-fold shells attributed to the shops of Brian Wilkinson (left), fig. 23, and Samuel Harding (right), fig. 56.

Figure 2 Details showing flat shells attributed to the shops of Brian Wilkinson (left), fig. 50, and Samuel Harding (right), fig. 60.

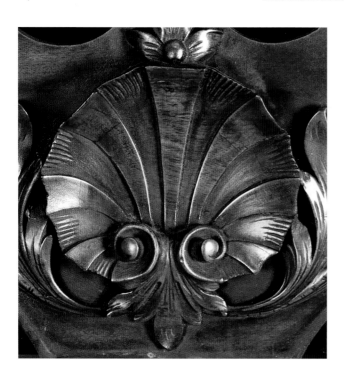 

Figure 3 Details showing leafage on furniture
appliques attributed to the shops of Brian Wilkinson
(left), fig. 50, and Samuel Harding (right), fig. 56.

Figure 4 Details showing leafage on
architectural appliques attributed to the shops
of Brian Wilkinson (top) and Samuel Harding
(bottom).

Appendix B

Figure 1   Desk-and-bookcase, Philadelphia, 1735–
1745. Mahogany with tulip poplar and yellow
pine. H. 89", W. 41⅛", D. 24". (Private collection.)
The shield ornament on this desk-and-bookcase
is the earliest Philadelphia example known.
Given the probable date of this object, Anthony
Wilkinson is a likely candidate for its carver.

Figure 2   High chest of drawers, Philadelphia,
1745–1755. Walnut and walnut veneer with tulip
poplar, white cedar, and yellow pine. H. 85⅝",
W. 43", D. 24". (Private collection; photo,
Museum of Early Southern Decorative Arts.)
The carving on this chest is stylistically related
to that from the Wilkinson and Harding shops,
but the leafage is crude by comparison.

Figure 3 High chest of drawers, Philadelphia, 1745–1755. Mahogany with white cedar and tulip poplar. H. 91½", W. 43 3/8", D. 24". (Courtesy, Maryland Historical Society.)

Figure 4 Dressing table, Philadelphia, c. 1750. Mahogany with white cedar, tulip poplar, and yellow pine. H. 31", W. 33½", D. 21". (Private collection; photo, Gavin Ashworth.) This dressing table is one of the most fully developed examples of its era. As the details shown in figs. 5 and 6 reveal, the leaf carving on the knees is superior to that on the drawers and most closely resembles work associated with the Wilkinson shops.

Figure 5 Detail of the carving on the drawer of the dressing table illustrated in fig. 4. (Photo, Gavin Ashworth.)

Figure 6 Detail of the carving on a leg of the dressing table illustrated in fig. 4. (Photo, Gavin Ashworth.)

Figure 7   Side chair, Philadelphia, c. 1750.
Walnut. H. 41^1/$_2$". (Courtesy, Christie's)

Figure 8 Side chair, Philadelphia, c. 1750.
Walnut. H. 42¹/₂". (Courtesy, Christie's)

Figure 9 Detail showing the knee carving on the
side chair illustrated in fig. 8.

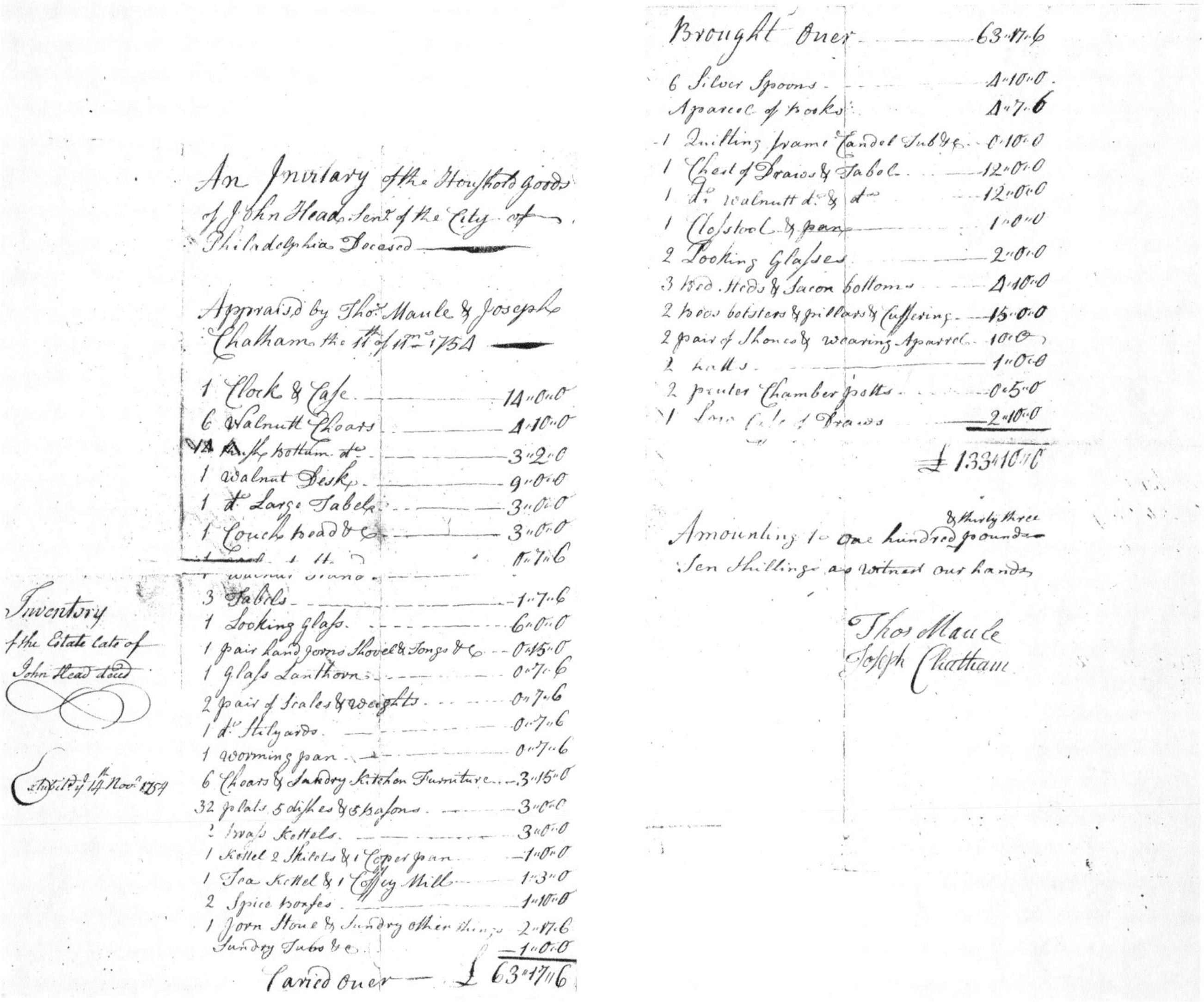

Figure 1   "An Inventory of the Household Goods of John Head Sen. of the City of Philadelphia Decesed Appraisd by Tho. Maule & Joseph Chatham the 11th of 11mo 1754." (Courtesy, Philadelphia City Archives and Historical Society of Pennsylvania.)

Jay Robert Stiefel

An Inventory of the Household Goods of John Head

▼ COMPLEMENTING THE RECENT monograph on the account book of Philadelphia joiner John Head (1688–1754) is the discovery of his probate inventory (fig. 1). Unavailable when Head's other original probate records were microfilmed, the long-sought document finally came to light in 2019 during the relocation of the Philadelphia City Archives.[1]

After a long and successful career as a cabinetmaker and merchant, John Head died at age sixty-six on October 6, 1754. His final will, signed on May 11 of that year, describes him as "being indisposed as to Health." The inventory of his goods was taken on November 11, 1754. Entries in the account book become sparse after Head began winding up his furniture business in December 1744 and liquidating his stock of goods, supplies, and materials over the next four years. By the time of his death, no shop goods may have been left to value; thus, his probate inventory appraised only his household goods. As was customary, the inventory valued none of Head's real estate holdings. (His will lists seven properties, six of them in the city and one, his country seat, along the Frankford Road.) Below is a transcription of the two-page inventory.[2]

An Inventory of the Household Goods of John Head Sen. of the City of Philadelphia Decesed Appraisd by Tho. Maule & Joseph Chatham the 11th of 11mo 1754

1 Clock & Case	14.0.0
6 Walnutt Choars	4.10.0
14 Rushe Bottum do	3.2.0
1 Walnut Desk	9.0.0
1 do Large Tabel	3.0.0
1 Couch Bead &c	3.0.0
1 Walnut Stand	0.7.6
3 Tabels	1.7.6
1 Looking Glass	6.0.0
1 pair hand irons Shovel & Tongs &c	0.15.0
1 glass Lanthorn	0.7.6
2 pair of Scales & Weights	0.7.6
1 do Stilyards	0.7.6
1 worming pan	0.7.6
6 Choars & Sundry Kitchen Furniture	3.15.0
32 plats 5 dishes & 5 Basons	3.0.0
2 Brass Kettels	3.0.0
1 Kettel 2 Skilets & 1 Coper pan	1.0.0
1 Tea Kettel & 1 Coffey Mill	1.3.0
2 Spice Boxses	1.10.0

1 Iron Stove & Sundry other things	2.17.6
Sundry Tubs &c	1.0.0
Caried over	£63.17.6
Brought over	63.17.6
6 Silver Spoons	4.10.0
A parcel of Books	4.7.6
1 Quilting frame Candel Tub &c	0.10.0
1 Chest of Draws & Tabel	12.0.0
1 do walnut do & do	12.0.0
1 Closstool & pan	1.0.0
2 Looking Glasses	2.0.0
3 Bed Steds & Sacon bottoms	4.10.0
2 Beds bolsters & pillars & cuffering	15.0.0
2 pair of Shoues & wearing Aparrel	10.0
2 hatts	1.0.0
2 peuter Chamber potts	0.5.0
1 Low Case of Draws	2.10.0
	£133.10.0

Amounting to one hundred & thirty three pounds Ten shillings as witnest our hands

Thos Maule
Joseph Chatham

Interpretation of Head's probate inventory is aided by his account book. The appraisers, both joiners, did business with Head and have accounts in his book. Among other things, Head charged Joseph Chatham (fl. ca. 1740–1754) for a frame and "five ledges [legs] for a Chest of drawers." Thomas Maule appears to have been Head's apprentice. Upon the latter's retirement from cabinetmaking, Maule purchased a joiner's bench and furniture hardware from him. As furniture usually comprised the most expensive goods in an estate, having first-hand knowledge of what Head's furniture was worth made Chatham and Maule obvious choices as appraisers.[3]

Head's probate inventory is especially useful in identifying the property he held at his death. Apart from "a Clock & Case" bequeathed to his daughter Rebecca Jones (1713–1787), his will is unspecific as to furniture or other household goods; they were collectively dispersed to his widow and another daughter. As only one clock is listed in the inventory, valued at £14.0.0, it was that for Rebecca.[4] Observations regarding other items in the inventory follow.

The "Walnut Desk" appraised at £9.0.0, even second-hand, must have been substantial, specially embellished, or of elaborate design. For his most popular model of new desk, Head charged only £6.0.0. For a "Larg" walnut desk he got £8.10.0, the same as he charged for each of two in mahogany. Only one of Head's desks cost more, £12.0.0, and was the last sold.[5]

The "Couch Bead &c" valued at £3.0.0 may be one of the two "Couch[es]" or daybeds he had bought for £1.4.0 from chair maker Solomon Cresson (1674–1746) on October 7, 1729, only one of which Head had sold. Head made no couches or other seating furniture himself. He did record "mending a Couch" for merchant John McComb Jr. (fl. 1720–1726) on April 25, 1721, at a cost of £0.0.6. One popular covering for seating furniture was leather. Head had provided a "Couch Hide" to cordwainer William Clare (1675–1741) on February 18, 1723, at a price of £0.3.0.

The "pair hand irons Shovel & Tongs &c" valued at £0.15.0 may have included the "payer of hand irons" that Head had purchased from George Kelley (fl. 1742–1744) for £1.0.0 on December 18, 1742.[6]

Given their low collective valuation of £1.10.0, the two "Spice Boxses" listed among other kitchen metal ware were presumably of like material and not similar to either of the two wooden spice boxes that Head made in his shop. One, at £2.10.0, sold on April 15, 1735, to his best customer, James Steel (ca. 1671–1742), the receiver general. The other, at £1.10.0, sold on July 25, 1736, to Samuel Burrows Sr. (fl. 1727–1738).[7]

"A parcel of Books," inventoried at £4.7.6, is intriguing. Although Head built bookcases for others, there are no entries in his account book for books. Nor is there a record of Head's being a member of a subscription library, such as the Library Company of Philadelphia, founded in 1731. A devout Quaker,

Figure 2 High chest and dressing table, Philadelphia, 1726. Black walnut with hard pine and Atlantic white cedar. High chest: H. 64½", W. 42", D. 23¼". Dressing table: H. 28¾", W. 33½", 23⅜". By the shop of John Head (1688–1754) and debited in his account book, p. 87 left, on June 14, 1726, to Caspar Wistar (1696–1752). (Courtesy, Philadelphia Museum of Art; photo, Gavin Ashworth.)

one would expect religious tracts to be among his possessions or, possibly, Thomas Chalkley's (1675–1741) travel journal, a work often listed in contemporary Philadelphia inventories. Regrettably, the appraisers listed no titles.[8]

The inventory entry for "1 Quilting frame Candel Tub &c ," valued at £0.10.0, is a reminder of the utilitarian items that John Head's shop supplied both for households and to his fellow tradesmen. He charged shipwright Nathaniel Pool (fl. 1709–1727) £0.7.6 on February 9, 1722, for a "Qwilting frame & Trusels [trestles]," and merchant Alexander Wooddrop (1685–1742) £0.7.0 on April 7, 1722, for a "Candle Trof [trough]."[9]

The two entries for a walnut "Chest of Draws & Tabel," each valued at £12.0.0, were no doubt en suite pairs of high chests and dressing tables at least as fine as the pair in highly figured black walnut (fig. 2) ordered from Head by Caspar Wistar—together with an oval table—at a cost of £10.0.0 on June 14, 1726, three weeks after Wistar's marriage to Catherine Johnson (1703–1786) of Germantown and paid for by her father on June 15. On April 30, 1730, Head also sold Wistar a clock case, for £4.0.0. It is the earliest known, fully documented Philadelphia tall-case clock, and has its original eight-day tide dial movement by William Stretch (1701–1748). [10]

The inventory entries for "3 Bed Steds [bedsteads] & Sacon [sacking] bottoms," at £4.10.0, and for "2 Beds bolsters & pillars [pillows] & cuffering [covering]," at £15.0.0, complement the entries for fifty-two "Badstads" in Head's account book, some of which were ordered two at a time, suggesting their use as pairs. Some of Head's bedsteads included charges for curtains and cornices. He also sold items required for beds, such as feathers and sacking bottoms. The £15.0.0 valuation for two of the beds in Head's household is unsurprising given that beds and their furnishings, along with clocks and their cases, were typically the most expensive items appraised in colonial inventories.

A silver cann by Philadelphia silversmith Joseph Richardson Sr. (1711–1784) and various documents have been passed down in John Head's family. As yet no furniture of his has been identified as having similarly descended, notwithstanding that over sixty pieces can be documented or attributed to his shop. Also unaccounted for is his daybook, from which entries were transferred into his account book. Such items may one day also be discovered, complementing the fortuitous survival of John Head's account book and probate inventory.[11]

ACKNOWLEDGEMENTS For assistance with this article, the author thanks Adam Bowett, Donald Fennimore, Patricia O'Donnell, Margaret Maxey, and Christopher Storb. This article is dedicated to the memory of Robert S. Cox.

1. Jay Robert Stiefel, *The Cabinetmaker's Account: John Head's Record of Craft and Commerce in Colonial Philadelphia, 1718–1753*, Memoir 271 (Philadelphia: American Philosophical Society, 2019); the will of "John Head . . . Joyner," signed May 11, 1754, with a codicil signed September 19, 1754, and proved October 18, 1754, Philadelphia Wills 1754-136. The Philadelphia City Archives opened at its new location, 548 Spring Garden Street, on December 6, 2018. Thanks to Margaret Maxey of the Historical Society of Pennsylvania, a copy of the probate inventory was

made and is now available in its autograph collection (#22) under "Head, John (1688–1754)": John Head will and inventory of household goods, 1754 [copies], Collection DO476/22A, Historical Society of Pennsylvania, Philadelphia, Pa. Prior to the inventory's disappearance, one of its entries had been cited by another researcher in 1964. Stiefel, *The Cabinetmaker's Account*, pp. 12, 17n4.

2. John Head's last entry for furniture was on December 27, 1744, for a "walnut chest of drawers—in 3 parts" which, together with "a Little Chest of Drawers," cost blacksmith John Rouse (d. ca. 1778) £18.0.0. Twenty days prior, Head had sold "a Joyners Bench" to Thomas Maule (b. 1720; fl. 1744–1755). Between 1744 and 1747 Head also sold off to Maule large quantities of furniture hardware. On May 24, 1748, Head's son-in-law Benjamin Hooton (1719–1792) bought thousands of board feet of lumber from him. Stiefel, *The Cabinetmaker's Account*, pp. 254–255.

3. Ibid., pp. 65–66, 135, 170.

4. Ibid., pp. 12, 91, 218–226; Philadelphia Wills 1754-136.

5. Stiefel, *The Cabinetmaker's Account*, p. 233.

6. Ibid., p. 129.

7. Ibid., p. 243.

8. Ibid., p. 234; Thomas Chalkley, *A Collection of the Works of Thomas Chalkley* (Philadelphia: Printed by B. Franklin, and D. Hall, 1749).

9. Stiefel, *The Cabinetmaker's Account*, p. 245.

10. Ibid., pp. 151–157, 179–186.

11. Ibid., pp. 2, 13–17, 47–49, 255.

Figure 1 Side chair illustrated on page 252, cat. 52, in Benno M. Forman, *American Seating Furniture, 1630–1730: An Interpretive Catalogue* (New York: W. W. Norton for the Winterthur Museum, 1988). The wood of this chair is cataloged as "American beech." Species of beech cannot be separated microscopically.

Figure 2 Heading of the catalog entry for the side chair illustrated in fig. 1.

52.
CANE CHAIR WITH CARVED TOP
Boston, Massachusetts
1689–1705
WOOD: American beech (*Fagus grandifolia*)
OH 51⅞" (131.8 cm)
SH 19" (48.3 cm), SW 18¼" (46.4 cm), SD 15¼" (38.7 cm)
PROVENANCE: South Shore of Boston; family of Samuel F. B. Morse; Roland B. Hammond; museum purchase
73.382

Harry A. Alden

Misconceptions and Mistakes in Wood Identification and Furniture Scholarship: Corrections to Benno M. Forman's *American Seating Furniture, 1630–1730*

▼ BENNO M FORMAN'S *American Seating Furniture 1630–1730*—an "interpretive catalogue" of the Winterthur Museum's collection of chairs, stools, couches, and other forms—is one of the more frequently cited sources in books and articles on that subject. When his work was published in 1988, the author of this article was employed as Wood Researcher at Winterthur and was credited with making "minor corrections to the chapter on woods." Those corrections were neither minor nor ambiguous, and the author was not made privy to the final draft of that chapter nor to the wood identifications in the catalog entries. Because incorrect and misleading wood identifications made in Forman's book continue to be repeated by furniture scholars and academics (fig. 1), this article will provide corrections and discuss the value of scientific evidence over unfounded opinions, conclusions, and problematic methodologies.[1]

Author's Credentials
- Graduated magna cum laude from Millersville University with a B.S. in biology in 1981.
- Received M.S. in botany specializing in plant anatomy, plant morphology, and plant growth and development from the University of California, Davis in 1984.
- Received Ph.D. in biology from Florida State University in 1993.
- Trained in wood identification at the Center for Wood Anatomy Research at the USDA Forest Products Laboratory in Madison, Wisconsin, with two years in temperate wood identification (Donna J. Christensen) and three years in tropical wood identification (Dr. Regis B. Miller).
- Employed as Wood Researcher/Wood Identification Specialist at the Winterthur Museum from 1986 to 1989, identifying over 1,700 samples.
- Employed as a microscopist (microscopic analysis of objects from archaeological and fine arts contexts, teaching in microscopy and microscopic analysis, digital image analysis), GS-401-12, Smithsonian Center for Research and Education, Smithsonian Institution, Museum Support Center, Suitland, Maryland.
- Founded Alden Identification Service in 1987, performing numerous wood identifications for the past thirty-three years. For a complete list of the author's publications and C.V., see https://wood-identification.com.

Corrections to Catalog Entries and Illustrations by Wood

Background: The wood identifications for *American Seating Furniture, 1630–1730* were done by Gordon Saltar and are identified by being in italics (fig. 2). With the exception of black walnut, *none* of the species separations made by Saltar can be done microscopically.

Nomenclature: The abbreviation for single species is sp. The abbreviation for species in the plural is spp.

SOFTWOODS

White Pine (*Pinus strobus*) should read White Pine Group (*Pinus* sp.).
Figures 33, 170.
Pages 150–19, 182-38, 185-40, 192–44.

HARDWOODS

American Ash – Black Ash – Red Ash should read Ash (*Fraxinus* sp.).
Figures 30, 33, 46, 52, 89.
Pages 93-2, 96-3, 98-4, 101-5, 103-6, 105-7, 108-9,118-12,124-15, 185-40, 317-67.

Red Oak (*Quercus rubra*) should read Red Oak Group (*Quercus* sp.).
Figure III.
Pages 148-18, 152-20, 180-35, 180-36, 214-45, 216-46, 308-64, 311-65, 314-66, 320-69, 320-70, 325-71, 333-75, 335-76, 363-87.

Post Oak (*Quercus stellata*) should read White Oak Group (*Quercus* sp.).
Page 182-37.

White Oak (*Quercus alba*) should read White Oak Group (*Quercus* sp.).
Figure 89.
Pages 105-7, 114-11, 122-14, 150-19, 180-36, 190-43, 220-48, 338-77, 340-79.

European Field Maple (*Acer campestre*) should read Soft Maple Group (*Acer* sp.).
Page 120-13.

Red Maple (*Acer rubrum*) should read Soft Maple Group (*Acer* sp.).
Pages 124-16, 241-45, 216-46, 304-61, 304-62, 306-63, 344-80.

American Silver or Red Maple (*Acer saccharinum* or *Acer rubrum*) should read Soft Maple Group (*Acer* sp.).
Pages 182-38, 325-71, 338-77.

American (Striped) Maple (*Acer pennsylvanicum* [*sic*]) should read Soft Maple Group (*Acer* sp.)
[*pensylvaticum* is misspelled].
Figure 158.
Pages 268-56, 279-60, 311-65, 331-74.

Sugar Maple (*Acer saccharum*) . . . a Maple of the Soft Group should read Hard Maple Group (*Acer* sp.).
Pages 226-50, 308-64, 335-76.

American Beech (*Fagus grandifolia*) should read Beech (*Fagus* sp.).
Figures 126, 142.
Pages 251-52, 254-53, 268-55, 328-73.

European Beech (*Fagus sylvatica*) should read Beech (*Fagus* sp.).
Figures 99, 116, 126, 163, 173.
Pages 278-59, 279-60.

Ohio Buckeye (*Aesculus glabra*) should read Horse Chestnut (*Aesculus* sp.).
Page 96-3.

Hickory (genus *Carya*) should read either True Hickory Group or Pecan Hickory Group (*Carya* sp.).
Pages 105-7, 112-10, 120-13, 128-17.

American Elm (*Ulmus fulva*) or White Elm (*Ulmus americana*) should read Elm (*Ulmus* sp.) [*Ulmus fulva* is an archaic species epithet designation for Slippery Elm (*Ulmus rubra*)].
Pages 108-9, 340-78.

American Black Cherry (*Prunus serotina*) should read Cherry (*Prunus* sp.).
Pages 114-11, 118-12.

Fig. 3 The image on the right is labelled "transverse plane." This is clearly the tangential plane.

Corrections to Chapter 2 with Comments on Wood Identification

PAGE 23:

In the second full paragraph, Forman makes several erroneous statements.:(1) walnut from Salem, Massachusetts, looks the same as walnut from Norfolk, Virginia, or any other place within its growth range; (2) wood from a tree growing on the dry top of a hill will look the same as the same species growing beside a stream at the bottom of the hill; (3) the absence or presence of minerals in the soil does not impart different colors in the same species. In the third full paragraph, Forman states that "Micro-analysis is practiced by the professional botanist who is a microanatomist." Microanatomist is a poor term and too general—it should be a plant anatomist, with additional training in wood identification.

PAGE 24:

Softwoods are conifers and not their "close relatives." Forman may have been referring to gymnosperms, which include conifers. The "close relatives" of conifers do not produce wood. In figure 5, the wood wedge drawn by Robert Blair St. George and Wade Lawrence has a blatant error. The regions of each growth ring (D) use archaic terms: spring growth should be earlywood (D_1) and summer growth should be latewood (D_2). Even worse, the drawing has the earlywood produced last in the ring and latewood produced first, which is backwards. In the drawing to the right, the cambium (B) points to the bark (C). At the bottom of the first full paragraph, Forman states that red oak (*Quercus rubra*) is native only to North America. While this is true, there is a Turkish oak (*Quercus cerris*) native to Europe that looks exactly like *Quercus rubra*. Also in this paragraph, Forman describes early growth as composed almost entirely of pith and bark. This is not true; it has some pith but is composed mostly of primary xylem (vessels/pores) with primary phloem (inner bark) and bark. The cambium develops between the primary xylem and primary phloem. This is basic undergraduate botany. In addition, secondary phloem does have anatomical features useful in identification and is not insusceptible. There is also an error in figure 6. Tyloses are not resinous, but are cellulosic extensions of adjacent parenchyma cells. Also, the presence of tyloses in the separation of red and white oak groups is not useful because the sapwood of white oaks is devoid of tyloses, and some species of red oaks have tyloses.[2]

PAGE 25 AND FIG. 5, OAKS SECTION:

In describing rays in oaks, the word "gigantic" should be replaced with "wide" and "fine" should be replaced with "narrow" (or, better, with "uniseriate"). In the fifth full paragraph, tylosis should be replaced with tyloses (the plural form); and tyloses do not dry out, as they are neither liquid nor resinous.

PAGE 28, CONIFERS SECTION:

Thuja occidentalis is not a pine, and it is called northern white-cedar, not to be confused with Atlantic white cedar (*Chamaecyparis thyoides*). Also, the yellow pine that grows in the Connecticut River Valley *is* pitch pine (*Pinus rigida*). In the fourth full paragraph, firs (*Abies* spp.) can sometimes be separated by continent.[3]

PAGE 29, TULIPWOOD SECTION:

First, tulipwood is a species of rosewood (*Dalbergia frutescens* [Vell.] Britton). Second, it is unlikely that tulip poplar was cultivated anywhere, and it grows naturally in southern Massachusetts (see map at the end of this article).

PAGE 29, MAPLES SECTION:

Species within each group (Hard Maple and Soft Maple Groups) look exactly alike microscopically. *Acer pseudoplatanus* should be Hard Maple Group. *Acer saccharum cannot* be distinguished from other species in the Hard Maple Group. The same goes for *Acer campestre* and the Soft Maple Group. Again, with reference to Gordon Saltar, no species separations are possible. Striped maple (*Acer pensylvaticum*) should not appear here, because it is a very small understory tree and was not used for anything but small items, like inlays or veneers (see Appendix A).

PAGE 30, BEECH SECTION:

Species of beech *cannot* be separated microscopically, and Saltar's "test" was fallacious. His anatomical features for separating beech species were the presence of crystals, ray height/width, and the presence of "tandem" rays. According to Saltar, American beech has "crystals minute of the rays," tandem rays, and "short rays," whereas English beech has "long (tall) rays" and "visible small (narrow) rays." He describes these as "reliable though elusive factors." Crystals exist in both species but are rare. The term "tandem rays" was apparently invented by Saltar, as the author has never heard of them or encountered that term in scientific literature. The feature Saltar refers to is artefactua, and is a single wide ray bisected by fibers that appears to be two rays. More importantly, Saltar does not use the presence of crystals in beech as a positive character. That is, its presence (to him) indicates American origin, while its absence (to him) indicates English/European origin. This is faulty logic, as crystals (and other features in wood identification) are correctly treated as positive characters, especially when they are scarce. They only can be used in a positive sense, while their absence indicates that the unknown sample could be either species/species groups. This applies to crystals in spruce (*Picea* spp.) and fir (*Abies* spp.), and to storied rays and specific gravity in the True Mahogany Group (*Swietenia* spp.).[4]

PAGES 30–31, WALNUT SECTION:
The reference to *Juglans regia* in the third paragraph is incorrect. *Juglans regia* is not native to England or Europe, but rather to the Balkans and from Iraq eastward to the Himalayas and southwestern China; its proper common name is Persian walnut. The characterization of American walnut on page 31 should read "American walnut exhibits an irregular thickening of the vessel walls (called gashes) and short chains of calcium oxalate crystals in the axial parenchyma."

PAGE 32, ASH SECTION:
All species within the genus *Fraxinus* (ash) look exactly alike microscopically.

PAGE 33, BIRCH SECTION:
Birch is not always a cold-loving tree. The river birch (*Betula nigra*) grows in the southern United States to Florida (see Appendix A). Species separations are not possible microscopically.

PAGE 37, NOTES SECTION:
The editor's note for number 34, stating that "Saltar's tests for American Beech have been confirmed by Her Majesty's Forest Products Laboratory at Prince's Risborough England but they have not been published by Saltar," is patently false. The author has a copy of Saltar's explanation of his methodology, and it would never have been published by a peer-reviewed journal. The statement that "research is currently being undertaken to verify Saltar's techniques" is also false, as the author was the Wood Researcher at Winterthur at the time and expressly informed the editors that species separations of beech could not be made microscopically.[5]

Other Questionable Identifications by Gordon Saltar and Others

Gordon Saltar's "identifications" in other publications should be questioned. A web search found six:

> 1. Tomas Ryder, "Two Historic Carriages," *Carriage Journal* 27, no. 3 (Winter 1989): 118.
>
> 2. Scott Odell, "The Identification of Wood Used in the Construction of 17th and 18th Century Keyboard Instruments," *Bulletin of the American Group. International Institute for Conservation of Historic and Artistic Works* 12, no. 2 (1972): 58–61.
>
> 3. Frances Gruber Safford, *American Furniture in the Metropolitan Museum of Art. I. Early Colonial Period: The Seventeenth-Century and William and Mary Styles* (New Haven, Conn.: Yale University Press for the Metropolitan Museum of Art, 1985), p. 90.
>
> 4. Morrison Heckscher, *American Furniture in the Metropolitan Museum of Art. II. Late Colonial Period: Queen Anne & Chippendale Styles* (New York: Random House for the Metropolitan Museum of Art, 1985), p. 113.
>
> 5. Roderic H. Blackburn and Ruth Piwonka, *Remembrance of Patria: Dutch Arts and Culture in Colonial America. 1609–1776* (Albany, N.Y.: Albany Institute of History and Art., 1988), p. 262.
>
> 6. Nancy Goyne Evans, *Windsor Chair Making in America: From Craft Shop to Consumer* (Hanover, N.H.: University Press of New England for the Winterthur Museum, 2006), p. 114.

There are also dubious species assignments made by J. Thomas Quirk (deceased). The author worked with Quirk at the Forest Products Lab. He was not a wood anatomist, but a mechanical engineer transferred to the wood anatomy section. After retiring from the Forest Products Lab, Quirk started a wood identification business. Like Saltar, he often assigned false American species designations.

Microscopic wood identification is a complex process that initially involves the precise preparation of samples, the recognition of cellular characteristics, and the arrangement of cells within the tissue called wood. Secondarily, these cellular characters are then used in: 1) a dichotomous key; 2) entered onto punch-cards; or, 3) into a multivariate computer array (InsideWood, 2004–onwards, published on the internet, http://insidewood.lib.ncsu.edu/search). Finally, potential taxa generated are compared to reference samples for a final positive identification.

The establishment of new ways to separate genera in tropical woods or species separations in temperate genera requires thorough scientific data collection and analysis, followed up with submission to peer-reviewed journals such as the *IAWA* [International Association of Wood Anatomists] *Journal*.

Data from Bruce Hoadley, Regis Miller, and Scott Kitchener indicate that the presence of fusiform ray extensions on radial resin ducts that are 100 microns tall or more indicate deal (*Pinus sylvestris*), but those authors' research is only about 70% accurate. While the basic approach is good, the accuracy rate is poor and the sample size needed is impractical for small samples.[6]

There is also a graduate thesis dealing with species separation of ash (*Fraxinus* spp.). Not all species were examined, the structure and collection of data were poor, and the sample size needed was impractical and is of no use in wood identification. The author has shared a copy of that thesis with the editor of a peer-reviewed wood anatomy journal for comments. The response was that the thesis was unworthy of publication and had questionable scientific value.

Efforts to separate species microscopically with good science are continuing, but there is a limit to how far things will progress. First, species assignments are based on the plants' (trees') floral and foliar (leaf) characteristics and, for the most part, wood anatomy at this level is evolutionarily conservative. Second, there are many genera where the anatomical characters of species overlap—in the rosewoods (*Dalbergia* spp.), for example—making species separations mostly impossible. One must use other features such as specific gravity or density, heartwood colors and their patterning, and chemical tests (water and ethanol extracts color and their color under long-wave UV fluorescence). These latter features require a large sample of approximately 6 x 4 x 1 inches.

Appendix A

Generic Descriptions Alphabetically by Common/Trade Name

NORTHERN WHITE-CEDAR (*Thuja* L./*Cupressaceae*) is composed of about six species worldwide and is native to North America (2) and Asia (4). Northern white-cedar (*T. occidentalis* L.) is found in southeastern Canada and northeastern United States to the Lake States region (fig 3).

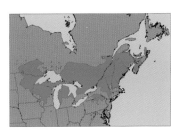

Figure 3 Northern White-Cedar (after Little, Jr.)

Elbert L. Little, Jr., *Atlas of United States Trees*, vol. 1, *Conifers and Important Hardwoods*, U.S. Department of Agriculture Miscellaneous Publication 1146 (Washington, D.C., 1971), 9 pp., 200 maps.

WESTERN RED CEDAR (*Thuja plicata*) ranges from southeastern Alaska to northwestern California and also in the northern Rocky Mountain region. The heartwood of *T. occidentalis* is a pale brown with a faint but characteristic cedar odor; the heartwood of *T. plicata* is reddish or pinkish brown to dull brown with a much stronger and spicy aroma.

WESTERN RED CEDAR (*Thuja plicata*) and northern white-cedar (*Thuja occidentalis*) can sometimes be separated based on their microscopic anatomy (B. Francis Kukachka, "Identification of Coniferous Woods," *Tappi* 43 [1960]: 887–896). The word *thuja* comes from the Greek *thuia*, an aromatic wood (probably a juniper).

PINE (*Pinus* spp./*Pinaceae*) is composed of at least ninety-three species worldwide and can be separated into three groups based on their microanatomy: the Red Pine Group, the White Pine Group, and the Yellow or Hard Pine Group.

WHITE PINE GROUP contains twenty-one species that grow in Asia (10), Europe (3), Central America (1), and North America (7). All species in this group look alike microscopically. Unless imported as ship masts or crating, the presence of all species other than *Pinus strobus* would be highly unlikely in American furniture made before the nineteenth century. *Pinus strobus* is native to the northeastern United States and Canada.

Eastern North America		Europe	
Common Name	Scientific Name	Common Name	Scientific Name
Eastern white pine	*P. strobus*	Swiss stone pine	*P. cembra*
		Italian stone pine	*P. pinea*
		Balkan pine	*P. peuce*
Western North America			
Whitebark pine	*P. albicaulis*		
Mexican white pine	*P. ayacahuite*		
Chiapas pine	*P. chiapensis*		
Limber pine	*P. flexilis*		
Sugar pine	*P. lambertiana*		
Western white pine	*P. monticola*		
Southwestern white pine	*P. strobiformis*		

ASH (*Fraxinus* spp./*Oleaceae*) is composed of between forty and seventy species, with perhaps twenty-one in Central and North America and fifty in Eurasia. All species look alike microscopically except for Manchurian ash (*F. mandshurica*)*. The commercial ashes are, to my knowledge:

Eastern North America		Europe	
Common Name	Scientific Name	Common Name	Scientific Name
Black ash	*F. nigra*	Common ash	*F. excelsior*
Blue ash	*F. quadrangulata*	Flowering ash	*F. ornus*
Green ash	*F. pennsylvanica*	Narrow-leaved ash	*F. angustifolia*
Pumpkin ash	*F. profunda*		
White ash	*F. americana*		

*Manchurian ash (*Fraxinus mandshurica* Rupr./*Oleaceae*) is also known as ash, Asiatic ash, "Chinese Oak," curly ash, *damo, frassino giapponese, frene du Japon, fresno japones*, Japanese ash, *Japanse es, japansk ask, mandschurische esche, shioji, tamo, ya chidamo*, and *yachi-damo*. It is native to northeastern Asia in northern China, Korea, Japan, and southeastern Russia. It is a medium-sized to large tree reaching heights of 30 meters, with trunk diameters of up to 50 cm.

BEECH (*Fagus* spp./*Fagaceae*) contains eight species that grow in Asia (4), Europe (*F. sylvatica*), and North America (*F. grandifolia*). All species look alike microscopically.

Eastern North America		Europe	
Common Name	Scientific Name	Common Name	Scientific Name
American beech	*F. grandifolia*	European beech	*F. sylvatica*

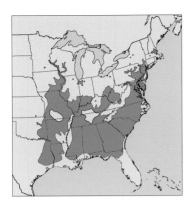

Figure 4 Current Range for River Birch (*Betula nigra*)

Elbert L. Little, Jr., *Atlas of United States Trees,* vol. 1, *Conifers and Important Hardwoods,* U.S. Department of Agriculture Miscellaneous Publication 1146 (Washington, D.C., 1971), 9 pp., 200 maps.

BIRCH (*Betula* spp./*Betulaceae*) is composed of between thirty and fifty species growing in Asia (12), North America (4), and Europe (4). All species look alike microscopically. The common commercial species are to my knowledge:

Eastern North America		Europe	
Common Name	Scientific Name	Common Name	Scientific Name
Gray birch	*B. populifolia*	Hairy birch	*B. pubescens*
Paper birch	*B. papyrifera*	Silver birch	*B. pendula*
River birch	*B. nigra*		
Sweet birch	*B. lenta*		
Yellow birch	*B. alleghaniensis*		

CHERRY, etc. (*Prunus* spp./*Rosaceae*). The genus *Prunus* contains between 200 and 400 species distributed in most parts of the world, especially the northern temperate regions (North America, Asia, Europe, and the Mediterranean). This genus includes cherries, plums, peaches, almonds, and apricots. All species look alike microscopically; however, woods in this genus with a reddish cast (light or dark red) with a light ray fleck are assumed to be cherry. Some samples are more highly figured due to the rays being wider than normal and at a greater concentration than normal. This figure is probably due to the sample coming from an older tree or from parts close to the ground. The tree-size species are, to my knowledge:

Eastern North America		Europe	
Common Name	Scientific Name	Common Name	Scientific Name
Black cherry	*P. serotina*	Blackthorn	*P. spinosaspinose*
		Cherry plum	*P. cerasiferaP. spinosa*
		Sour cherry	*P. cerasusP. cerasifera*
		Wild cherry	*P. aviumP. cerasus*

Elm (*Ulmus* spp./*Ulmaceae*) contains between eighteen and forty-five species native to Asia (11), Europe and the Mediterranean region (6), South and Central America (7), and North America (7). There are species on both sides of the Atlantic that look alike microscopically.

North America		Europe	
Common Name	Scientific Name	Common Name	Scientific Name
American elm	*B. populifolia*	English elm	*U. procera*
Rock elm*	*B. papyrifera*	Fluttering elm	*U. laevis*
Slippery elm	*B. nigra*	Smoothed-leaved elm	*U. minor*
Winged elm*	*B. lenta*	Wych elm	*U. glabra*
Cedar elm*	*B. alleghaniensis*		

* Hard elms

HICKORY (*Carya* spp./*Juglandaceae*) is composed of at least sixteen species native to Asia (4), Central America (4), and North America (11) (including southeastern Canada). The European species became extinct during the Ice Age. With a large enough sample, this genus can be split into the True

Hickory Group and the Pecan Group based on microanatomy (see M. A. Taras and B. Francis Kukachka, "Separating Pecan and Hickory Lumber," *Forest Products Journal* 20, no. 4 [1970]: 58–59).

True Hickory Group		Pecan Group	
(earlywood w/out banded parenchyma)		(earlywood with banded parenchyma)	
Common Name	Scientific Name	Common Name	Scientific Name
Shagbark hickory	*C. ovata*	Pecan	*C. illinoensis*
Pignut hickory	*C. glabra*	Water hickory	*C. aquatic*
Shellbark hickory	*C. lacinosa*	Nutmeg hickory	*C. myristicaeformis*
Mockernut hickory	*C. tomentosa*	Bitternut hickory	*C. cordiformis*
Red hickory	*C. ovalis*		

HORSE CHESTNUT (*Aesculus* spp./*Hippocastanaceae*) contains about thirteen species, which grow in the United States (6), Mexico (1), and Eurasia (6). Species cannot be separated based on microanatomy. The name *aesculus* is a Latin name of a European oak or other mast-bearing tree.

MAPLE (*Acer* spp./*Aceraceae*) contains between seventy and 120 species with sixteen species in Asia, eight in North America and eleven in the European/Mediterranean region. The maples can be separated into two groups based on their microscopic anatomy (ray width), the Soft Maple Group and the Hard Maple Group. Species within each group look alike microscopically.

The commercial species (with respect to American vs. English/European) are to my knowledge:

HARD MAPLE GROUP

Eastern North America		Europe	
Common Name	Scientific Name	Common Name	Scientific Name
Black maple	*A. nigrum*	Norway maple	*A. platanoides*
Sugar maple	*A. saccharum*	Sycamore*	*A. pseudoplatanus*

* *Acer pseudoplatanus* is known as "sycamore"" in England but is not to be confused with the American sycamore, *Platanus* spp., which carries the common name "plane tree" in England.

SOFT MAPLE GROUP

Eastern North America		Europe	
Common Name	Scientific Name	Common Name	Scientific Name
Red maple	*A. rubrum*	Field maple	*A. campestre*
Silver maple	*A. saccharinum*		

Striped Maple (*Acer pensylvaticum*) is a small deciduous tree growing to 5–10 meters (16–33 ft.) tall, with a trunk up to 20 cm. (8 in.) in diameter. The wood of the species is diffuse-porous, white, and fine grained, and on occasion was used by cabinet makers for inlay material. Botanists who visited North America in the early eighteenth century found that farmers in the American colonies and in Canada fed both dried and green leaves of the species to their cattle during the winter. When the buds began to swell in the spring, they turned their horses and cows into the woods to graze on the young shoots

(William J. Gabriel and Russell S. Walters, "Striped Maple," https://www.srs.fs.usda.gov/pubs/misc/ag_654/volume_2/acer/pensylvanicum.htm).

Common Uses: Veneer, paper (pulpwood), boxes, crates/pallets, musical instruments, turned objects, and other small specialty wood items. Striped maple is so called because of its distinct green-striped bark. It is much smaller than most other maple species, and with trunk diameters measured in inches, rather than feet, it is seldom used for lumber (Eric Meier, The Wood Database, 2008–2020, https://www.wood-database.com/striped-maple/).

OAK (*Quercus* spp./*Fagaceae*) contains between 275 and 500 species and can be separated into three groups based on their microanatomy: the Live or Evergreen Oak Group, the Red Oak Group, and the White Oak Group. Species within each group look alike microscopically. For colonial American objects, Live and Red Oak Groups are indicative of American origin, whereas the White Oak Group could be from either side of the Atlantic Ocean.

Species of the White Oak Group were used in American and English furniture. To my knowledge, species in the Red Oak Group were not commercial timbers in Europe and England during the seventeenth and eighteenth centuries. *Quercus cerris* (Turkish oak), a species in the Red Oak Group, was introduced into England in the late 1730s from the Mediterranean region as an ornamental tree. Its appearance in furniture would be astronomically rare. Based on these assumptions, furniture of the seventeenth and eighteenth centuries containing wood of the Red Oak Group is most likely American in origin.

RED OAK GROUP (*Erythrobalanus*)

Eastern North America		Europe	
Common Name	Scientific Name	Common Name	Scientific Name
Black oak	*Q. velutina*	Turkish oak	*Q. cerris*
Blackjack oak	*Q. marilandica*		
Laurel oak	*Q. laurifolia*		
Northern red oak	*Q. rubra*		
Pin oak	*Q. palustris*		
Scarlet oak	*Q. coccinea*		
Shumard oak	*Q. shumardii*		
Southern red oak	*Q. falcata*		
Water oak	*Q. nigra*		
Willow oak	*Q. phellos*		
Western North America			
California black oak	*Q. kelloggii*		
Interior live oak	*Q. wislizenii*		
Coast live oak	*Q. agrifolia*		

Eastern North America		Europe	
Common Name	Scientific Name	Common Name	Scientific Name
Chestnut oak	*Q. prinus*	Algerian oak	*Q. canariensis*
Chinkapin oak	*Q. muehlenbergii*	Cork oak	*Q. suber*
Overcup oak	*Q. lyrata*	Downy oak	*Q. pubescens*
Post oak	*Q. stellata*	Durmast oak	*Q. petrea*
Swamp chestnut oak	*Q. michauxii*	Holm oak	*Q. ilex*
Swamp white oak	*Q. bicolor*	Hungarian oak	*Q. frainetta*
White oak	*Q. alba*	Pedunculate oak	*Q. robur*
		Portuguese oak	*Q. faginea*
		Pyrenean oak	*Q. pyrenaica*
		Round-leaved oak	*Q. rotundifolia*
		White oak	*Q. polycarpa*

Western North America	
Valley oak	*Q. lobate*
Oregon oak	*Q. garryana*
Blue oak	*Q. douglasii*

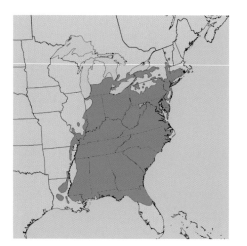

Figure 5 Current distribution of Tulip Poplar (*Liriodendron tulipifera*).

Elbert L. Little, Jr., *Atlas of United States Trees*, vol. 1, *Conifers and Important Hardwoods*, U.S. Department of Agriculture Miscellaneous Publication 1146 (Washington, D.C., 1971), 9 pp., 200 maps.

TRUE POPLAR GROUP (*Populus* spp./*Salicaceae*) *Populus* sp. is a genus of thirty-five species that contains poplar, cottonwood, and aspen. Species in this group are native to Eurasia/North Africa (25), Central America (2), and North America (8). All species look alike microscopically.

Eastern North America		Europe	
Common Name	Scientific Name	Common Name	Scientific Name
Balsam poplar	*P. balsamifera*	Aspen	*P. tremula*
Bigtooth aspen	*P. grandidentata*	Balsam poplar	*P. gileadensis*
Eastern cottonwood	*P. deltoides*	Black poplar	*P. nigra*
Quaking aspen	*P. tremuloides*	Gray poplar	*P. canescens*
Swamp cottonwood	*P. heterophylla*	White poplar	*P. alba*

TULIP POPLAR (*Liriodendron* spp./*Magnoliaceae*) contains two species, the yellow poplar/tulip poplar of North America (*L. tulipifera*) and the Chinese tulip tree (*L. chinensis*). Both species look alike microscopically.

WALNUT/BUTTERNUT GROUP (*Juglans* spp. L./*Juglandaceae*) contains about twenty species (walnuts and butternuts) that grow in South America (6–11), Eurasia (5), and North America (4). If the sample is large enough, tropical walnuts (6–11 spp.), American black walnut (*Juglans nigra*), common English/European/Persian walnut (*Juglans regia*), and the butternuts (4 spp.) can be separated from each other based on microanatomy. Microscopic characters needed for a positive *Juglans nigra* identification are: 1) irregular wall thickenings in latewood vessels ("gashes"); and, 2) calcium oxalate crystals in axial parenchyma cells in short chains of 1–4 (see Regis B. Miller, "Wood Anatomy and Identification of Species of *Juglans*," *Botanical Gazette* 137, no. 4 [1976]: 368–377). I currently have no anatomical information on California walnut (*Juglans hindsii*).

Eastern North America		Europe/Middle East	
Common Name	Scientific Name	Common Name	Scientific Name
American black walnut	*Q. prinus*	Common (English European/Persian) walnut	*Q. canariensis*
Butternut	*Juglans cinerea*		
Asian Walnuts		Tropical Walnuts	
Japanese walnut	*J. ailantifolia*	See below	
Chinese walnut	*J. mandshurica*		

With regards to color, *Juglans nigra* and the Tropical Walnuts usually have a dark brown to red-brown colored heartwood. Asian Walnuts and *Juglans regia*, on the other hand, have a heartwood that is usually a light tan but can range in color to dark brown.

TROPICAL WALNUTS

J. australis Griseb. (*J. brasiliensis* Dode)—Argentine walnut, Brazilian walnut

J. boliviana (C. DC.) Dode—Bolivian walnut, Peruvian walnut

J. hirsuta Manning—Nuevo León walnut

J. jamaicensis C. DC. (*J. insularis* Griseb.)—West Indies walnut

J. mollis Engelm—Mexican walnut

J. neotropica Diels (*J. honorei* Dode)—Andean walnut, *cedro negro, cedro nogal, nogal, nogal Bogotano*

J. olanchana Standl. & L.O. Williams—*cedro negro, nogal,* walnut

J. peruviana Dode—Peruvian walnut

J. soratensis Manning

J. steyermarkii Manning—Guatemalan walnut

J. venezuelensis Manning—Venezuela walnut

1. Benno M. Forman, *American Seating Furniture, 1630–1730: An Interpretive Catalogue* (New York: W. W. Norton for the Winterthur Museum, 1988).

2. Harry A. Alden and Alex C. Wiedenhoeft, "Qualified Determination of Provenance of Wood of the Firs (*Abies* spp. Mill.) Using Microscopic Features of Rays: An Aid to Conservators, Curators and Art Historians" (poster presentation, 26th American Institute of Conservation Annual Meeting, Arlington, Va., June 1–7, 1998).

3. Author's personal observation at the USDA, Forest Service, Forest Products Research Laboratory, Center for Wood Anatomy Research. I examined all of the *Quercus* specimens in the MADw and SJRw collections with a hand lens. These are the two collections making up the largest research wood collection in the world. I found several species of the Red Oak Group with tyloses. Also, species in the White Oak Group with sapwood showed no tyloses, as they are features of the heartwood.

4. Memo from Gordon Saltar, 1978, Joseph Downs Collection and the Winterthur Archives, Winterthur, Del.

5. Ibid.

6. R. Bruce Hoadley, Regis B. Miller, and Scott Z. Kitchener. "Distinguishing *Pinus resinosa* Ait. and *Pinus sylvestris* L. on the Basis of Fusiform Ray Characteristics," *IAWA Bulletin* 11, no. 2 (1990): 126.

Book Reviews

Edward S. Cooke Jr. *Inventing Boston: Design, Production, and Consumption, 1680–1720*. New Haven and London: Paul Mellon Centre for Studies in British Art, 2019. ix + 222 pp.; numerous color and bw illus., index. $60.00.

Bostonians at the end of the seventeenth and beginning of the eighteenth centuries reshaped their town and their world. They built their homes and churches with brick made with clay from the surrounding riverbanks, but designed those structures partially on English models. They sat on chairs carved from New England wood, upholstered with fabric from England, leather from Russia, or caned with Indian rattan. Boston's skilled carpenters crafted chests of drawers to store cloth woven in India, England, or Portugal, often after a Boston woman had made the fabric her own by embroidering it with silken thread from China in a popular South Asian motif. Bostonians dined off plates made in Portugal or Holland on patterns borrowed from China, and smoked pipes from West Africa. They stored their Caribbean sugar in silver boxes made from coins taken in trade or by privateering from Spanish Peru. They marked their graves with slate quarried from beneath their feet, carved by local craftsmen, who often shipped their stones to other colonial outposts. This small place engaged with the rest of a wide world.

Edward S. Cooke Jr. first began thinking of this book in 1986 when he set out to buy a chest-on-chest. It was not an ordinary chest, and Cooke was not an ordinary furniture shopper. At the time he was an associate curator at the Museum of Fine Arts, Boston, and for them he was acquiring a nine-drawered chest-on-chest built in Boston in about 1720. The chest's high level of cabinetwork intrigued him. The "accomplished technical repertoire of this craftsman" (p. 97) and the choices of wood—veneered rather than solid drawer fronts and case sides, for example—made him wonder why other scholars of furniture had paid little attention to the craftsmen, their supply chains, and the choices they made to overcome disruptions and fluctuations.

That curiosity has led Cooke to investigate the six basic materials Bostonians used to shape their world—brick, slate, wood, textiles, ceramics, and silver. Over the past decades he has shared his findings on the materials, the craftsmen who shaped them, and the people who bought and used them in lectures and articles. Now in this book he elaborates on each, providing a permanent, elegant, beautifully illustrated (185 pages of text, 218 illustrations), and indispensable volume.

Cooke challenges long-cherished notions. The slate gravestones scholars have used to mark a "Puritan way of death" Cooke shows to represent something more interesting. Drawing on more recent Puritan scholarship, which looks more to the laity's practice than the divines' preaching, Cooke introduces us to the stone carvers—and reminds us that Boston's burying grounds were secular, not affiliated with a particular parish. Congregationalists were buried beside Quakers, Baptists, Anglicans, and French Huguenots (Catholics and Jews were not buried in Boston before the nineteenth century). These stones do not so much mark a "Puritan way" as a Boston way, and Boston's native-born stonecutters exported their work to other places in the British Atlantic. Boston's carvers also invented side-borders, echoing the printed borders of book frontispieces—Puritanism was a way of the book—and reminding us that Boston had more printers at work than all other North American towns combined.

Boston's chairmakers also modified standard English styles into an "innovative local expression" (p. 78), translating the molded-back form imported from England into something distinctively Boston. They modified the cane-bottomed chairs, which they had made identical to the English models, by turning the front stretcher (rather than carving it) and using a sawn-out skirt-rail with a cyma profile below the front seat rail, which gave the appearance of a chair with an upholstered slip seat. They still used the rattan (*Calamus rotang*) imported by the East India Company from South East Asia, but modified the design. The surviving examples, with nine different designs on the crest rail and two options for the stretcher arrangement, show common construction features but with variations suggesting a close coordination among Boston's shops and craftsmen.

Boston's upholsterers began to work in the middle of the seventeenth century, first using imported German webbing and osnaburg, a linen and jute fabric, to support the marsh grass and horsehair fillings. Later, the upholsterer would use Russian leather, softer and more pliable than that provided from local tanneries. A later adaptation was to use Turkey carpets—either from the Ottoman Empire, or "Turkey work," woven in Yorkshire or Norwich. This woven upholstery came first. The chair frame would be custom-sized to fit. When wool became more common after 1705, a new seating form emerged, the easy chair. One bill for a 1729 chair shows that a third of the cost came from the wood and the labor; more than half the cost was in imported material, including the stuffing, nails, and cover.

Cotton, mostly produced in India, flexible, soft, washable, and cheaper than silk or linen, became the global fabric of choice in the seventeenth century. Imported cotton threatened to drain specie from England, and the sudden taste for chintz, a painted Indian cotton fabric popular for bed hangings, led English cotton and linen manufacturers to petition for Parliamentary protection. Wrought fabrics from Gujarat featured a chain-stitching style that inspired English and colonial women in their decorative, genteel needlework. Susanna Hiller's embroidered cupboard cloth, which she stitched about 1700, demonstrates a familiarity with embroidered Bengali colchas, which had become popular in Portugal after that empire opened trade with India. By the time Susanna Hiller was stitching hers in Boston, these embroidered quilts were also being woven in England. Her linen base came from England, the yellow silk likely from China, and her design, two peacocks flanking a floral arrangement, is an English interpretation of the South Asian colcha motif.

Textiles occasionally are well documented, but few examples remain. On the other hand, we have many surviving pieces of ceramics but little documentation. Few pieces of Chinese porcelain have been found in Boston, but ceramic shards found in Boston archaeological sites include much Dutch and Portuguese work inspired by the Chinese porcelain motifs. The ownership of ceramics, Cooke shows, speaks to the fluidity of Boston's commerce. Unlike in other colonies, Boston's economy was not based on a staple crop or the export of raw material. But Boston prospered through trade. New England merchants and ship captains traded in different forms of ceramics as they traveled through the Atlantic world, acting as "cultural brokers who "absorbed, discarded, and combined" different ceramic offerings (p. 147).

Cooke puts the shards together, showing how the fragments found in Katherine Wheelwright Nanny Naylor's privy or the site of John Carnes's house match surviving patterns found in other parts of the wider world, and how Bostonians were part of this wider world of commerce. It comes as no surprise to find bits of pottery made in Charlestown or in Boston, but finding these domestic shards along with necks of Spanish botijas, fragments of plates from Devon or Staffordshire, a plate with the Portuguese Royal Coat of Arms, a pipe from West Africa, and bowl fragments from Pisa show us the world from which Boston set its table. Cooke also notes what is not here: no tin-glazed earthenware from Seville or much in the Spanish tradition.

Bostonians did not import Sevillian ceramics, but they brought home in abundance another Spanish export, silver. Before 1670 fewer than half a dozen silversmiths worked in Boston. The trade drawing pottery and textiles also brought in silver, but so did privateering, particularly in the years of war between Britain and Spain. Much of the silver refashioned in Boston came in the form of Spanish coins, "anglicized" into sugar bowls, tankards, casters, porringers, monteiths, tobacco boxes, chocolate pots, punch bowls, candlesticks. Boston's merchants simultaneously griped about not having enough circulating currency while melting down every Spanish coin they found to furnish their increasingly elegant tables.

Cooke tells us much about Bostonians and the things they built, bought, and used, and his well-chosen illustrations show us these objects, reminding us that the objects contain the essence of their owners and makers. Through the depth of his research and the clarity of his prose Cooke tells us much about who made these things—the stone-carvers, house-builders, carpenters, and silversmiths—allowing us to see Boston's economic activity from the shop floor to the place where each would be used. Bostonians were creating and buying useful things: bricks, chairs, grave-markers, curtains and cupboard cloths, plates and bottles, teapots and casters.

But this is more than a book about things Bostonians made and used. His title is not "Making and Buying Things in Boston," but *Inventing Boston*. In his concluding essay, "Affirming Bostonness," Cooke shows how the choices Bostonians made, in what they made, bought, and used in this "period of dynamic creativity," demonstrate their "aspirations within a new political relationship with Britain" (p. 180). Within a shared British culture, Bostonians were developing a distinctive style and flavor, connecting British trappings with influences from the wider world, and forging their own identity, a hybrid one that would have profound ramifications not only for Boston, but for the British Empire and the world. It is not a coincidence that in these years Boston saw the births of Thomas Hutchinson, the merchant, historian, and unfortunate colonial governor who would in the 1760s and 1770s oversee the collapse of British power in Massachusetts, and Benjamin Franklin, who might better than any other individual reflect this hybridization of Boston culture and transform it into an American culture.

The objects that Cooke shows us illustrate that transformation. The craft and artistry that went into creating these utilitarian objects have allowed them to endure as works of art. It is not surprising that a curator at the Museum of Fine Arts, Boston, would purchase a three-hundred-year-old chest-on-chest for its aesthetic value, not its provenance or utility. Like the pieces of clay, wood, cloth, slate, and silver that Cooke displays here, each laden with meaning that he helps us to see, *Inventing Boston* will endure as a work of historical value and lasting beauty.

Robert J. Allison
Suffolk University, Boston

Cybèle Gontar. *Chasing the Butterfly Man: The Search for a Lost New Orleans Cabinetmaker, 1810–1825*. New Orleans, La.: Louisiana Museum Foundation, 2020. 238 pp.; numerous color illus. $60.00.

Chasing the Butterfly Man: The Search for a Lost New Orleans Cabinetmaker, 1810–1825, adds to a growing list of scholarly publications centered on Louisiana furniture history. The book focuses on a group of seventeen armoires believed to be from the same unknown maker, nicknamed the "Butterfly Man." With no shop records or shared provenance to tie these pieces together, the author uses physical evidence to confirm the attribution. Many of the armoires share similar decorative elements, such as elaborate inlays with leaf-and-vine and bellflower motifs, a bottom skirt that incorporates a swag or scallop-and-spur pattern, and scratch beading on the edges of doors, shelves, and drawers. Other shared construction characteristics include flush door panels separated by a false center stile, a middle belt of three drawers, and a six-panel back with pinned joints. Mahogany, cherry, and walnut serve as primary woods, with poplar, cypress, and occasionally walnut used for the cornice, back panels, and interiors. The unidentified cabinetmaker gained his catchy moniker for the butterfly-shaped, double dovetail that he used to strengthen the armoires' side panels. This feature is now seen as the Butterfly Man's unique fingerprint, as no other area cabinetmakers incorporated this feature into their armoires.

How does one go about writing a book focusing on a cabinetmaker who remains unidentified? The author creates a smartly laid out narrative that provides the context and motivations behind the production of these armoires before moving into a discussion of the most likely suspects in this furniture whodunit.

No furniture is produced in a vacuum, and first the author thoughtfully details the landscape surrounding nineteenth-century furniture production in New Orleans, where all seventeen of the armoires have been discovered. She begins with the question: "Was the Butterfly Man a French Creole or émigré, an African-American (*homme de couleur libre* or slave), or an Anglo-American transplant?" (p. 10). In the energetic backdrop of the French Quarter, an influx of immigrants and transplants brought with them designs from the French Caribbean, Europe, and the Mid-Atlantic. Between 1810 and 1825 the number of cabinetmakers in the French Quarter doubled, and shortly thereafter, more than one hundred cabinetmakers could be found in city directories. These armoires are a product of this diverse environment, marrying French West Indian design with federal Anglo-American inlay.

To provide a wider context, the author also presents a general history of the armoire. The narrative is presented as a stroll through its earliest international sightings, centering on its evolution from a thirteenth-century chest to the form we expect today. Gontar's analysis also reviews its inclusion in art and design books, a satisfying approach not unlike the survey found in David L. Barquist's *American Tables and Looking Glasses in the Mabel Brady Garvan and Other Collections at Yale University* (1992). The reviewer wishes Gontar had extended this appealing train of thought to an analysis of the armoire specifically in the nineteenth-century New Orleans home and both its prevalence in house inventories and frequency as a form. This would place the Butterfly Man's armoires into a more localized context of use and value. The chapter concludes with a full eleven-page reprint of French historian Henry Harvard's 1887 encyclopedic survey of the armoire, which presents as a complete history of the armoire unto itself. Its inclusion is interesting but would have benefited from more analysis by Gontar regarding Harvard's tome.

Periodically throughout the book, the author includes these unexpected surprises that add to the robustness of the volume. An essay by scholar and cabinetmaker Stephen Latta about inlay maker George Dewhurst dives into the minutia of nineteenth-century inlay production. A section devoted to the armoires' construction includes many detail photographs and benefits from the voice of furniture restorer Steven Huber, whose involvement allows the conversation to delve into the physicality of the pieces in a way that only a furniture conservator can provide. A six-page compilation of furniture makers collected from New Orleans newspapers is a wonderful resource for scholars. The amassed group includes cabinetmakers, joiners, turners, upholsterers, and wood merchants listed between 1805 and 1824.

Archival items—from newspaper clippings to invoices and inventories—are included with as much prominence as the furniture itself. Most are printed at a large scale, allowing their script to be fully legible and inviting the reader to plunge into these primary materials. Taken together, these elements support the author in creating a richer account of the Butterfly Man's armoires.

At the center of the book is a directory of cabinetmakers who could have laid hands on these armoires during their production. To be included, the makers had to fit three criteria: they produced furniture in the decades leading up to 1825; they had stable, productive workshops; and they trained apprentices, suggesting a high level of skill and success. The author concludes that these criteria are needed to account for the 1800-to-1830 period in which the Butterfly Man's armoires were produced and the proficiency needed to finish the pieces. Gontar presents twenty-three cabinetmakers who match these parameters, with the list set alphabetically. The author does not go as far as to prioritize any of these cabinetmakers (with the exception of George Dewhurst) as the more likely candidates for being the Butterfly Man.

Each entry summarizes the known information about the cabinetmaker and, in many cases, includes primary documents and a copy of his signature, which adds a personal quality to the entries. Some describe address changes within the city, while others outline genealogical information. Within this directory, there are delightful elements to be found, like the 1835 newspaper advertisement that reads, "AUGUSTE DOUCE invites connoisseurs and judges to visit a BEDSTEAD and an ARMOIRE, manufactured in his Work-shop, 267 Royal st." (p. 98). Cabinetmaker Auguste Douce is presented with ten pages of archival materials relating to his workshop, including invoices, a probate workshop inventory, and a household inventory. Taken together, these exceptional cabinetmaker biographies paint a picture that supports the author's accounts of New Orleans as a lively center of furniture production.

Gontar notes that the cabinetmaker responsible for the case construction may be a different person than the inlay producer. George Dewhurst is presented as the most likely maker behind the inlay on the Butterfly Man's armoires. As such, Dewhurst is given the most comprehensive narrative. English-born Dewhurst lived in Boston, Baltimore, and then Lexington, Kentucky, before landing in New Orleans by 1817. In his accompanying essay, Stephen Latta chronicles Dewhurst's movements with exacting precision. Latta also describes the high demand for inlay in Boston and Salem during the late eighteenth and early nineteenth centuries, coinciding with the specialization of shops in specific aspects of the trade. The Boston shop of Dewhurst and Son was noted as "stringing makers" in 1806 and 1807 directories, providing local cabinetmakers with inlay and eventually exporting their work as well. Latta recounts how migratory patterns and expanding business in growing East Coast cities lured cabinetmakers like Dewhurst to move with these tides. Latta expertly uses physical evidence—in the form of highly sophisticated inlays—to provide a road map of Dewhurst's movements down the Eastern Seaboard, the presence of these unique inlays keeping in step with the maker's relocations. Several inlay patterns are specifically linked to Dewhurst, including the "domino" and "toothed" banding. By 1817 Dewhurst had settled in New Orleans, and around that time both of these banding patterns show up on the Butterfly Man's armoires, providing tantalizing evidence that Dewhurst was involved in their production. Gontar also notes the uniqueness of several inlay uses that are atypical for Louisiana craftsmanship, suggesting the hand of an Anglo-American maker. One example of this is in the incorporation of bellflowers and stringing along the mitered joints of an armoire's door frames. Another is a sophisticated inlay urn medallion on an armoire that relates to the inlay design on a Boston card table. The narrative provided by Gontar and Latta regarding the probable importance of Dewhurst to the Butterfly Man's story is compelling. Their thesis is made stronger by each other's insights.

The book concludes with a catalogue of thirteen of the Butterfly Man's armoires (four more are noted but not pictured). Each piece is allotted several pages, including a conservation history and any known provenance. The catalogue begins with plainer examples and progresses to ornately inlaid pieces. Also included are photographs of the armoires in situ in their contemporary homes. Room interior shots and photos showing personal use remind us that these pieces continue to have a history that grows. The photography in this section is artistically presented, which highlights the beautiful detailing of each armoire.

In all, this book delivers on a well thought out narrative. It sets the stage for why these armoires were produced as well as the how and where. The author concludes by noting, "Many discussions have ensued between me, Jack, Steve, and Mercedes about whether the maker was one person, whether he worked in partnership, whenever he was from the West Indies, or perhaps a northeast transplant" (p. 237). Gontar stops short of giving her best educated thoughts regarding who produced the cases, and the reviewer felt vested enough in the narrative that she would have found that more satisfying. By including a history of the armoire and a wider-view presentation of the cabinetmaking industry in New Orleans, Gontar lays important groundwork for the Butterfly Man's story. As such, this book will be a go-to resource for information beyond this group of armoires. A few logistical additions would have helped create a smoother read. The figures are not numbered, which makes keeping track of their references in the text challenging. The addition of an index, bibliography, and full citations for the archival materials would aid those wishing to go further into this story.

At the end of her book, Gontar describes a memory of being in the workshop of Steven Huber with a fully dismantled armoire after it survived Hurricane Katrina but needed restoration. In her recounting of this experience and the subsequent years of work on the project, diving into its smallest details, it is clear she has brought her excitement and thoughtfulness to the Butterfly Man's story. That energy exudes from this volume and makes for a compelling, enjoyable read that is as much an important scholarly work about New Orleans cabinetmaking as it is an intimate portrait of this connected group of armoires.

Christie Jackson
The Trustees of Reservations

Brian Fagan and Nadia Durrani. *What We Did in Bed: A Horizontal History*. New Haven: Yale University Press, 2019. xiii + 224 pp.; bw illus., bibliography, index. $26.00.

Brian Fagan and Nadia Durrani's most recent collaboration has yielded an insightful and entertaining book on the subject of beds, aptly described by the authors as "one of humanity's most overlooked artifacts" (p. 8). Structured around the use of beds and their cultural significance, *What We Did in Bed: A Horizontal History* covers a broad swath of human activity associated with them. Spanning from Paleolithic bed pits to the digitally connected beds of the future, the publication's scope is as broad as the second part of its title implies. Themes such as the nature of human sleep, sex, birth, death, mobility, and the role of the bed in public and private life frame an exploration of its importance across cultures and throughout time. From the carved and gilded beds of Egyptian pharaohs and French kings, to hammocks adopted by sailors in the British Navy as early as the sixteenth century (and later used by astronauts on the Apollo lunar module), to John Lennon and Yoko Ono's week-long Bed-In for Peace at the Amsterdam Hilton in 1969, Fagan and Durrani use broad strokes to paint a compelling picture of the history of the bed.

The initial two chapters chronicle the evolution of the bed and how sleep itself has changed for humanity over time. Our earliest ancestors ventured down from the canopy to huddle together around fires two million years ago, creating close family ties and pair bonding. After setting this prehistoric stage, Fagan and Durrani contrast the light, wood-frame beds with feet used in ancient Egypt, Greece, and Rome with the raised platform beds used in Chinese and Ottoman courts. While frame beds with layers of mattresses begin to appear in Europe in the twelfth century, poorer peasants literally just "hit the hay," fortunate to have even a straw-filled sack on a platform. The industrial period changed Western society's relation to the bed with the production of factory-made iron bedsteads with metal springs, horsehair mattresses, and layers of more affordable sheets and pillows. When British designer Terrance Conrad introduced the Swedish duvet cover in the 1970s, the bed, which had already been confined to the most private areas of the house, could be made quickly—an important feature in the second half of the twentieth century, when most households did not have servants. The authors describe how this period of industrialization pulled Western society out of its propensity for a segmented or biphase pattern of sleep, illustrated by Chaucer's references to "fyrste sleep." The consumption of products that promise uninterrupted sleep began as early as 1903, when Veronal, the first synthetic barbiturate, was introduced.

For elites in Western European culture, the bed and bedchamber were quasi-public spaces where the consummation of marriage played out. While conceiving children traditionally occurred on a bed, childbirth usually occurred away from the actual bed—although in a private space—with the aid of birthing chairs or stools dating as far back as Mesopotamia. The mother and newborn child would then use a bed for the thirty-day period of isolation. The rise of the male-dominated field of obstetrics in the eighteenth and nineteenth centuries led to the establishment of lying-in hospitals, institutions that displaced traditional midwives and encouraged women to give birth in a reclined position on a bed. The discovery of the anesthetic properties of chloroform in the 1840s dramatically changed childbirth, but the use of antibiotics in the 1940s finally lowered the mortality rate, which even by the late 1930s was one maternal death for every two hundred successful deliveries.

Given that much of what is understood about beds in ancient societies stems from archaeological artifacts and images found in burial sites, the authors' observation that these burial sites contain human remains arranged in positions of sleep (on their sides, in fetal position, etc.) is an indication of the universality of the state of sleeping being like death. In 1700 BCE there were numerous bed burials in the Nubian Kingdom of Kush, and today, in that same region now known as Sudan, the dead are often carried to their graves on beds during funerals. Although there is little archaeological evidence of death beds in ancient Greek grave sites, by the eighth century BCE, the *klinē* deathbed was the most common icon found on funerary vases. The deathbed could be a social place, as it was often the locus of succession where the next Chinese emperor or Indian maharajah could be named. A measure of the degree to which the passing of loved ones has become a secluded, private event is seen in the recent online posting of a postmortem photograph of Queen Victoria on her deathbed by the British government, which has been described as "shocking." At Queen Victoria's death in 1901, a staged photograph of the body of an older woman surrounded by flowers and mementos of her family would have been recognized as part of a longstanding European tradition of a wife being painted with her family surrounding her at her deathbed.

A concise chapter on the commonplace sharing of beds among travelers utterly unknown to each other and the sharing of beds among family members is followed by an expansive chapter titled "The Moving Bed." The authors' far-reaching approach to the subject begins with a discussion of how monarchs and their courts moved constantly within their domain to assert power, which entailed servants' reassembling household furnishings constantly, including large beds. By juxtaposing King Tutankhamun's traveling bed from the fourteenth century BCE with the blocks of sleeping platforms used by forty or fifty laborers at a time built, by craftsmen constructing the pyramids of Giza in a town just south of the great monuments, Fagan and Durrani push their history of the bed beyond court culture. In perhaps one of the most striking passages in the book, they point out that most workers in ancient Egypt just slept on the ground, like "mil-lions of migrant workers and travelers around the world do to this day" (p. 126). From the campaign furniture of Julius Caesar, to the charpoys (from the Persian *chihar-pai*, meaning four feet) brought by Sikh soldiers from India to the Sudan, to the first sleeping bags or "Euklisia rugs" that were mass-produced by a Welsh entrepreneur in the late nineteenth century, this chapter moves swiftly across time and the globe. After describing the derivation of the word hammock from the Arawak and Taino "hamaka" for a stretch of cloth between two points, the authors observe that only a century after Christopher Columbus's encounter with these two groups of Native Americans this most portable of beds was adopted by seamen in the Royal Navy. The authors conclude by recounting the rise of the Pullman sleeper cars that eventually led to the introduction of the RV by Winnebago in 1967.

The last few chapters of this publication explore the development of royal beds at the center of European court life. Their intimate proximity to the body of the monarch placed them at the center of power in a bedchamber, where they functioned as a key object in theatrical royal births, marriages, christenings, and deaths. King Louis XIV's state bed in the Palace of Versailles was the apotheosis of the royal bed, while Queen Victoria's shutting the door of the royal bedchambers to the court reflected the growing desire for privacy in domestic life. While the growing specialization of domestic spaces and furnishings in the nineteenth century has long been a subject of scholarship, Fagan and Durrani contextualize the phenomenon with anecdotes of Winston Churchill holding meetings in his bedroom wearing a dressing gown during the Second World War and the 1930s Hays Code that dictated separate twin beds for on-screen couples. As beds and bedrooms have moved away from the center of public view to more private, tucked-away places in the home, they may become socially revitalized through virtual connections like USB ports. The controversy surrounding Tracy Emin's *My Bed* installation created in 1998 for the Tate Modern, replete with crumpled and stained sheets and the detritus of life, illustrates the strong sense of the private nature of the bed and bedroom in modern life. The authors also fold in a discussion of the high cost of living space in urban areas that has led to the successful marketing of the Murphy bed and its twenty-first-century offspring, the Nomad Living futurist folding bed designed by the Dutch architecture practice Studio Makkink en Beyhas. Whether looking at the works of art from the past half century that feature the prosaic but universal bed, the rise of the water bed in the United States in the 1980s, or futuristic bed and bedding designs, the authors of *What We Did in Bed* guide us through the use of the bed across cultures and millennia, enlivening their speculations on how the most universal of artifacts will continue to service humanity in the future (p. 180).

Clearly, a subject this complex benefits from multiple authors. Annie Carlano and Bobbie Sumberg's *Sleeping Around: The Bed from Antiquity to Now*, published by the Museum of International Folk Art in 2006, comes closest to *What We Did in Bed* in the range of cultures and time periods it surveys. Carlano and Sumberg's extensively illustrated exploration of the topic is based on decorative art objects, with supporting imagery from paintings, photography, and film. Although *Sleeping Around* delves deeper into twentieth- and twenty-first-century design than *What We Did in Bed*, both publications incorporate contemporary works of art to demonstrate the enduring universality of the bed and sleep. The closing chapters of *Sleeping Around*—one on cradles, infant carriers, and family sleeping arrangements, followed by another on diverse cultural associations between death and sleep—are in keeping with the broad anthropological underpinnings of the Museum of International Folk Art and its rich holdings in the decorative arts. *Bed Hangings: A Treatise on Fabrics and Styles in the Curtaining of Beds, 1650–1850*, originally published by the Society for the Preservation of New England Antiquities (now Historic New England) in 1961 under the aegis of Abbott Lowell Cummings, contrasts with the other two bed publications for its definitively deep dive on a narrower slice of the subject. The third printing, issued in 1994, includes a foreword by Jane Nylander that acknowledges the important contributions of women such as Florence M. Montgomery, once keeper of textiles at the Henry Francis du Pont Winterthur Museum, and Nina Fletcher Little, who brought a deep knowledge of American material culture to an analysis of pictorial sources in the original publication.

Given the amount of time spent at home in close proximity to our beds over the last year, this new book on the subject of beds and their use is especially relevant. Although the range of material and visual evidence used by the authors of *What We Did in Bed* exceeds previous explorations of the subject, this engaging publication adds to the strong foundation established more than half a century ago.

Jennifer Swope
Museum of Fine Arts, Boston

[Stanley Weiss]. *Fine American Antiques in the Stanley Weiss Collection*. Foreword by Brock Jobe. [Providence, R.I.: Stanley Weiss], 2019. 305 pp.; 800+ color illus. $35.00.

The lane occupied by books, catalogues, and pamphlets published by dealers is one avenue among the many roads leading to an understanding of American furniture, broadly conceived. *Fine American Antiques in the Stanley Weiss Collection* is the latest addition to this genre and follows comfortably in the established mode for such works.

The ten volumes and other attendant publications issued by the firm of Israel Sack from the 1960s into the 1990s are perhaps the most well known earlier examples of this genre. Many other shops have added to the conversation over time with their own occasional published catalogues and brochures, including Bernard and S. Dean Levy, Hirschl and Adler, C. L. Prickett, and numerous others. While these works are essentially group advertisements, as a genre they provide a lasting record of objects that, in many cases, have come from private collections and, also in many instances, will return there shortly. Thus, like auction catalogues, dealers' publications provide the field with at least a glimpse of, and a published record for, many objects that might otherwise be submerged below the level of historical scrutiny. Individual advertisements in trade journals and newspapers also provide these important snapshots of important (and perhaps not so important) objects, but it is much more convenient, even in the digital age, to have them grouped together in volumes such as the one under consideration here.

Dealers have also contributed monographs to the literature that illustrate and discuss objects other than ones they have put on the market. The three-volume *Furniture Treasury* issued in the 1920s and 1930s by Wallace Nutting (who, among many other things, was also a dealer) was considered as the bible for many early collectors. Albert Sack's *Fine Points of Furniture*, issued in 1950 and in revised form in 1993 and again in 2007, served collectors as a guide for making subjective aesthetic value judgments for years, even creating two categories that were somehow considered better than "best."

With its more than eight hundred color illustrations, *Fine American Antiques* documents a large body of furniture that has passed through the hands of Stanley Weiss, who has operated a shop in Providence, Rhode Island, for about the last thirty years. Like the aforementioned Wallace Nutting, Weiss has worn many hats in his life, as recounted in his personal reminiscence that serves as the introduction to this volume. His love for old furniture stems in part from his background as a violinist, in which he learned to appreciate the fine qualities and grains of the woods used in their creation. After a successful career in the realms of finance and real estate, he began the flourishing antiques business that is commemorated here.

The catalogue is arranged in two principal sections: "Colonial" and "Classical." Each is further subdivided by region, with some hard-to-classify objects inserted here and there. For some reason, objects that would typically be considered federal or early neoclassical in style, and that date well after Independence, can be found in both the Colonial and the Classical sections. The Classical section also contains a few unexpected surprises, such as a cluster of objects by Pottier and Stymus and Herter Brothers from the late nineteenth century (pp. 232–33), and other late objects also pop up now and then. Fireplace equipment is also included, along with a healthy batch of mirrors and looking glasses.

Each object is illustrated with a beautiful silhouetted photograph by Marc Beaulac and a short caption. The floppy, 8½ by 12 inch paperback format allows for several objects to be included on each page. The headings for the captions are in the form much beloved by auction houses, where the actual name of the object is swaddled by six, seven, or more descriptors, as in "A Figured Maple Chippendale Six-Drawer Dished Top Tall Chest with Fan on Dovetailed Bracket Feet" (p. 13). The primary wood is noted for each object, and on occasion the secondary wood, and the overall height and width (but not depth) of each piece is also provided. For some objects, very brief comments mention provenance information and make reference to previous publications that have included the object. Endnotes amplify this material in some cases and often refer the reader to the Weiss website (www.

stanleyweiss.com), where detailed reports and technical notes by conservators and consultants can be found. (The headings to these "Additional Notes" frequently provide inaccurate cross-references to page numbers.) Readers with a particular interest in an object will need to use this book in conjunction with the website.

Depending on their interest, most readers will find some favorite objects in these pages. Furniture attributed, with a healthy dose of superlatives, to many prominent makers, such as the Seymours, Phyfe, Lannuier, Quervelle, and others, is abundant. But many lesser-known cabinetmakers and shops are also represented, such as Amariah T. Prouty and John Sailor of New York, and Jonathan Fairbanks of Harvard, Massachusetts. Although it is only mentioned in the front matter, a few examples in the book have migrated to public collections, including the Greene family early baroque high chest of drawers (p. 1) now in the Rhode Island Historical Society and other pieces acquired by the Philadelphia Museum of Art (p. 240) and the White House (p. xii).

Surfing through this book provides an opportunity to reflect back on the earlier days of the literature on American furniture. Even the title ("*Fine American Antiques . . .*") is something of a throwback. As Brock Jobe, professor emeritus at the Winterthur Museum, notes in his foreword, lavishly illustrated picture books of this type are not necessarily the norm in the field these days. But even in the age of the Internet, a catalogue such as this provides one of the lasting building blocks that will inform more interpretive studies for years to come.

Gerald W. R. Ward
Museum of Fine Arts, Boston

Recent Writing on American Furniture: A Bibliography

Compiled by
Gerald W. R. Ward

▼ THIS YEAR'S LIST primarily includes works published in 2019 and roughly through September 2020. As always, a few earlier publications that had escaped notice are also listed. The short title *American Furniture 2019* is used in citations for articles and reviews published in last year's edition of this journal, which is also cited in full under Luke Beckerdite's name.

Once again, many people have assisted in compiling this list. I am particularly grateful to Luke Beckerdite, Marc Beaulac, Jay Cantor, Dennis Carr, Deborah M. Child, Jonathan Fairbanks, Patricia E. Kane, Joshua Klein, Robert W. Lang, Mariah Nielson, Matt Thurlow, and Barbara McLean Ward, as well as to the scholars who have prepared reviews for this issue. I am also indebted to the librarians of the Museum of Fine Arts, Boston, the Portsmouth Athenaeum, the Massachusetts College of Art and Design, and the Portsmouth Public Library for their ongoing assistance. Preparing this annual survey has been more challenging than usual this year. The pandemic has curtailed publishing to at least some degree, more titles are only available as eBooks, and physical access to libraries has not been possible since mid-March 2020.

Thus, even more so than in the past, I would be glad to receive citations for titles that have been inadvertently omitted from this or previous lists. Information about new publications and review copies of significant works would also be much appreciated.

Abbott, James A., et al. *Evergreen: The Garrett Family, Collectors and Connoisseurs*. Baltimore, Md.: John Hopkins University Press, 2017. xiv + 255 pp.; illus., bibliography, index.

Adams, Marc. *The Difference Makers: The Fourth Generation*. Covington, Ky.: Lost Art Press, 2019. xiv + 244 pp.; color illus.

Albertson, Karla Klein. "Chasing the Butterfly Man: Exploring a Mysterious Maker at the Cabildo in New Orleans." *Antiques and the Arts Weekly* (February 14, 2020): 1C, 12C–13C. Color illus.

———. "Photography and Folk Art: Looking for America in the 1930s at the Art Institute of Chicago." *Antiques and the Arts Weekly* (November 29, 2019): 1C, 30–31. 1 color and 13 bw illus.

American Period Furniture: Journal of the Society of American Period Furniture Makers 18 (2018): 1–120. Numerous color illus., line drawings. (See also individual articles cited elsewhere in this list.)

American Period Furniture: Journal of the Society of American Period Furniture Makers 19 (2019): 1–120. Numerous color illus., line drawings. (See also individual articles cited elsewhere in this list.)

Attfield, Judy. *Wild Things: The Material Culture of Everyday Life*. 2000. 2nd ed. London and New York: Bloomsbury Visual Arts, 2020. 242 pp.; bw illus., bibliography, index.

Aymes, Carla, and Gustavo Curiel. *Carpinteros de la sierra: el mobiliario taraceado de la Villa Alta de San Ildefonso, Oaxaca (siglos XVII–XVIII)*. 2 vols. México: Universidad Nacional Autónoma de México, Instituto de Investigaciones Estéticas, 2019. Numerous color and bw illus., maps, bibliographies. ("This publication, in its first volume, studies a wide variety of furniture for civil use . . . made in the 17th and 18th centuries with a unique marquetry technique of its kind and made exclusively in the area mountain range of Oaxaca, in the Villa Alta de San Ildefonso. In the furniture of the Villa Alta there was a taste for building scenes that resemble engravings through the use of contrasting and sculpted woods filled with a black paste that was called zulaque. In the workshops of Analco, one of the two prominent neighborhoods of the Villa Alta, numerous European engravings, mainly flamenco, were on hand, which served as a source for the representation of the images displayed on the furniture. The second volume is a Catalogue of all the production that was located, both in Mexico and abroad.")

[Banks, William N., Jr. collection]. *Single Owner Auction: The Estate of William N. Banks, Jr.: Newnan, Georgia: September 12, 2020*. Asheville, N.C.: Brunk Auctions, 2020. 300+ lots; color illus. Online auction catalogue at https://www.brunkauctions.com (accessed August 26, 2020). (Includes contents of Bankshaven, his residence.)

Beach, Laura. "The Gentleman from Georgia: Writer and collector William N. Banks Jr., Remembered." *Antiques* 187, no. 5 (September–October 2020): 66–75. Color and bw illus.

———. "In Pursuit of History: A Lifetime Collecting Colonial American Art and Artifacts." *Antiques and the Arts Weekly* (January 24, 2020): 1C, 30–32. Color and bw illus.

———. "Material Georgia, 1733–1900: Two Decades of Scholarship." *Antiques and the Arts Weekly* (January 17, 2020): 1C, 30–31. Color and bw illus.

Beckerdite, Luke, ed. *American Furniture 2019*. Milwaukee, Wis.: Chipstone Foundation, 2019. vii + 261 pp.; numerous color and bw illus., index. Distributed by Oxbow Books. (See also individual articles cited elsewhere in this list.)

"Bingham Desk Redux: Fraud Escapes Prison Sentence for Faux Folk Art." *Antiques and the Arts Weekly* (October 16, 2020): 37.

Black Craftspeople Digital Archive. http://www.blackcraftspeople.org (accessed September 1, 2020).

Boudreau, George W., and Margaretta Markle Lovell, eds. *A Material World: Culture, Society, and the Life of Things in Early Anglo-America*. University Park: Pennsylvania State University Press, 2019. x + 331 pp.; 22 color and 109 bw illus., bibliography, index. (See, in particular, Paul G. E. Clemens and Edward S. Cooke Jr., "Clock-Making in Southwestern Connecticut, 1760–1820," and Jennifer Van Horn, "'Painting' Faces and 'Dressing' Tables: Concealment in Colonial Dressing Furniture.")

Brewster, Nathaniel. "A Chair Called Henry." *Mortise & Tenon Magazine* 6 (2019): 36–43. Color and bw illus.

British and Irish Furniture Makers Online. https://bifmo.history.ac.uk/ (accessed October 29, 2019).

Brown, Michael A. *Art & Empire: The Golden Age of Spain*. San Diego, Calif.: San Diego Museum of Art, 2019. 198 pp.; numerous color illus., bibliography, index.

Budinger, Meghan. "Furnishing Ferry Farm." *American Period Furniture: Journal of the Society of American Period Furniture Makers* 19 (2019): 72–83. Color illus.

[Byrdcliffe]. "Current and Coming: Looking Back at Byrdcliffe." *Antiques* 187, no. 3 (May–June 2020): 20. 2 color illus. (Re exhibition originally scheduled for the Milwaukee Art Museum.)

Cantor, Jay E. *Random Observations 2019*. [New York]: privately printed, 2019. 65 pp.

Chu, Petra ten-Doesschate, and Jennifer Milam, eds. *Beyond Chinoiserie: Artistic Exchange between China and the West during the Late Qing Dynasty (1796–1911)*. Leiden and Boston: Brill, 2019. xv + 323 pp.; color and bw illus., bibliography, index.

Clancy, Jonathan. "Things Wrought by the United Crafts: An Expression of Modern Life." Online exhibition, May 30, 2020–January 3, 2021. https://www.stickleymuseum.org (accessed June 15, 2020).

Connors, Thomas. "Rooms with a Viewpoint." *Antiques* 187, no. 5 (September–October 2020): 42–43. 5 color illus. (Re period rooms at the Minneapolis Institute of Arts.)

Couch, Dale L., ed. *Material Georgia, 1733–1900: Two Decades of Scholarship*. Athens: Georgia Museum of Art, University of Georgia, 2019. 240 pp.; illus., bibliography.

Dapkus, Mary Jane. "More on Clock Maker James Cross (1794–1867) of Rochester, Somersworth, and Peterborough, NH." *Watch and Clock Bulletin* 61, no. 6 (November/December 2019): 499–500. 4 color illus.

Darby, Elisabeth. *Re-Issue, Re-Imagine, Re-Make: Appropriation in Contemporary Furniture Design*. London: Lund Humphries, 2020. 152 pp.; color and bw illus., bibliography, index.

Davidson, Benjamin, and Pippa Biddle. "Object Lesson: All About the Windsor Chair." *Antiques* 187, no. 3 (May–June 2020): 30–32, 34, 36, 38. 8 color illus.

———. "Object Lesson: Rose Valley Furniture." *Antiques* 187, no. 1 (January/February 2020): 82–84. 6 color illus.

DeKay, James T., et al. *The Stephen Decatur House: A History*. Washington, D.C.: Decatur House Museum, 2018. 1 vol. (various pagings); illus.

Compston, Christine, Stephen Senge, and Walter McDonald. *Rewarding Work: A History of Boston's North Bennet Street School*. Boston: North Bennet Street Industrial School, 2018. 440 pp.; color illus., bibliography.

Dervan, Andrew H. "Herman Miller Clock Co. and Howard Miller Clock Co." *Watch & Clock Bulletin* 61, no. 5 (September/October 2019): 412–26. 24 color and bw illus.

Dervan, Andrew H. "Wallace Goodwin, North Attleboro, MA." *Watch & Clock Bulletin* 61, no. 4 (July/August 2019): 322–27. 10 color illus., 2 tables.

Dietrich, H. Richard, III, and Deborah M. Rebuck, eds. *In Pursuit of History: A Lifetime Collecting Colonial American Art and Artifacts*. Philadelphia: Dietrich American Foundation in association with the Philadelphia Museum of Art, 2019. 303 pp.; 215 color illus., timeline. Distributed by Yale University Press, New Haven and London. (Includes chapter on furniture by Edward S. Cooke Jr.)

Dietrich, H. Richard, III, and Deborah M. Rebuck. "In Pursuit of History: A Lifetime Collecting Colonial American Art and Artifacts." *Antiques and Fine Art* 19, no. 1 (spring 2020): 106–13. 12 color illus.

Di Mauro, Damon. "Henry Harmson of Marblehead." *Watch & Clock Bulletin* 61, no. 5 (September/October 2019): 458–65. 8 color illus.

Erbes, Scott. *Making Time: The Art of the Kentucky Tall Case Clock, 1790–1850*. Louisville, Ky.: Speed Art Museum/Butler Books, 2019. 124 pp.; color illus.

Erby, Adam T. "'Mostly new, and very elegant': The Several Lives of George William and Sally Fairfaxes' London-Made Furniture." *American Furniture 2019*, 1–77. 62 color illus., appendix.

———. "Recreating George and Martha Washington's Front Parlor: Interpreting the Documentary Evidence." *Antiques and Fine Art* 19, no. 2 (summer 2020): 54–61. 11 color illus.

[Esherick, Wharton]. *The Pennsylvania Sale: The Hedgerow Theatre Collection*. Auction 1686. Philadelphia: Freeman's, October 28, 2020. Online auction catalogue available at http://www.freemansauctions.com (accessed October 21, 2020). (See lots 131–42.)

Eversmann, Pauline, comp., et al. *Guide to Winterthur Museum, Garden, & Library*. Winterthur, Del.: Winterthur Museum, Garden, and Library, 2019. 111 pp.; color and bw illus.

"Examination of a Grain-Painted Chest-over-Drawers." *Mortise & Tenon Magazine* 8 (2020): 88–95. Color illus.

"Examination of an Early 18th-Century High Chest of Drawers." *Mortise & Tenon Magazine* 7 (2019): 106–15. Color illus.

"Examination of an 1804 Painted Cupboard." *Mortise & Tenon Magazine* 6 (2019): 56–65. Color illus.

"Examination of an 1815–1830 New England Rocker." *Mortise & Tenon Magazine* 9 (2020): 70–79. Color illus.

Fagan, Brian, and Nadia Durrani. *What We Did in Bed: A Horizontal History*. New Haven: Yale University Press, 2019. xiii + 224 pp.; bw illus., bibliography, index.

Fernandez, Kathleen M. *Zoar: The Story of an Intentional Community*. Kent, Ohio: Kent State University Press, 2019. xiii + 298 pp.; illus., bibliography, index.

Ferrigno. Kevin G. "Hartford's Hockey Stick Stands." *Maine Antique Digest* 48, no. 9 (September 2020): 73–75. 11 color and bw illus.

Finamore, Daniel, and George Schwartz. "At Sea: The New Maritime Galleries at the Peabody Essex Museum." *Antiques and Fine Art* 19, no. 2 (summer 2020): 62–71. Color illus.

Frishman, Bob. "The *Other* Simon Willard, Clockmaker." *Maine Antique Digest* 47, no. 12 (December 2019): 152–53. Color illus., bibliography.

———. "Professor Bond at the 1851 London World's Fair." *Watch & Clock Bulletin* 61, no. 4 (July/August 2019): 320–21. 1 color illus.

Frost, Canlin J. "The Master is Free: The Legendary Skill of John Hemmings." *Mortise & Tenon Magazine* 9 (2020): 98–109. Color illus.

Fuller Craft Museum. *Acquisitions to the Permanent Collection, July 1, 2018–June 30, 2019*. Brockton, Mass.: Fuller Craft Museum, 2019. Unpaged; color illus. (Includes furniture by Christine Enos and Stephen Litchfield.)

Garnier, Richard, and Leo Hollis. *Innovation and Collaboration: The Origins and Early Development of the Pendulum Clock in London*. Isle of Man: Fromanteel, 2019. 413 pp.; numerous illus., appendices, bibliography, index.

Gaskell, Ivan, and Sarah Anne Carter, eds. *The Oxford Handbook of History and Material Culture*. New York: Oxford University Press, 2020. xiv + 664 pp.; illus., bibliography, index.

Giaquinto, Jessica. Review of *The Cabinetmaker's Account: John Head's Record of Craft and Commerce in Philadelphia, 1718–1753*, by Jay Robert Stiefel. In *Watch & Clock Bulletin* 61, no. 4 (July/August 2019): 318–19. 1 color illus.

Glisson, James, ed. *Becoming America: Highlights from the Jonathan and Karin Fielding Collection of Folk Art*. San

Marino, Calif.: Huntington Library, Art Museum, and Botanical Garden; New Haven: Yale University Press, 2020. 264 pp.; color illus., bibliography, index.

Gontar, Cybèle. *Chasing the Butterfly Man: The Search for a Lost New Orleans Cabinetmaker, 1810–1825*. New Orleans, La.: Louisiana Museum, 2020. 238 pp.; numerous color illus.

Grant, Daniel. "Top Museum Acquisitions: 2019 in Review." *Antiques and Fine Art* 19, no. 1 (spring 2020): 96–105. 15 color illus.

Hadd, Arnold, with commentary by Joshua A. Klein and Michael Updegraff. "As Part of a Life Lived: A Shaker's Perspective in His Community's Craft." *Mortise & Tenon Magazine* 7 (2019): 72–89. Color and bw illus.

Hannan, Leonie, and Sarah Longair. *History through Material Culture*. Manchester, England: Manchester University Press, 2017. xvi + 183 pp.; illus., bibliography, index.

Havenhand, Lucinda Kaukas. *Mid-Century Modern Interiors: The Ideas that Shaped Interior Design in America*. London: Bloomsbury Visual Arts, 2019. 145 pp.; illus., bibliography, index.

Heckscher, Morrison, Femke Speelberg, and David Snowdon. *Chippendale's Drawings for The Director*. Newburgh, N.Y.: Thornwillow Press, 2019. 229 pp.; illus., facsimiles. (Limited edition in various formats based on the collection of drawings at the Metropolitan Museum of Art.)

Henderson, Amy Hudson. "French & Fashionable: The Search for George and Martha Washington's Presidential Furniture." *American Furniture 2019*, 76–155. 68 color illus.

Hendren, Sara. *What Can a Body Do? How We Meet the Built World*. Englewood Cliffs, N.J.: Prentice-Hall, 2020. 228 pp.; illus., bibliography.

Henion, Paul. "Engraved Images: A Historical Look at Their Development and Use in Clock Tablets." *Watch & Clock Bulletin* 62, no. 1 (January/February 2020): 8–91. 208 color illus., 2 tables.

"Hirschl & Adler Staff Sampler: Staff Picks to Stimulate and Delight." Online exhibition, June 8–19, 2020. Available on social media and at https://www.hirschlandadler.com (accessed June 26, 2020). (Includes two pieces of furniture.)

Hubbard, Bruce. "This Guy Can Help You . . . A Lot!" *American Period Furniture: Journal of the Society of American Period Furniture Makers* 18 (2018): 12–17. (Re Cartouche Award winner James [Ray] Journigan.)

Hurst, Ronald L., and Margaret Beck Pritchard. "British Masterworks: Ninety Years of Collecting at Colonial Williamsburg." *Antiques and Fine Art* 19, no. 2 (summer 2020): 82–91. Color illus. (Includes one of the Chinese Chippendale side chairs with a Portsmouth, N.H., history, from the set that is mainly at the Moffatt-Ladd House and Garden.)

Jobe, Brock. "The Cabinetmaker's Shop: Breathing New Life into an Old Trade." *Mortise & Tenon Magazine* 6 (2019): 114–27. Color illus.

Journigan, James. "What Are You in It For?" *American Period Furniture: Journal of the Society of American Period Furniture Makers* 18 (2018): 18–25. Color illus.

Kane, Patricia E. "Mahogany: New Research on the Wood of Choice for Early Rhode Island Furniture." *Yale University Art Gallery Bulletin* (2019): 69–77. 4 color illus.

Kawamura, Yayoi, Alicia Ancho Villanueva, and Berta Balduz Azcárate. *Nambam Lacquer: Japanese Shine in Navarre: Supplement*. Pamplona, Spain: Government of Navarre, Department of Culture, Sports, and Youth, 2016. 92 pp.; color illus.

Kennedy, Kate, and Hermione Lee, eds. *Lives of Houses*. Princeton, N.J., and Oxford: Princeton University Press, 2020. xvii + 297 pp.; bw illus., index. (See esp. Alexandra Harris, "Moving Houses," pp. 3–17.)

Kirtley, Alexandra Alevizatos. "A Scholarly Appetizer of Scallops." *Antiques* 187, no. 3 (May–June 2020): 52–53. 2 color ilus.

———. Philadelphia Furniture: Design, Artisans, and Techniques. https://www.philafurniture.com (accessed May 20, 2020). (Website devoted to American furniture, 1650–1840, in the Philadelphia Museum of Art.)

Klein, Joshua A. "A Fresh & Unexpected Beauty: Understanding David Pye's 'Workmanship of Risk.'" *Mortise & Tenon Magazine* 7 (2019): 24–33. Color illus.

Klein, Joshua A., ed. *Mortise & Tenon Magazine* 6 (2019): 1–144 pp.; numerous color and bw illus. (See also individual articles cited elsewhere in this list.)

———. *Mortise & Tenon Magazine* 7 (2019): 1–144 pp.; numerous color and bw illus. (See also individual articles cited elsewhere in this list.)

———. *Mortise & Tenon Magazine* 8 (2020): 1–144 pp.; numerous color and bw illus. (See also individual articles cited elsewhere in this list.)

———. *Mortise & Tenon Magazine* 9 (2020): 1–144 pp.; numerous color and bw illus. (See also individual articles cited elsewhere in this list.)

Kries, Mateo, and Jochen Eisenbrand, eds. *Atlas of Furniture Design*. Weil-am-Rhein, Germany: Vitra Design Museum, 2019. 1,026 pp.; 2,852 color and bw illus., glossaries, bibliography, index.

[Lamb, Peter]. "A Partnership with Nature: An Interview with Peter Lamb." *Mortise & Tenon Magazine* 7 (2019): 8–23. Color and bw illus.

Lane, David. "William Morris, George Nakashima: Finding the Middle Landscape." *Mortise & Tenon Magazine* 6 (2019): 44–55. Color and bw illus.

Lanza, Katherine. "Current and Coming." *Antiques* 187, no. 1 (January/February 2020): 40–41. 2 color illus. (Includes reference to Wendell Castle exhibition at R and Co., New York.)

Levy, Bernard, and S. Dean Levy, Inc. *Gallery Catalog XVII (2020)*. New York: by the gallery, 2020. 33 pp.; color illus.

Lome, Erica P. "The Many Reproductions of William Brewster's Chair." *Decorative Arts Trust Magazine* 5, no. 2 (winter 2019): 20–21. 6 color illus.

[Lumbard, Nathan]. "Old Sturbridge Village Receives Nathan Lumbard

Chest." *Antiques and the Arts Weekly* (October 16, 2020): 9. 1 bw illus.

Lytle, Lulu, and Elizabeth Wilhilde. *Rattan: A World of Elegance and Charm.* New York: Rizzoli, 2020. 223 pp.; color and bw illus., index.

Magazine Antiques, Editors of, comp. "Curious Objects." In [Catalogue of] *The Winter Show 2020,* pp. 56–64. New York: East Side House, 2020. Color illus. (Includes sofa, Boston or North Shore, ca. 1765, offered by Bernard and S. Dean Levy, Inc.)

Manca, Joseph. *Shaker Vision: Seeing Beauty in Early America.* Amherst and Boston: University of Massachusetts Press, 2019. x + 391 pp.; color and bw illus., maps.

Marcus, George H. *Introduction to Modern Design: Its History from the Eighteenth Century to the Present.* London: Bloomsbury Visual Arts, 2019. 227 pp.; illus., bibliography, index.

Mascelli, Mike. "Decoding Diderot: Can These Tools Really Be for Upholstery?" *American Period Furniture: Journal of the Society of American Period Furniture Makers* 19 (2019): 65–71. Color illus.

McConnell, Jim. "A Painted Chest in the Pennsylvania-German Tradition." *Mortise & Tenon Magazine* 6 (2019): 84–95. Color illus.

Meier, Eric. *Wood: Identifying and Using Hundreds of Woods Worldwide.* [United States]: The Wood Database, 2018. 266 pp.; numerous color illus., 3 appendices, bibliography, index.

[Metropolitan Museum of Art]. "Met Gets Gift of Late Nineteenth Century Decorative Arts and Paintings." *Antiques and the Arts Weekly* (December 13, 2019): 34. 1 bw illus. (Re Wigmore collection.)

———. "The Met's 150th Anniversary Celebrated with Major Gift." *Antiques and Fine Art* 19, no. 1 (spring 2020): 56. 5 color illus. (Re Wigmore collection.)

Milosch, Jane, and Nick Pearce, eds. *Collecting and Provenance: A Multidisciplinary Approach.* Lanham, Md.: Rowman & Littlefield, 2019. xxi + 428 pp.; 103 bw illus.

Minardi, Lisa. "Center for Pennsylvania German Studies Opens." *Antiques and Fine Art* 19, no. 1 (spring 2020): 114–23. Color illus.

Morgan, Hollie L. S. "Bedfellows." Review of *What We Did in Bed: A Horizontal History,* by Brian Fagan and Nadia Durrani. *History Today* 70, no. 1 (January 2020): 101–2. 1 color illus.

Morris, Kathleen M. "An 'American' Mirror at the Clark Art Institute." *Decorative Arts Trust Magazine* 6, no. 2 (winter 2019–20): 33. 1 color and 1 bw illus. (Re a ca. 1820 mirror attributed to Salem, Massachusetts, that proved to have the label of a German maker.)

Mueller, Shirley M. *Inside the Head of a Collector: Neuropsychological Forces at Play.* Seattle: Lucia/Marquand. 2019. 191 pp.; color and bw illus., bibliography, indexes.

Mueller-Maerki, Fortunat. Review of *From Celestial to Terrestrial Timekeeping: Clockmaking in the Bond Family,* by Donald Saff. In *Watch & Clock Bulletin* 61, no. 4 (July/August 2019): 319–20. 1 color illus.

[Nakashima, George]. *George Nakashima, Woodworker: The Documentary.* Produced and directed by John Nakashima. 2020. New Hope, Pa.: Nakashima Foundation for Peace, 2020. DVD, 90 minutes. (Available on DVD and streaming at https://nakashimadocumentary.com.)

Nielson, Mariah, and Åbäke, eds. *JB Blunk.* Inverness, Calif., and London: Blunk Books/Dent-De-Leone, 2020. 224 pp.; 71 color and 73 bw illus., chronology, bibliography, index. (Includes contributions by Glenn Adamson, Alyssa Ballard, Fariba Bogzaran, Rene Bustamente, Louise Allison Cort, Rita Lawrence, Lucy R. Lippard, Mariah Neilson, Isamu Noguchi, and Rick Yoshimoto.)

"Old Sturbridge Village Acquires Important Chest by Alden Spooner." *Antiques and the Arts Weekly* (November 29, 2019): 42. 1 bw illus.

Orr, Emily M. *Designing the Department Store: Display and Retail at the Turn of the Twentieth Century.* London and New York: Bloomsbury Visual Arts, 2020. xii + 193 pp.; color and bw illus., bibliography, index.

Pavlak, Bill. "The Weight of the Past: Unearthing the 18th-Century Cabriole Leg." *Mortise & Tenon Magazine* 7 (2019): 34–45. Color and bw illus.

Pool, Rachel. "A Rare Glimpse into Two Masters' Lives: Exploring the Charles and Ray Eames House." *Decorative Arts Trust Magazine* 6, no. 2 (winter 2019–20): 22–23. 4 color illus.

Powers, Alan. *Bauhaus Goes West: Modern Art and Design in Britain and America.* New York: Thames and Hudson, 2019. 280 pp.; color and bw illus., bibliography, index.

Price, Jim. "Chauncey Jerome's Oversized Steeples with Their Four Unique Movements." *Watch & Clock Bulletin* 61, no. 5 (September/October 2019): 438–54. 49+ color illus.

Priddy, Sumpter, III. "Cabinetmaker John Brown and the Tall Case Clocks of Wellsburg, Virginia, 1800–1825." *Journal of Early Southern Decorative Arts* 40 (2019). https://www.mesdajournal.org (accessed October 9, 2019). 24 color and bw illus.

Quinn, Stephen. "Characteristics of a 'Jacob Graff' Tall Case Clock?" *Watch and Clock Bulletin* 61, no. 6 (November/December 2019): 537–42. 22 color illus.

Racknitz, Joseph Friedrich Freiher zu. *A Rare Treatise on Interior Decoration and Architecture: Joseph Friedrich zu Racknitz's Presentation and History of the Taste of Living Nations.* Translated and edited by Simon Swynfen Jervis. Los Angeles, Calif.: Getty Research Institute, 2019. 360 pp.; color and bw illus., bibliography, index. Distributed by University of Chicago Press.

"Rhode Island Historical Society Exhibits Weiss Furniture Gifts." *Antiques and the Arts Weekly* (March 6, 2020): 25. 1 bw illus. (Re objects owned by the Greene family.)

Ring, Madelia Hickman. "Q & A: Philip Morris, Jr." *Antiques and the Arts Weekly* (March 20, 2020): 1, 10. 3 bw illus. (Re account book, 1814–1853, of William Painter of Connecticut, a clock-dial painter.)

Ritok, Christine. Review of *Hands Employed Aright: The Furniture Making of Jonathan Fisher, 1768–1847,* by Joshua A. Klein. In *American Furniture 2019*, 234–37.

——. Review of *Inventing Boston: Design, Production, and Consumption, 1680–1720*, by Edward S. Cooke Jr. In *New England Quarterly* 93, no. 2 (June 2020): 325–29.

Rivas-Perez, Jorge F., ed. *Circulación: Movement of Ideas, Art, and People in Spanish America*. Mayer Center Symposium, Readings in Latin American Studies. Denver, Col.: Denver Art Museum, 2018. 216 pp.; color illus., bibliography. (See in particular Gustavo Curiel, "Flemish Imagery in Oaxacan Furniture: Villa Alta Cabinetmakers of the Zapotec Mountains, 17th–18th Centuries," pp. 40–63.)

Ryan, Zoë, ed. *In a Cloud, In a Wall, In a Chair: Six Modernists in Mexico at Midcentury*. Chicago: Art Institute of Chicago, 2019. 235 pp.; color and bw illus.

Saunders, Richard. "Strange Bedfellows: Samuel Colt's Other Claim to Fame." *Maine Antique Digest* 48, no. 5 (May 2020): 122–23. 12 color and bw illus. (Re wicker furniture.)

Scherer, Barrymore Laurence. "Aesthetic Appeal." *Antiques* 187, no. 1 (January/February 2020): 90–99. 16 color illus. (Re Wigmore collection.)

Schiff, Richard. *Sensuous Thoughts: Essays on the Work of Donald Judd*. Berlin: Hatje Cantz Verlag; Marfa, Tex.: Marfa Book Co., 2020. 295 pp.; color and bw illus.

Self, Robert L. "'I Have a Job of 4. Pembroke Tables on Hand at Monticello': Five Tables Made for Thomas Jefferson's Poplar Forest by Joiners James Dinsmore and John Hemmings." *Journal of Early Southern Decorative Arts* 41 (2020). https://www.mesdajournal.org (accessed July 31, 2020). 35 color illus. and line drawings.

Shaykin, Rebecca. *Edith Halpert: The Downtown Gallery and the Rise of American Art*. New York: Jewish Museum, 2019. 232 pp.; bw and color illus., bibliography, index. Distributed by Yale University Press.

Slough, William. "2019 Crafts Competition." *Watch and Clock Bulletin* 61, no. 6 (November/December 2019): 560–65. Color illus.

Solis-Cohen, Lita. "The Center for Pennsylvania German Studies Opens." *Maine Antique Digest* 47, no. 11 (November 2019): 154–55. 3 color illus. (Re facility in Trappe, Pennsylvania.)

——. Review of *American Furniture 2018*, edited by Luke Beckerdite. In *Maine Antique Digest* 48, no. 4 (April 2020): 134–35. 1 color illus.

"Southern Secretary Holds All the Riches at Brunk." *Antiques and the Arts Weekly* (September 27, 2019): 36. 1 bw illus. (Re secretary-linen press with signature of John Gough, an African American craftsman from Charleston, S.C.)

[Speed Art Museum]. "'Shaker Commonwealth' Celebrates Kentucky Shaker Art & Faith: Dual Exhibitions Combine Nineteenth Century Design and Contemporary Performance." *Antiques and the Arts Weekly* (September 18, 2020): 44. 7 bw illus.

Sprague, Laura F. "Rufus Porter's Curious World: Art and Invention in America, 1815–1860." *Antiques and Fine Art* 19, no. 1 (spring 2020): 140–47. Color illus.

Sprague, Laura F., and Justin Wolff, eds., with a contribution by Deborah A. Child. *Rufus Porter's Curious World: Art and Invention in America, 1815–1860*. University Park: Pennsylvania State University Press; Brunswick, Me.: Bowdoin College Museum of Art, 2019. xiii + 137 pp.; numerous color illus., appendix, bibliography, index.

Stevenson-Futch, Liane. "An Inherited Chest of Joiner's Tools." *American Period Furniture: Journal of the Society of American Period Furniture Makers* 19 (2019): 5–11. Color illus. (Re career of 2019 Cartouche Award recipient Robert Glen Stevenson Jr. See also Stevenson's article, "Federal Style Breakfront," in the same issue, pp. 16–23.)

Storb, Christopher. "Dietrich American Foundation: A John Brocas High Chest." *Antiques and Fine Art* 19, no. 3 (autumn 2020): 104–9. 5 color illus.

Stuart, Hal. *Virginia Sectional Furniture: 1800 to 1860: Furniture Designs for a House Divided*. 2016. Rev. ed. Aurora, Col.: Written Words Publishing, 2019. 254 pp.; color and bw illus., bibliography, index.

"Talking Antiques: The Winter Show." *Antiques* 187, no. 1 (January/February 2020): 44–55. (Includes some furniture.)

Tejuca, Celia Rodriguez. "The Folded Spaces of Two Pueblan Colonial Desks." *Decorative Arts Trust Magazine* 6, no. 2 (winter 2019–20): 26–27. 6 color illus.

Temkin, Ann, ed., with contributions by Erica Cooke, Tamar Margalit, Christine Mehring, James Meyer, Annie Ochmanek, Yasmin Raymond, Ann Temkin, and Jeffrey Weiss. *Judd*. New York: Museum of Modern Art, 2020. 304 pp.; color and bw illus., bibliography.

Tigerman, Bobbye, and Monica Obniski. "Fjord and Function." *Antiques* 187, no. 3 (May–June 2020): 86–93. 13 color illus. (Re influence of Scandinavian design in America; see also catalogue listed below.)

Tigerman, Bobbye, and Monica Obniski, eds. *Scandinavian Design and the United States, 1890–1980*. Los Angeles: Los Angeles County Museum of Art; Munich and New York: DelMonico Books-Prestel, 2020. 336 pp.; numerous color and bw illus., bibliography, index.

Turino, Kenneth C., and Max A. Van Balgooy, eds. *Reimagining Historic House Museums: New Approaches and Proven Solutions*. New York: Rowman and Littlefield, 2019. 312 pp.; bw illus., bibliography, index.

[Two Red Roses Foundation]. "Four Rare Frank Lloyd Wright Chairs Acquired by Two Red Roses Foundation." *Antiques and the Arts Weekly* (January 31, 2020): 6. 1 bw illus. (Re dining chairs from the Ward W. Willits House, Highland Park, Ill., ca. 1902.)

Updegraff, Michael. "Scribes of Nature: Dendrochronology and the Deeper Story of Wooden Objects." *Mortise & Tenon Magazine* 9 (2020): 50–69. Color illus.

——. "Tool Marks Tell Stories." *Mortise & Tenon Magazine* 8 (2020): 112–27. Color illus., appendix.

Vesentini, Andrea. *Indoor America: The Interior Landscape of Postwar Suburbia*. Charlottesville: University of Virginia

Press, 2018. xviii + 321 pp.; color and bw illus., bibliography, index.

Vignon, Charlotte. *Duveen Brothers and the Market for Decorative Arts, 1880–1940.* New York: Frick Collection in association with D. Giles, 2019. 320 pp.; numerous color illus., biographies, bibliography, index.

Waddington, Chris. "Museum Visit: Parlor Room Talk." *Antiques* 187, no. 3 (May–June 2020): 40, 42. 3 color illus. (Re period room at New Orleans Museum of Art featuring rococo revival furniture retailed by Hubbell and Curtis of Bridgeport, Connecticut.)

Walker, George. "Axioms of Pre-Industrial Craft." *Mortise & Tenon Magazine* 7 (2019): 130–37. Color and bw illus.

Wagner von Hoff, Dorothee. *Ornamenting the "Cold Roast": The Domestic Architecture and Interior Design of Upper-Class Boston Homes, 1760–1880.* Bielefeld, Germany: Transcript, 2013. 338 pp.; illus., bibliography. (Originally presented as author's doctoral thesis, Universität München, 2012.)

Ward, Barbara McLean. "An 18th-Century Parlor Brought to Life: The Artful Restoration of New Hampshire's Moffatt-Ladd House." *Decorative Arts Trust Magazine* 7, no. 1 (summer 2020): 16–19. 12 color illus.

Ward, Gerald W. R. *Family Treasures: 175 Years of Collecting Art and Furniture at the New England Historic Genealogical Society.* Boston: New England Historic Genealogical Society/AmericanAncestors.org, 2020. xv + 160 pp.; numerous color illus., bibliography, index.

———. Review of *The Art of Display: The American Pedestal, 1830-1910*, by Conner-Rosenkranz et al. In *American Furniture 2019*, 237–39.

Ward, Gerald W. R., comp. "Recent Writing on American Furniture: A Bibliography." In *American Furniture 2019*, 246–51.

Waterhouse, George. "William Markham, Jr., and His Overpasted Southern Labels on Connecticut-Manufactured Clocks." *Watch and Clock Bulletin* 61, no. 6 (November/December 2019): 492–97. 18 color and bw illus.

[Weiss, Stanley]. *Fine American Antiques in the Stanley Weiss Collection.* Foreword by Brock Jobe. [Providence, R.I.: Stanley Weiss], 2019. 305 pp.; 800+ color illus.

Wendell Castle: A New Vocabulary. New York: Friedman Benda, 2019. http://www.friedmanbenda. com (accessed October 22, 2020). (Exhibition catalogue.)

Westgarth, Mark. *The Emergence of the Antique and Curiosity Dealer in Britain, 1815–1850: The Commodification of Historical Objects.* Abingdon, England, and New York: Routledge, Taylor and Francis Group, 2020. x + 191 pp.; 36 bw illus. (Also available as an eBook.)

Westman, Annabel. "Baroque Exuberance." *Antiques* 187, no. 1 (January/February 2020): 114–19. 8 color illus, (Excerpt from book cited below by the same author.)

———. *Fringe, Frog, and Tassel: The Art of the Trimmings Maker in Interior Decoration.* London: Bloomsbury/Philip Wilson, 2019. xv + 272 pp.; illus., bibliography, index.

Wiltse, Heather, ed. *Relating to Things: Design, Technology, and the Artificial.* London: Bloomsbury Visual Arts, 2020. xv + 281 pp.; 68 bw illus. (Also available as an eBook.)

[White House]. *Furnishing the White House: The Decorative Arts Collection.* Special issue of *White House Quarterly*, no. 56 (winter 2020): 1–108. Numerous color and bw illus. (See especially Melissa Naulin, "A Suite for the Nation Restored to Its Original Splendor: Regilded and Reupholstered, the Historic White House Bellangé Suite Begins Its Third Century," pp. 6–23; Lauren McGwin, "Davenport & Company Furniture Designs for Theodore Roosevelt's White House Renovation: An Architectural Treasure Trove in the White House Collection," pp. 42–63.)

Widmer, Kemble. Review of *The Cabinetmaker's Account: John Head's Record of Craft and Commerce in Colonial Philadelphia, 1728–1753*, by Jay Robert Stiefel. In *American Furniture 2019*, 239–45.

Wouters, Gina J. "The Electrifying Art and Spaces of Robert Winthrop Chan-

ler." *Antiques and Fine Art* 19, no. 2 (summer 2020): 92–99. 13 color illus. (Re painted screens and other works by Chanler [1872–1930].)

Wouters, Gina J., and Andrea Gollin, eds. *Robert Winthrop Chanler: Discovering the Fantastic.* Miami, Fla.: Vizcaya Museum and Gardens; New York: Monacelli Press, 2016. 254 pp.; color and bw illus., bibliography, index.

Yale University Art Gallery. "Selected Acquisitions, July 1, 2018–June 30, 2019: American Decorative Arts." *Yale University Art Gallery Bulletin* (2019): 100–103. 6 color illus. (Includes tea table, Newport, R.I., 1760–90, and lady's secretary and bookcase, Emery Moulton, Lynn, Mass., 1814.)

Zapf, Marilyn, ed. *Forging Futures: Studio Craft in Western North Carolina.* Asheville, N.C.: The Center for Craft, Creativity & Design, [2017]. 94 pp.; color and bw illus., bibliography.

Zimmerman, Philip D. "A Beekman Legacy: 1819 French Tapestry Chairs by John Banks of New York." *American Furniture 2019*, 156–213. 58+ color and bw illus., four appendices.

———. "Early Eighteenth-Century Swedish-American Furniture from Wilmington, Delaware." *American Furniture 2019*, 214–33. 19 color and bw illus.

———. Review of *Claggett: Newport's Illustrious Clockmakers*, by Donald L. Fennimore and Frank L. Hohmann III. In *New England Quarterly* 93, no. 1 (March 2020): 138–41.

Index

Lion's head, carved, 66(fig.)
Little, Elbert L., 184(fig.)
Little, Nina Fletcher, 197
Little Navigator (King), 68(fig.)
Live or evergreen oak group, 183
Livingston, Robert R., 35–36
Lock, Mathias, 91, 106(&fig. 30)
Locust, desk, 27
Logan, James, 155
Logan, William, 155
London, desk-and-bookcase, 143(fig.)
The London Tradesman (Campbell), 100, 105
Long Wharf (Boston), 58–59
Lord, Ivory, 71
Loring, David, 30–31
Lotter, Matther A., 125(fig. 6)
Louis XIV, 196
Low, Nathaniel, 72
Lucas, Nathan, 15, 49, 52–53, 55
Lucius Smith and Company, 37
Luyker, Matthew or Matthias, 123

Madeira Islands, as shipping destination, 56
Madison, James, 60
Magnus (ship), 70
Mahogany: armoires, 190; card tables, 109(figs.); chest-on-chest, 147(figs.); counter top, 37–38; countinghouse desk, 30; desk-and-bookcases, 148(fig.), 153(figs.), 154(figs.), 162(fig. 1); dressing tables, 96(fig. 11), 163(figs.); easy chair, 108(fig.); high chests of drawers, 96(fig. 10), 156(fig. 64); pier tables, 142(fig. 40), 144(fig.); side chairs, 94(fig. 6), 95(fig. 8), 97(figs. 13 & 14), 98(figs.), 100(figs.), 107(fig.); store counter, 26; tall case clock, 138(figs.); tea tables, 140(figs.), 142(fig. 38)
Mahogany furniture, in inns, 42, 47
Maintenance, woodworkers and business site, 10–15
Malcolm, James Peller, 124(fig.)
Manchurian ash, 180
Maple, 176, 182; hard maple group, 174, 176, 182; pembroke table, 71; as secondary wood in signs, 3; side chair, 97(fig. 13), 98(fig. 15); soft maple group, 174, 176, 182; striped, 176, 182–83
Mariner's compass, 67–68
Maritime History (Morison), 34

Maritime trades, woodworkers and, 55–78; fabrication of sea chests, 62; furnishings for steamboats on eastern waters, 75–78; sailmakers and rope makers, 62–64(&figs. 45 & 46); ship carvers, 64–67(&figs. 48 & 49); ship equipment, 67–71(&figs. 50 & 51); ship furniture, 71; ship repairs and painting, 72–73
Marselis, Peter, 25
Martha Cadwalader (Peale), 113(fig. 43), 114
Martin, Nathaniel F., 49, 53
Mary (ship), 121
Materia Medica, 23
Maule, Thomas, 171n2; appraisal of household goods inventory of John Head and, 166(fig.), 167–68
McComb, John, Jr., 168
McDowell, Patrick, 72
McElheney and Van Pelt, 22
McIntire, Samuel, 66
McLean, John, 49
Medical box, for ships, 69
Medicine case, 24
Medicine chest, 24–25
A Merchant's Counting House (Lawson), 32(fig.)
Merrifield, G. W. and C. F., 12–13
Metal-working trades, 21
Metropolitan Museum of Art, 74(fig.)
Microscopic wood identification, 178–79
Mifflin, John, 33
Miles and Lyons, 26
Miller, Henry W., 38
Miller, Joseph, 33
Miller, Lewis, 22(fig. 15), 25(figs.), 38(fig.), 43(fig.), 54
Miller, Regis, 178
Miller, Samuel, 24
Mill flume, 49, 52–53
Milliners, 15, 17–19
Mills, Richard, 72
Mills, woodworkers and, 48–55; cider mills, 54–55(&fig.); gristmills, 48, 51–54(&fig. 53); sawmills, 48–50(&fig. 36), 51(fig.)
Millstones, 53
Minerva (mythological figure), 66, 87n82
Miranda, Francisco de, 44(fig.), 45, 48, 59
Montesquieu (ship), 70(&fig.)
Montgomery, Florence M., 197
Mooney, William, 123, 142, 144
Moravian inn (Sun Inn), 42(fig.), 43–45

Mordecai, Jacob, 8
Moreau de Saint-Méry, Frédéric Louis, 7
Morgan, John, 73
Morison, Samuel Eliot, 34
Morris, John, 24
Morris, Robert, 36–37
Morse, Jedidiah, 54
Morss, Phillip, 13
Moulton, A. W., 13
Mount Pleasant Furnace, 136(&fig. 26)
Moyers, Thomas J., 6
Mrs. Hersh's Tavern (Miller), 43(fig.)
Mucklevain, William, 4
Muhlenberg, Frederick Augustus, 9(fig.)
Munroe, John, 12
Murphy bed, 196
Museum of Fine Arts, Boston, 187, 190
Museum of International Folk Art, 196, 197
My Bed (Emin), 196
Mythological figures, 87n80; vessels and figureheads named after, 65

Napoleon, 60
Naylor, Katherine Wheeler Nanny, 189
Nests of drawers/cases: for physicians and apothecaries, 23–24; for stores, 26
A New Bedford Merchant (Hathaway), 64(fig.)
A New Book of Ornaments, Thos. Johnson Carver, Design'd for Tables & Friezes, 93(fig. 4)
Newcomb, Reuben, Jr., 71
New Lutheran Church, in Fourth Street Philadelphia (Birch), 9(fig.)
Newman, John, 23–24
New Orleans, search for "Butterfly Man," 190–94
Newport Mercury (newspaper), 65
New-York Revised Prices for Manufacturing Cabinet and Chair Work, 31
New York Weekly Journal, 21
Nichols, Samuel, 77
Nicholson, John, 121
Nomad Living folding bed, 196
Norris, Charles, 140
North America (ship), 67
Northern Star (steamboat), 75
Northern white-cedar, 176, 179(&fig.)
Nubian Kingdom of Kush, 195
Nutting, Wallace, 198
Nylander, Jane, 197

Oak, 183–84; desk-and-bookcase, 143(fig.); as secondary wood in signs, 3;